HOW WILL OUR CHILDREN LEARN?

How Will Our Children Learn?

Choosing Better Schools:
Educational Excellence
in Every Postcode

Michael Hewitson

Publisher's Apprentice

Published 2013 by Publisher's Apprentice (An imprint of Connor Court Publishing Pty Ltd)

Copyright © Michael Hewitson 2013

ALL RIGHTS RESERVED. This book contains material protected under International and Federal Copyright Laws and Treaties. Any unauthorised reprint or use of this material is prohibited. No part of this book may be reproduced or transmitted in any form or by any means, electronic or mechanical, including photocopying, recording, or by any information storage and retrieval system without express written permission from the publisher.

PO Box 224W
Ballarat VIC 3350
sales@connorcourt.com
www.connorcourt.com

ISBN: 9781922168788 (pbk.)

Cover design by M. Giordano

The cover photo was taken by Michael Hewitson, William is his 11th grandchild.

Printed in Australia

CONTENTS

	Preface	vii
	Acknowledgements	ix
	Synopsis *What this book shows about education in Australia*	xi
1	When state schools were king	1
2	The hidden curriculum *What schools are really about*	19
3	Entering tiger country *Allowing a choice for parents*	32
4	Impossible tales *Learning what parents want*	48
5	Teetering beginnings *The opening of Trinity College*	64
6	Survival or extinction? *Trinity College, 1985*	77
7	"Burn the lot!" *Shaping the character of a school*	98
8	Demand grows, but obstruction wins *How parents' wishes are frustrated*	117
9	Pressure grows at home *Trinity expands southwards*	126
10	Drugs and sex *What's a headmaster to do?*	137
11	Academic failure *Change takes time*	158
12	The octopus grows *Trinity becomes a threat*	175
13	All-out attack *Who really runs state schools?*	193
14	Industrial relations *Seven days a week*	209
15	Flooded with money *Funding not the main game*	228
16	Fundamentalism and bankruptcy *The Investigator College story*	237
17	Change and real teaching *Do the lessons of this story stand up to teaching today?*	260
18	Rescuing Australian schooling *Educational excellence for all, in every postcode*	277
	Appendix: How to choose a school for your child	295
	Endnotes	297

Preface

Inside stories of a headmaster and teacher

All with an interest in a child's future should read this story. The school a child attends is one of the most important determinants of who the child becomes. Indeed the schools we choose will change the country. Choosing better schools is a theme of the book. It will help you choose.

The author is a teacher, a past director of the Salisbury Education Centre, the founding principal of the largest school in Australia, a Fellow of the Australian College of Education and, in the past decade, a practising maths and science teacher.

Public education fails in the lower socio-economic areas of Australia: this story reveals what we need to know in order to provide effective schools for our children, and what parents need to know to choose an effective school. State schooling has declined to the extent that rich areas have good state schools, but the entrée card to them is owning prohibitively expensive real estate. Parents from poor communities cannot afford the entry fee of a residence in the area, yet they are increasingly stymied in seeking to do something better for their children.

How Will Our Children Learn? asks big questions: How will our children know what is important? How will we know that our children have at least learnt the basics? How did one state school for a decade become the property of the unionised staffroom? Why did parents choose a new school in a dusty paddock – a school without traditions, money or resources? Why did the enrolment at this school grow to more than 3000 children within 15 years and still not meet the demand?

Using actual experiences and personal stories, the story of the decline of public state schooling is revealed without bureaucratic PR spin. The aim of the story is tell it the way it is, and to suggest how we can choose and run schools to benefit each child and the nation. For those who prefer to cut to the chase, my main conclusions about what is needed to rescue Australian schooling are summarised in the synopsis.

Public education of our children will be the story of our country. Some believe that Australian children in lower socio-economic areas are automatically condemned to poor educational results, but this book gives the lie to that claim. It outlines a compelling vision: in every postcode of Australia, educational excellence for all.

Bruce Hobby Photo   Thanks to our family pictured in 2011

Acknowledgements

Unley Council

Cr Peter Hughes, past principal of Jamestown Primary School; Cr Mike Hudson, journalist and editor.

Trinity College

Dr Rupert Thorne, college council from 1988, chair 1994–2004; Geoff Gordon, chair 1984–1994; Rosslyn Hewitson, head of R–4 1984–2004; Michael Slocombe, principal of South; Chris Short, college council 1984–88, building manager 1989–2011; David Smith, deputy college principal 1985–2003; Kevin Whittington, principal of Blakeview School 1991–1998.

Professional

Len Woodley: publishing advice; Anna Nakos, deputy principal of Temple Christian College; Caroline Pritchard, Trinity student 1985–1997, English teacher Tatachilla Lutheran, daughter and editor; Don Grimmett, principal of Investigator College 2002 (input to chapter 16); Jill Boundey, secretarial preparation of text; Owen Salter for the final edit. My thanks are also owed to numerous others from tertiary education and schools.

To the **general readers** who read this book in draft form as a story, knowing nothing of the background yet encouraging me by their enthusiasm and pushing me to finish the next chapter – my thanks. To the many unnamed parents, students and staff who have contributed to the story and to my understanding of how to live and how we should run schooling in Australia – thank you.

A synopsis of the principles emerging from this story

This book is about public education, its importance and how to better provide it. It tells of the decline of learning in our poorest schools and how to provide a state school system that would build a better country.

A. To achieve real change and school improvement three things need to be recognised:

1. **That more money thrown at a non-performing system of schools does not, and will not, increase student access to quality schooling.**

   Australia has increased real spending on schools by nearly 50% in the past decade, yet standards have fallen. Appallingly, one-quarter of all our Year 4 students do not meet minimum international literacy proficiency benchmarks. Both sides of politics detail this failure.

   Spending more on a school system that fails is just more expensive. Good teachers are important, but in badly governed schools where no one is clearly responsible for a student's learning, they will burn out, and – being skilled competent professionals – they will find jobs outside teaching. This book explains how a school with only 65% of the money (per child) of a state school, in the lowest achieving region of South Australia, was able to outperform independent and state schools nationally.

2. **That school governance is the core problem which must be addressed.**

   The best schools are those where parents, teachers and the school philosophy are in harmony. The key issues to

governance (in both state and independent schools) are:
a. Who determines whether a school is successful?
b. Who is actually responsible to ensure success?

Educational experts often design expensive, sophisticated measuring tools which, if introduced as 'the solution', will merely distort what passes as education to win government funding. This book demonstrates how informed parents, not the state, are the best determiners of a quality education.

3. **That *all* parents, both rich and poor, must have access to a choice of schools.**

   Parents want:
   - good teachers
   - good academic standards
   - safe schools
   - good values.

   Therefore they need to be able to choose between schools which are contesting in all these areas: academics, pastoral care and a definable value system underpinning the school's educational approach.

B. **Action is required in several key areas:**

The stories in this book demonstrate the effectiveness of the following achievable approaches:

1. **A choice of schools requires the establishment of independent state schools.**

   A new category of school could be funded in all lower economic areas in all states of Australia. To ensure competition in all areas of education, including values, independent state schools could be sponsored by both education departments and non-government providers. Only by this mechanism will parents have real choices in all important areas of schooling.

Chapter 18 describes how these schools can be governed and established. Enrolment is non-selective and open to all. Because students have no say in whether they attend school or not, proselytising of any faith system expecting student compliance is unacceptable.

2. **Effective governance requires an autonomous school board/council with the responsibility of principal selection, review and support, with an independent external umpire.**

This board/council should provide clarity as to:
- what school principals need
- who is going to actually be responsible for the schooling of students
- what authority an individual classroom teacher needs.

3. **Appointment of an effective principal.**

The work of the principal is vital for every successful school. As well as the daily management of the school, principals need to have the authority and responsibility for staff, students and curriculum. They must enjoy the support of the school community and be keen to strengthen and support the school's philosophical foundations. Schools offering what parents wish for their children are over-run with demand.

4. **Adherence to the core curriculum.**

Primary schooling in the core curriculum is an essential foundation in poor areas for good Year 12 results. Time on English, spelling, grammar and writing, together with number skills and mathematics, needs to be allocated as a priority. Parents value common testing and honest reporting.

5. **Provision of an all-day, 8.00 am to 6.00 pm timetable.**

   Parents would like many other things from a school. Families, with both parents working, or a single-parent family seeking to work, would wish for a longer school day to cater for cultural and sporting opportunities. The book describes how to provide an 8.00 am to 6.00 pm school day.

6. **Permitting bankruptcy.**

   It is important that schools which fail are allowed to become bankrupt. This forces change and does not mean that the facilities of a bankrupt school are wasted. Changing the culture of a bankrupt school is described in chapter 16.

Applying the above principles will enable all parents, rich or poor, to ensure that their child (and hence every child) receives an education that will build our families and communities, and therefore our nation.

The story begins ...

1
When state schools were king

Penguin, officially known as the Rev John Caulfield Miller, headmaster of St Peter's College, had asked me to attend a meeting.

What had gone wrong? I was a boarding house tutor at St Peter's and was completing a Diploma of Education. 'Saints' regarded itself as, and probably was, South Australia's leading school. We were brought up on the Nobel Prize winners and Rhodes scholars who had gone there. Premiers from all sides of politics and even the leader of the Communist Party were old scholars.

What had happened? What had the boys discussed within the school? Why did the headmaster want to meet a boarding house tutor? There was unrest amongst the staff and the 1960s student revolution was in the air. Plenty could go wrong in a boarding school. Was it on my watch? Was I to be pumped for information about the staffroom?

Problems had arisen at Westminster School the year before. As a resident master (essentially the same as a boarding house tutor), I knew that the housemaster had been rightly dismissed. The boarding houses were subsequently reorganised. I had learnt of behaviour within a school community and boarding school that would have greatly upset the respected Christian leader and principal of Westminster. Yet the possibility of scandal at St Peter's, with a housemaster of the stature and integrity of Dick Potter, was not even a possible thought.

Nonetheless, the impending interview was worrying.

Saturday eventually arrived and I was ushered into the Head's office in a state of general anxiety. On a dais at the far end of the double classroom-sized room was the headmaster's huge desk and chair. Light streamed through the bay windows. The form of the headmaster at work could be made out. But as I entered, he rose and walked around the large boardroom table and chairs in front of wall-to-ceiling panelled bookcases to meet me.

"Michael, I want you to join the staff of Saints as a biology master next year," he said.

This was a surprise to me because the school rarely employed fresh-out-of-college teachers. I had completed a science degree with a broad range of maths, physics, chemistry and biology. I had sized up that the then rapidly growing science of microbiology was one that would be in great demand, and the Microbiology Department at Adelaide University had been recruiting students with a background of maths, physics and physical and inorganic chemistry. We were invited to do a major and subsequently an honours degree in microbiology. This new science required people with number skills, an understanding of technology and a grasp of molecular chemistry.

I had intended to join the Education Department as a matter of course. There were only four of us in microbiology honour's year, and we were indeed sought after, with job approaches and salaries discussed about double that of a teacher. Being young and idealistic, education had an attraction for me as I believed that teaching the next generation would shape the future of our country.

"Sir, do I have the experience required to contribute to Saints?" I asked. "I attended St Peter's College from Reception to Year 12, of course, but I've only had one year as a resident master at Westminster College. It might be good for my ability to teach to gain wider experience." Probably I was more awkward and may have messed up the thought with some ungracious statement.

"I've thought of that, Michael. That's why we would like you to apply to take up the position for two years at St Peter's, followed by two years in England in a leading public school. Following the two years in England you would be welcomed back as a member of staff with international experience." As I remember the exchange, he continued after what seemed a considerable time but was probably instantaneous, "In order to consider this offer, you may like to know that St Peter's has had some applications from teachers in state schools. Indeed, I am making an appointment of a teacher who is a senior master in the Education Department." I was given the weekend to think it over.

The Education Department of South Australia gained the best teachers. Those with permanent status, and particularly senior master status, rarely applied to independent schools. During this time state schools were king. Teachers sought to be part of them and were loyal to them. Many other independent schools were in financial trouble and not all their teachers had recognised degrees or qualifications for their subject areas.

Discussion in the Saint's staffroom reckoned that Saints was the only independent school likely to survive financially in South Australia. With the 'Baby Boom' passing through the schooling system there was a teacher shortage. The state school system had a scholarship program which attracted the top 20 per cent of students to sign up for a degree and gain their Diploma of Education, after which they were bonded to teach for three years in the state school system. The only alternative for working and middle-class families was for their child to win a rare Commonwealth Scholarship. For most, a teacher's scholarship was the only way a university course could be considered.

I did not like the idea of being bonded for three years following university, so I entered as a free agent. My first year there was indeed a struggle, paid for by fruit picking, frugal living and a generous arrangement of board with a family friend. I won a Commonwealth Scholarship which covered the university fees, but unlike the teacher's scholarship, it did not provide income to live on. To students making their own way, those in the State Teachers' University Training Program were rich.

At the time I found there was a distinct element of class attitude in others' responses to this decision. To the generally upper class students with whom I went through school, teaching was a low-status profession because teachers lacked financial status. State schools contracted the best teachers before they were even qualified.

Returning for the weekend to my parents' home in country Kadina, I thought about the offer from St Peter's. After church on Sunday morning, Jim Giles, Area Director of Education, came up to me to discuss my future. I suspect my father, rector of the parish, had spoken with him.

"Michael, if you really want to broaden your education and improve your capacity to teach, you won't take up the two years at Saints and two years in a similar English school overseas," he said. "You'll join the least popular school in the South Australian Education Department and learn how the others live. You'll widen your education and gain experience of their needs. State schools educate the state, not just the select few. See how our least popular schools operate. You'll learn far more."

Such an appeal to altruism and a challenge to enter unknown territory was attractive. My application went into the South Australian Education Department for the least popular school in the state. Looking back, this was the move of an idealistic, naive young man. Yet without this choice, I would never have come to understand the importance of public education or be able to tell the story describing the decline of state schooling – a story that impacts us all.

My Whyalla experience

The least popular school to teach at in South Australia, or at least the school to which the Education Department wished to send me, was Eyre High School, Whyalla West.

Whyalla was a rapidly growing mining town with steel manufacture and shipbuilding as its backbone. On certain summer days, with a strong north-westerly blowing red dust up the streets and the temperature soaring above 40°C, a stranger in town would tell stories of visiting hell. On other days when the wind changed, smoke blowing across the city kept the illusion alive. Whether it was this occasional searing heat, dust and smoke from pluming industrial chimneys, or just the fact that Whyalla lived up to its Aboriginal name as the meeting place of the winds, no one wanted to teach there. This reluctance was fuelled by a teacher shortage across the state – student numbers were stretching teacher numbers to breaking point. Whyalla's five-hour separation from Adelaide also contributed to its undesirability.

Teachers who went there faced a huge task. The following year my new wife, Rosslyn, joined another Whyalla school, Memorial Oval Primary School, as teacher of a combined Reception/Year 1 class of about 50 five-year-olds. In 1971, with a teacher fresh out from college, a class with 50 Reception children was considered too large, so Ros was given a double classroom to teach in. Six weeks into Term 1, with the arrival of a new teacher, the class was reduced to 38, although during the year it grew to 40.

How did the Education Department cope with this kind of demand? Did real learning take place in the classrooms? Without good discipline and an organised curriculum, teaching and learning were not possible.

Eyre High School, Whyalla West, was a new school in the poorer migrant and working class part of Whyalla. Whyalla High was the established secondary school in town. Eyre High catered for students from Year 8 and was starting Year 11 and subsequently Year 12 for the first time. When visiting the school the year before starting, I was given the job of helping prepare the order list for equipment for the physics, chemistry and biology departments. The senior staff members of physics and chemistry at that time did not have degrees in their subject areas, and they told me they were unsure what the equipment on the lists was and what to order. As a new graduate appointee, I had the challenge of setting up the biology program and ordering all the equipment without any experienced senior biology staff.

The school was serving a difficult area. Today such schools would probably be struggling for control and hence little learning would be taking place. But this school was well ordered, well disciplined. This was a time when state schools were respected, especially in the more challenging parts of the state. Even in these areas, as long as teachers earned it they were given respect and classroom discipline was readily maintained. The situation in primary schools was even more favourable. Ros taught in a number of primary schools across Whyalla and discipline was not an issue.

In the secondary school, discipline had to be earned. This is illustrated by an incident in which Year 8 students were shooting shanghais at the French teacher.

"All of those students who were shanghaiing the French teacher" – a pause follows as I think – "please, you have a choice. Those of you with the guts to own up, line up on the right hand side of the door. Those who are innocent or not prepared to take the responsibility, line up on the left hand side of the door. Those who have been shanghaiing the French teacher will be given one stroke of the cane."

I am addressing about 45 students in my 1970 Year 8 class. The classroom is new. As their maths and science teacher, I also have the pastoral care role as their class teacher.

"You may think it is stupid to line up and admit your involvement and by so doing receive the cane. This is the honour system. Your honour and integrity is at stake. My grandfather at your age, the age of 12, lost an eye as a result of a student shooting shanghais. It is dangerous."

The mood in the classroom is slowly changing. "As Form Master of this Year 8 class it is my job to make sure this classroom is safe for all. Due respect must be given to teachers as well. If you own up, you know you will receive one cut of the cane, and that is the end of it. You will also gain respect for your own integrity, respect for the person you have to live with for the rest of your life."

This being my first year of teaching, I had already discussed the matter of the shanghaiing with the principal, Mr George Williams. Corporal punishment was the norm for serious offences. I was required to speak with the principal because, as a junior teacher, I had no authority to cane students. Canings had to be done with the authority of, or by, a senior teacher. Now I left the students to think about what I had said and went to Mr Williams' office. He wrote on a sheet of paper that I had authority to cane the students who admitted to the shanghaiing. Their names were of course unknown. No one might be prepared to own up.

With the authority in hand, I walked confidently back to the classroom. There I had the shock of my life. Out of the 45 students a number of girls had lined up with the expected numerous boys. My whole education from Reception to Year 12 had been in an all-boys' school. Both boarding houses had been all male. I had not believed that Year 8 girls would be shanghaiing the French teacher. Indeed, one of those girls was the daughter of the Regional Director of Education.

I knew that caning the boys with one whack across the backside would have a salutary effect. It hurt. But whilst I was brought up with corporal punishment, I was always uncomfortable administering it. My personal rule was to cane only those students who had accepted the punishment. The alternative may have been an after-school detention or worse. Another personal rule with students was to keep my promises. Fair, firm and friendly were the bywords of discipline. These three words were reinforced by the example and good practice of teachers during my student days. Consistency in treatment of students was a prerequisite for good classroom discipline.

By this time I was wondering how in the heck I was going to discipline the girls and keep my promise. I was caught between a promise and my values. I had promised one whack of the cane for those who owned up. They had had the courage to own up.

The boys had come and gone, one at a time, clearly sore and repentant. The girls were all in tears but there was no way they were going to receive the same treatment as the boys. So with the one-foot ruler in hand, flat side down, a tap on the hand was administered to the already crying and remorseful girls. Justice and honour were maintained. The classroom environment was drawn into line and the students were clearly proud of themselves. There was no more shanghaiing.

When I sent back the list of names caned to the principal, however, there was a very quick knock on the door, and an anxious Mr Williams asked me, "Did you cane all of those students on the list?" When I answered yes, he said, "You had better come and see me. Caning girls is forbidden by the Act."

I tell this story to give an insight into the way that even a first year out teacher who made a wrong commitment in dealing with discipline of girls was quietly supported. There were no parental complaints. The principal, whilst pointing out my error, gave me support. Such was the respect and authority of teachers in general in the community, and the respect for the principal of the school, that I was able to continue a teaching career.

Under-resourced but successful

Normal discipline in schools is essential for effective learning. In the 1960s and early 1970s even a state school loaded with migrants from the wrong suburb of Glasgow and migrants from Spain brought in to provide a workforce for BHP's steel works and shipbuilding, plus the most working-class Australian students, was a school of learning. Yet Eyre High School also had a smattering of upper-middle-class and professional-class students. The Area Director of Education (later to be the Director General of Education for the state) sent his own children there. Although it was a school without an established reputation, out west in Whyalla, the Area Director of Education had confidence that it would be successful and sent his own children there. If this was true for one of the least popular and prestigious schools in the state, then the state system could rightly, with all its difficulties, hold its head high. State schools were indeed king.

There were, of course, times of trouble. With the drastic teacher shortage, a class of 45 seemed normal. At one point, to make up the numbers, a failed first year medical student was appointed to teach. Another teacher, who in my opinion was cynical, lazy and behaved irrationally with students, was held in disdain by both the students and the school. He lined his classes up at the door so that when the bell went, he could rush out to play cards in the staffroom. One day a bucket of gravel was tipped from the roof two storeys up, and as he was rushing off to play bridge, the gravel landed on top of him. I don't know that the students were actually ever caught.

Looking back now, I see that this action was a challenge to the authority of all teachers. Yet back then I did not feel threatened. I knew that the tech studies master, backed by a deputy principal, Miss Grant, had the authority and discipline of the school in hand. Formal school detentions, cleaning up the yard and other forms of possible discipline

Eyre High School Year 10 combined level maths class, 1971

such as the cane were something students wished to avoid. Even the bottom class was disciplined.

Why did this school succeed? Today it would be regarded as outrageously under-resourced.

Curriculum in the '60s and '70s

The inspectors were coming. One was known to wipe his fingers over the top of the doorframes to check for dust.

It was not a good day for a Junior Class B teacher to be demonstrating physics by apparently lying on the front bench. There was no knock on the door. In walked the science inspector, Mr Russell. He was an experienced teacher and author of the biology content in the science textbooks.

The students had been told that the inspectors were coming to check up on them and how much they knew. This, of course, was strictly true. However, checking up on the learning also meant assessing the teacher. The students backed their teachers against the foreign inspector. Our programs were looked at and the testing was reviewed. The students felt a little embarrassed and yet pleased that they were important enough to be reviewed. The motto for the inspectors and the Education Department could well have been: "What you don't inspect, don't expect."

How thin can you spread? The curriculum of schools was yet to become crowded. Reading, 'Riting and 'Rithmetic were regarded as the three Rs and the basis for primary school education. Nature science, social studies and health education were taught and there were a few special days such as Arbor Day. But the pendulum was already swinging towards a broader curriculum. Learning by doing was challenging the pure rote learning of previous years. In themselves all the curricular additions sounded worthy and new subjects such as road safety, sex education, protective behaviour, anti-bullying, physical education theory, technology education and computing were added. Over the coming years, special days or weeks for indigenous education, world conservation, the Red Nose and Daffodil appeals, grandparents' day, school open days and other school-based activities would push into the curriculum. If there was a problem in the general community there was a growing expectation that schools would fix it. Yet schooling packed to solve all our societal problems risks overloading the curriculum, undermining those necessary skills of reading, writing and arithmetic.

Schools had a curriculum document that was content-based. Students learnt the phonics method with word groups such as mat–cat–rat. Spelling was seen as a progression with word lists for each year level. Science was a formal subject with a program. Maths covered number, space and measurement. Standards were high and inspectors visited the school to ensure that the curriculum was being taught and students were learning. Teachers felt valued. The modern discussion about teacher performance, inspection, pay and recognition was not an issue – these things were already in place. There were the superior 'Classification A' teachers and the lower 'Classification B' teachers. The visit was important to be promoted to Junior Class A. With the principal's recommendation and support of inspectors you were able to achieve Classification A status. Pay was involved, as was self-esteem.

In secondary schools the timetable was weighted heavily towards mathematics, science and English literature. From Year 8 both maths and science were timetabled with twice as many lessons as any other subject. A foreign language (French and/or German), home economics/art/tech studies, geography, history and religious instruction made up the program. I kept my Year 10 science overhead transparencies for 33 years and discovered I could use them in 2002 to teach Year 11 and 12 physics. In 1970 the Year 9 and 10 science program also had a double subject weighting. Like today, junior science was 19th century science; unlike today, it had an extensive mathematical foundation. Science had a belief that it was teaching hard facts. Experiments were performed, graphs drawn, mathematical equations written to explain the observations. The inclusion of biology into junior science was an innovation.

In terms of accountability, public examinations were the order of the day. "Public examinations are the only fair assessment in a democracy," we were told. "After all, the Chinese have used public examinations over thousands of years to establish a meritocracy in their Public Service." External assessment was done at Year 7 (Progress Certificate) to ensure all graduates to high school could read, write and do arithmetic. There were also public examinations at Years 10, 11 and 12. The schools had formal exams in Years 8, 9 and 10. Parents had confidence that their children were learning.

In June 2007 Professor Dean Jaensch wrote about the 1950s secondary school in an article entitled, "Lessons from the past can serve us into the future".[1] He attended a state country high school. The school and staff set high levels in academic and social matters. Jaensch writes, "We had external examinations in Years 10, 11 and 12 to establish whether we had achieved the standard. If we didn't, we failed and came back the next time. I failed Year 11 and repeated it with a much better expectation of what was expected."

The role of external examinations in the success of secondary schooling in the 1960s and '70s can easily be overlooked. These exams ensured much more than the fact that content had been taught and duly learnt. As a student you respected teachers because they were on your side. Teachers were critical in enabling you to pass the exam. Homework and academic standards were supported by this external threat. The public exam was the 100% measure for the whole year. It was a make-or-break written examination. If you were sick on the day it was unfair. The exams underpinned the academic rigour and classroom relationships.

Freedom to learn
While schools focused on basic academic skills and knowledge, they also had a lot of freedom for teachers to give students extensive social,

physical and spiritual skills as well. After-hours, school-based sport and other activities in state schools were normal.

Let me give a rather hair-raising example to illustrate the freedom given.

The Natural Science Society I ran at lunchtime and after school decided to go caving in the north-eastern Flinders Ranges. The best man at our wedding, David Bullock, came up to take us through some very narrow and frightening caves. He led us down into the pitch black and the students eagerly followed on their stomachs like snakes slithering down a hole. We only had carbide torches as we pushed through the narrow openings, using our feet as paddles. I was tail-end Charlie and no one was to be left behind unless I was stuck. Since I was somewhat bigger than the rest of the group, this prospect seemed all too real.

At the time I did not realise the enormous trust and confidence given to us newly out-of-college teachers by both the school leadership and the parents. Down in the cave I was wondering where this trust and confidence came from. We were heading into the unknown, yet students were learning leadership skills, teamwork and about 'us' as a collective rather than 'me' as an individual.

We were heading into the unknown in the classroom as well. The school curriculum, whilst prescribed, tested and reviewed, did not occupy all the learning time. In science, for example, we worked together to build telescopes. We ground an eight-inch (20 cm) lens from two circles of plate glass, which took many hours. This was achieved by an afternoon roster of students carefully grinding by hand on the end of a 44-gallon drum. The resultant concave lens was then silvered and inserted into the end of a rolled steel tube.

There was an expectation in state schools that there would be out-of-hours co-curriculum activity. I ran the Natural Science Society with about 54 students who went caving, camping and exploring and held evening lectures at which presentations were made to parents.

We had time after school hours to encourage exploration, thinking and teamwork. Students learnt that by working together they could achieve more. The learning achieved in such co-curricular activities cannot be underestimated.

Here is another example of the freedom schools enjoyed. In my third year at Eyre High School I was assessed as eligible to be appointed as a senior science master in another school. With shipbuilding and steel product manufacture growing, Whyalla was booming and a third high school was being built even further west. I was appointed to it as a senior master in my fifth year.

In the first week of teaching at Stuart High I got something of a shock. A student told me, "Sir, my mum makes drink at home in an open pot. Potato peelings and vegetable scraps all get chucked into it, we add some sugar and it bubbles and ferments and then we distil it." As a young teacher with a microbiological background, I was rather horrified by the potential production of retail alcohol along with methyl alcohol in this homemade brew. Methyl alcohol causes eventual blindness and is a major discouragement from drinking methylated spirits instead of vodka.

We grew wine grapes at our home in Whyalla. With our row of Rhine Riesling and Shiraz vines we made excellent Riesling. Using this experience and my microbiological background, I was given permission to develop a new course called 'Alcoholic Science'. If the students were going to make alcohol at home, at least they would understand the science and dangers of this potent brew. The course was written to teach the content of our existing science curriculum in a new way, which in 1974 was very radical. My wife had signed the anti-alcohol Temperance Union pledge as a state primary school student. Wine-making in schools was unthinkable. Yet in Whyalla I was allowed to proceed by John Lyon, the previous deputy principal at Eyre High, who was now principal of Stuart High.

Distant clouds gather

Such was the general climate in state schools in the late 1960s and early '70s, but it was not to last. Dark clouds were over the horizon, and the seeds of the future decline of state education were being planted. Some of the problems could be seen, even if only in hindsight, during my time in Whyalla..

With the great teacher shortage of the late '60s and early '70s, there were a lot of new appointments and rapid promotions. All senior staffing positions, including deputy principals and principals, were tenured for life. This meant that the vitality and contribution of energised professionals seeking to establish long-term careers was temporarily ensured. A tiny minority who sought appointments for income, personal gain and a feather bed for life were also entrenched. Soon the bright and able, along with those seeking just a salary, saw that the leadership positions were filled permanently. This system ensured that newcomers' career paths were limited. Young teachers quickly become disenchanted, and the heavy responsibilities of a teacher's load became a burden as the real work was shared unevenly. Resignations of those who could leave started as a trickle that grew.

This was also a time when people began to feel that the school curriculum was overly prescribed. The leadership of the Education Department may well have grown up in an era when the Director General of Education could stipulate that on Friday at 10.30 am, all Grade 5 students would turn to their arithmetic books and do page 53. By the late 1960s the pendulum was already swinging to local autonomy. With only about half the curriculum in each subject prescribed, there was great freedom for a teacher to decide what else to include. It was not long before the position of Inspector of Schools was removed. Schools began to vary their programs and offerings. Open space classrooms were introduced where larger numbers of students were placed with a group of teachers. In some cases, no specific teacher was responsible for the progress of the individual child, and some students stopped progressing.

With no testing and no inspections, the problems grew because teachers did not see the students who were falling behind. They were simply passed on to the next teacher since no one was allowed to fail.

Schools were given freedom, but the question arose: whose freedom? Who was in control? Students had freedom to learn by doing and exploring, but the trouble was there was a possibility students would share ignorance. It became possible for a child to miss being given a foundation in reading, writing and arithmetic. Students could miss number skill drills, miss an understanding of spelling and grammar, and miss out on developing the capacity to communicate in either mathematics or English. The curriculum was being expanded with subjects and activities designed to cure all social ills and needs. Sometimes new subjects with their own specialist teachers were added to the timetable, reducing the time available for core teaching. Sport became an activity within school hours. Interschool sporting competitions required lessons off and the best sporting students missed classes.

In the open learning classrooms students learnt the freedom of a self-exploratory curriculum, but some did not learn the basics. There is no doubt that different students learn best by different means, and for some students, this free self-discovery method of learning is indeed the best. But not for all. It is my contention that all students' education is enhanced by diverse approaches, but we still need to check that learning is taking place.

The teaching of reading also changed. The whole-word method was brought in whereby students were taught to read by recognising whole words. Phonetics – teaching by sound groups – began to decline. The phonetic method was looked on as old fashioned but the 'new' approach was not all that new – I can remember being taught by the whole word method in 1951 in St Peter's College. It was probably introduced by a teacher moving up the bureaucratic ranks.

Phonetic teaching enabled the overwhelming majority of students to learn to spell, read and communicate. In 1972, in at least two of the least popular schools in South Australia, all students could read and write and knew their tables. I taught the bottom students science in class 9H. The traditional high level abstract science program was beyond them, so I chose an English textbook with many short experiments and hands-on practicals, and this was successful. (Today this group of students would often not even attend school. They would be illiterate and violent.) At teachers' conferences other teachers did not raise concerns about poor student literacy and numeracy, or about absenteeism or systemic failure, so I believed that all Year 9 students in the most deprived schools in South Australia were at least as able as ours in Whyalla. They were literate and numerate.

Whilst the policy of the 1960s was on its own restrictive, it certainly worked. The curriculum was rigorously assessed, monitored and held accountable, with students and teachers working together to pass exams. This was backed-up by the capacity for self-discovery, adventure learning and a sense of fun, teaching students about teamwork rather than about just the individual.

Memorial Oval 1971, Rosslyn and Reception class with five absent

Lessons learnt

In Whyalla I discovered that some things worked and some were unhelpful to student learning. Here are the lessons I learnt from both the good and bad.

1. At Eyre High School, students had their own classrooms and teachers moved from one room to another. In contrast, teachers should be based in their own classroom and the students come to them because:
   a. This gives teachers time to tidy up and prepare for their next lesson.
   b. It gives students some exercise and fresh air.
   c. Teachers can have a variety of teaching aids and resources on hand, not just those they can carry from class to class.
   d. When there is no teacher in the room, sometimes students with idle time cause havoc, disrupting the start of the next lesson and putting the teacher on the back foot.
2. External exams were important and helpful.
3. A structured curriculum is important to students from lower socio-economic families. Parents have not always taught their children numeracy or literacy before attending school and may not have the educational resources or knowledge at home to reinforce or fill in the gaps in teaching at school.
4. The morale of teachers is not equated just to the level of resources.
5. The real possibility of failure is a vital stimulus for learning. Only those who pass core prerequisite skills to future learning should continue.
6. Industry catered for technical 'hands-on' students by offering jobs and apprenticeships at 15 years old. (Whyalla was building ships and manufacturing steel.)
7. The state school technical colleges in Adelaide were valued, leaving the high school able to provide an academic program for all of its students.

2
The hidden curriculum
What schools are really about

B-A-N-G! It is night time when glass shards splatter around the classroom. The ginger beer explodes. Another student experiment fails. The next day the rest of the brew is carefully placed under Perspex.

Hands-on learning is taking place; the students are learning to use yeast to make beverages such as ginger beer and wine. Why are they involved? A cartoon from the *Adelaide News* (below) told the story of a 1978 explosion in the Salisbury High School science laboratories. It is a story about *hidden curriculum* – a story that demonstrates that education is not so much about what is taught but what is caught.

At the cutting edge

I have already described how, as science senior master at Stuart High School in Whyalla, I wrote and taught a wine, beer and ginger beer making course in 1974. That early course was a strictly local effort, but this new 'Alcohol Education Program', involving eight Adelaide high schools and a Catholic secondary college, attracted the attention of everyone from the Assistant Director of the Education Department to the Adelaide newspapers.

Back in 1974 I naïvely thought promotions and appointments were decided by application to an often independent panel, and they were. But I had no idea how subtle the process could be. The Director General of the Education Department, Mr Alby Jones, knew me as president of the Whyalla Teachers Association, as well as the chair of the Whyalla Education Centre Committee. One day I received a letter from Mr Jones stating that he was my referee for the position as director of the Salisbury Education Centre but that he had not yet received my application! We had purchased our own house in Whyalla and made friends locally, but still I was encouraged to apply.

I did, and upon winning the position moved to Salisbury in northern Adelaide.

All involved in the Salisbury Education Centre were at the cutting edge of educational practice and innovation. Historically teachers had been regarded as tradespeople carrying out instructions; the Centre aimed to give them freedom to become genuine professionals. Included was the freedom to develop their programs and curricula. We developed courses for junior school science, mathematics, English literature, geography and art, and later, in 1982, the first computing courses for school students.

One area that still concerned me was teenage attitudes to alcohol. In the 1970s, just like today, student drinking and driving was a nightmare for parents and school leaders. Alcohol-affected car crashes were followed by the police knock on the door, and all parents knew it could be their child. Innocent people were killed. Some victims survived but were forever maimed.

We all know that young people from 12 to 20 are inherent risk-takers. Teenagers don't even know they take risks. Alcohol is often involved, but alcohol disconnects circuits at the front of the brain, the part that enables us to make judgments and decisions like "Is this a good thing? Is it right? Have I had enough drink?" If the prefrontal lobe is shut down by previous drinks, then the question "Have I had enough to drink?" can no longer be processed, allowing the drinker to drink even more.

How could schools respond to this challenge? The stakes, then as now, were high.

The Salisbury Education Centre was not under the direct authority of the Education Department. It was federally funded, and the federal government's innovations grant was enough to undertake a pilot study for an alcohol education program in schools. A teachers' group was set up in the Centre to develop the course. But the press heard about it and a reporter for the now defunct Adelaide newspaper *The News*, David Lewis, wrote in an article: "South Australian school students could be making wine, beer and ginger beer in the classroom if Mr Hewitson's idea ferments."[2]

The Assistant Director of Schools Curriculum in the Education Department, Jim Giles, was a strong supporter of the professional freedom operating at the Centre, but he had to react officially and firmly to the idea of making wine in classrooms. In the *News* the following day he wrote:

> **Corker Corked**
>
> The article entitled "The Corker Project" was entertaining but misleading …
>
> Mr Hewitson, Director of the Salisbury Education Centre, has developed an interesting course on Alcohol, but it is one we have a few doubts about. We are aware parents may share those doubts if the course was introduced into their school …

> Mr Hewitson has asked for approval to discuss his course with a number of teachers and schools. Before agreeing we shall want to be satisfied in some matters, and for this purpose Principal Education Officers in Secondary Science had discussions with Mr Hewitson.
>
> Perhaps the real place for the course, which in many respects is a fascinating one, is in the further education classes. In any event, its introduction to a school would also be subject to the decision of the school community.

Clearly, the Education Department wished to stop the use of the course in schools and relegate it to adult education classes. It had been gently but effectively banned.

The teachers' group behind the course was disappointed but challenged by the likely departmental refusal. Could we still gain approval? The most likely opponent of such a course would be the temperance union, and to any sensible person, a visit to the Temperance Alliance of South Australia might have seemed pointless. But we had nothing to lose. At least they shared my concerns about alcohol abuse. I also had a hidden asset: a strong teetotaller mother-in-law.

The Temperance Union comes to the party

My wife Rosslyn came from a very culturally different part of Adelaide to myself. I first met her briefly at a 21st birthday party and later tracked her down where she worked as a handicraft instructor with the Red Cross. After a few dates, I accepted the invitation to be part of her family's Sunday night tea. This involved attending their evening church service. There, in the inner western suburb of Allenby Gardens, I found a community quite different from the one in which I grew up in the eastern and south-eastern suburbs. It was like a foreign land and I was a stranger. They spoke differently, with a strong, distinctive Australian accent. And there was no alcohol.

Rosslyn and her family shared with me their values, arguments and perceptions of the world. Knowledge of this world became extremely important when I wrote the initial alcohol education course in Whyalla – I had written it, as it were, with my mother-in-law on my shoulder. The content had been discussed on our visits to Adelaide and I made sure she approved the arguments for abstinence. Moderate drinking and abstinence were both portrayed in the course as choices to be respected. The course also involved the opportunity for students to make non-alcoholic drinks such as ginger beer.

Given the initial opposition of the Education Department, I thought the support of the Temperance Alliance might prove to be the tipping point for them to reconsider and approve a trial. I visited the Alliance's Hutt Street premises. I had noted in the literature that if children in teetotaller families did drink, they often became problem drinkers. I suspected the Alliance had many personal stories of family alcoholism. Children from families with an alcoholic parent often became abusers themselves, or were passionate teetotallers. After a week's consideration, the Alliance gave their support in writing.

The Education Department agreed to reconsider, and eventually the authorities gave approval for a trial subject to the establishment of a review committee and a formal evaluation of the program. St Paul's Catholic College and eight government schools agreed to be involved.

For students, the proposed course was about excellent wine and beer making. The lessons about responsible drinking or abstinence were hidden, not overt. The information was included almost casually and enabled students, without preaching, to add two and two together and work out their own future.

Would the course work or make it worse?

From a pre-study of 4000 students we learned that, by Year 10 in 1976, one in eight students were consuming over 20 alcoholic drinks each weekend. We had to ask: would this course make the problem worse?

Until 1977, the history of other drug and alcohol education programs had not been promising. A few were ineffectual and most increased abuse.[3] A typical summary of the Continental, English and North American experiences was: "The general conclusion seems to be that drug education, as such and independently of method, has no effect or only minor positive effects at best, or has mixed or negative effects at worst."[4] In plain English, all failed.

Teaching about alcohol and drugs encouraged experimentation. Our children see adults drinking and enjoying alcohol. A negative program says, "You shall not drink until you are an adult", but children can see this as a direct challenge. Unrealistically we expect them to have adult wisdom and tell them they are not able to drink until they are adults. Yet teenagers need to see themselves as adults, so they take up the challenge to drink—sometimes in secret and without protection.

Seven months later, the story hit both the daily papers again and the front page of the local paper.

> **Alcohol Study for Schools**[5]
>
> Nearly 4000 children from seven northern suburban high schools will in the next few days begin studying the history of chemistry and other properties of alcohol. They will also learn how to make alcohol and, with parental approval, many will produce wine in their classrooms. A Roman Catholic Secondary School, St Paul's College, Gilles Plains, will also participate".
>
> It is to be classroom learning about how the brain is affected by continued heavy drinking, about sclerosis of the liver and about the financial costs to the community and the individual health costs. It is also about the health benefits of a little wine, meaning no more than two to three drinks in any day.
>
> It was also an affirmation of those who decided not to drink, that their decision required respect and acceptance.

Stewart Cockburn, a respected senior journalist, captured the course's approach when he described the original 1974 course in a full page article in *The Advertiser* before the new program started:[6]

The truth of alcohol

Michael Hewitson has taken advantage of his students' natural interest in alcohol to produce a science course with a new focus. Now the program is to be tested and sent to several metropolitan schools.

It all began when Michael Hewitson was Senior Science Master at Stuart High School, Whyalla in 1974. Three of his fellow teachers told him how in the course of normal science lessons they demonstrated fermentation processes of yeast which produced alcohol and other poisons.

But they found their students far from ignorant and another child with a father who was a home brew expert enthused, "I had 25 drinks of what he made and got sloshed". Incidents like this set Mr Hewitson, who also home brews some of his own alcoholic drinks, thinking deeply.

He reflected on the ingrained social pressures which lead to the abuse of alcohol; on the poor production controls which can turn ordinary alcohol to poison; on the desperate ignorance amongst most people about the real properties of alcohol.

With alcohol as a focus he wrote about the mathematics of equations, about the physics of specific gravity and about the biochemical pathways and assays. Then he reached over into aspects of botany, microbiology, cellular chemistry, and even farm economics. Very little new material was added to the curriculum but the approach and detail were very new. The students learned some practical social science. They were introduced into the basic functions of physiology, the brain, previously ignored.

Student drinking was not to be part of the course. However, one of the schools in the trial planned a night for parents to taste the wine with their students present and also tasting. The wine was then to be sent home with the parents.

The outcome

The outcomes of this experiment were not to be known for some months. Before students even started the program, however, the review committee, which included the Temperance Alliance, set a date for a public meeting in the Salisbury CAE Auditorium to release the results to those involved and interested. If a mistake had been made and we had turned 3000 children into drunkards, the parents needed to know. I believed parents had the prime responsibility for the education of their children and deserved to be told face to face.

My worries about the outcomes were shared by the review committee. The meeting was set for 7.30 pm on Tuesday, 4 July 1978. A large number of teachers and parents waited to hear the news, good or bad. We promised the truth.

When the time came, the review committee was puzzled. Five of the six schools in the program reported a clearly successful decline in student drinking. The sixth did not. This school's results were the same as those for the two control schools in the program, where students were taught the traditional alcohol and drug "health" program.[7] We asked why and discovered that the school had only just started the course in the week when the second round of student surveys was undertaken. This made it, unexpectedly, another control school, strengthening confidence in the assessment methodology.[8]

For the first time in the worldwide educational literature known to the State Library of South Australia,[9] we were able to report an effective program.[10] It was effective both for children from teetotaller families and those with moderate drinking parents. Not only were the numbers of binge drinkers reduced in the schools doing the program; those in Year 8 who were non-drinkers maintained their non-drinking status. In the control schools most of these became drinkers.

The power of the hidden curriculum

The story of the alcohol education program underlines the power of the hidden curriculum in education.

The overt curriculum of the program was about the proper manufacture of high quality wine, ginger beer and other yeast products. In order to make superb wines and beer, the students learned about the risk of producing poisonous alcohols which might send them blind. But there was also a hidden curriculum. Not only were students learning how to make wine, they were also learning the science of how alcohol affects the brain.

In education it is not what is taught that is important – it is what is learnt. The hidden curriculum is what students learn to live by. What is *caught* is often very different from the content *taught*. It is hidden because it is neither written down nor stated.

In previous drug education programs students were taught formally about the dangers of alcohol and what not to do. Students observed adult behaviour in their community, and being adolescents, wished to be seen as adults. The hidden curriculum in these courses had young people drinking freely – they met the challenges of alcohol consumption head-on through experimentation and heavier drinking. However, in this new course, students were given adult knowledge about the functioning of the brain, about the nature and chemistry of alcohol, and about alcohol's effect on society. They were taught to make excellent wine, beer and ginger beer and also discussed the financial and social costs of heavy drinking. On the surface there was no instruction on how they ought to behave. This lack of preaching enabled them to make their own informed decisions.

The hidden curriculum the students 'caught' was that it is sensible to be either a moderate drinker or a teetotaller, and to respect others' choices.

The hidden curriculum changes

For many years state Education Department schools had been educating children from both rich and poor backgrounds, and educating them well. If the hidden curriculum is so important, what was the hidden curriculum in state schools in the 1950s and '60s?

A reader of an early draft of this book grew up in the state system and became a state school principal. He wrote his answer at this point in the story: "It was male dominated, military, authoritarian and punitive." This is descriptive, and I think these features were to some extent overt rather than hidden. Certainly the state primary schools of the 1950s had each class march out to assemblies with school drum and fife bands, banners and the Australian flag flying. This certainly imbued a respect for 'Queen and country' and for order, and this was part of the hidden curriculum of the day.

I doubt whether most schools know their hidden curriculum, but its importance cannot be overemphasised. Why is public state education not as effective today in our lower socio-economic communities as it was forty years ago? Has the hidden curriculum changed?

In chapter 1 we saw how, in the 1960s, learning and content were assessed. Teaching was important and was externally inspected. Students who did not pass formal testing repeated the year – an immediate and visible consequence for not learning. There were public examinations for all in Year 10 (Intermediate), Year 11 (Leaving) and Year 12 (Leaving Honours). These tended to focus on the overt curriculum content for each subject. The *hidden* curriculum was that a student needed to learn and master a body of knowledge, and needed to work with teachers and classmates in a team to achieve this. With the growth of new educational approaches in the 1970s, however, this hidden curriculum changed significantly.

Another change to the hidden curriculum was in the spiritual life of the school. Rosslyn attended Allenby Gardens Primary School. This state school had prayers, Bible readings and hymns at its weekly assemblies. State schools of the 1950s and '60s were able to reflect the foundation of Australia: the Judaeo-Christian ethic. Religious instruction by the churches for members of their own communities in the state school was part of the scene. Children were divided into the Catholics, Anglicans, Non-conformists and a small group of others.

In 1875, when the South Australian Education Act for 'free, compulsory and secular' state schools was put in place, the Oxford Dictionary defined secular as 'non-denominational'. In the early years of the Education Department, reading of the Bible was specifically provided. The *Education Gazette* regularly published words and music to such hymns as "Sanctus", "Holy Night" and "The First Noel". Recently Ros and I went to lunch at the home of two Norwood High School 'old scholars'. We were surprised to have grace said and were told it was the first verse of the Norwood High school song:

> Father, hear the prayer we offer:
> Nor for ease that prayer shall be,
> But for strength that we may ever
> Live our lives courageously.

By 1968, however, the meaning of the word 'secular' was changing.[11] The now-dominant view that state education should be free of any religion was beginning to be reported in newspapers. Stories described how a minority of parents in one school caused Christmas carol services to be banned. Today South Australian state schools would not have Christian Easter and Christmas programs as part of their school's celebrations. Again, an aspect of the hidden, non-formal curriculum of state schools has changed.

Why not a Christian state school?

As director of the Salisbury Education Centre I sought to explore the hidden curriculum. We held public meetings on controversial topics and made radio programs from these. These were aired on a station at the Education Centre called 5PBA.

One of the topics was "Why not a Christian state school?"

Immediately there was strong public interest. About 200 attended a meeting and nominated members for a steering committee. The Para Christian Community Schools Association was formed and went on to found a new school. Its aim was to educate children in a way that was coherent with their parents' Christian faith. The founding committee believed this kind of education should be available for all, regardless of economic status or denominational affiliation: "We are committed to a low cost inter-denominational approach while holding as a longer term aim the desire to see the State accept responsibility for the provision of a Christian-based education, to all who desire it."

The Salisbury Education Centre became the school's office and the Para Christian Community School became one of the Centre's educational associations. As director of the Centre, I was able to arrange for a parcel of land from the surrounding College of Advanced Education. The CAE would then be co-located, not only with a state school (Salisbury East High School), but also with a low-fee interdenominational Christian school which was seeking in the long term to be part of the state system. Using this greater vision, the CAE board agreed on very favourable terms to provide sufficient acreage for the school to start. Today the school is called Tyndale College.

Why was there this drive from so many parents to face the arduous challenge of establishing a new school? There were many factors, but among them was the realisation that something very important had shifted in state education. The hidden curriculum in state schools had changed. Before it had been about 'God and country'; now it was about 'me' (the individual).

Many years later this transformation was underlined to me by two Australian state school teachers who had returned home after teaching in Japan for a year. "Do you know we are homesick for Japan?" they said. With nearly 40 years' teaching experience each, they commented how Australians made the slick statement when returning from overseas, "Well, Australia is the best place to live". "But Australians haven't seen the other side," my friends said. "In Japan, the children at school are happy. Ours are solemn. In Japan, school is about 'us'. In Australia, school is about 'me'."

The hidden curriculum of a school is an important key to motivating students and teachers whilst encouraging the support of parents. We may not know what it is, but it affects how we feel about our school. Although the hidden curriculum of South Australian public schools had changed from 'God and country' to 'me', this was not the only change.

Lessons learnt

1. The hidden curriculum of a school is at least as important as the overt stated curriculum.
2. Most schools will not know their hidden curriculum.
3. The hidden curriculum has the power to change lives.
4. State schools with an implicit Christian foundation and practice no longer exist.

3
Entering tiger country
Allowing a choice for parents

Reading your own primary school reports can be revealing. I should have read mine more carefully. My Grade 7 report stated, "Michael seems to instinctively swim against the tide". Stupidly, I thought this was a badge of honour. But this trait can be a great disadvantage when applying for rapid promotion in a tenured and seniority-based public service, as I found out.

The process started so politely, with an application in 1979 to become eligible to be appointed as a secondary school principal. In 1975 the Education Department had already confirmed my appointment as director of the Salisbury Education Centre to be a substantive permanent primary principal position, and in the 1970s this guaranteed a life-time salary at principal level. So my application was not about the money. I applied because school principals are the key to good schools, and I believed that schools should and could be better.

The department had recruited and promoted rapidly in the late '60s to meet growing student numbers as well as generational retirement. Back then promotion was by a system of eligibility and seniority. Even non-performing leaders at all levels were set for the next 35 years. This rapid scramble for promotion by many young teachers ended in the '70s, and the vitality and drive for excellence was at risk of sclerotic blockage. However, by 1979 promotion by merit was gaining a toehold. With a 'straight-A' assessment, applicants could jump the promotion waiting list by two years.

A panel to assess my application was appointed, with a past school inspector as the chair. One of the panel's three members was supposed to be my principal, but as CEO of the Salisbury Education Centre, I was the principal. So I sent in a list of secondary principals I had worked with in developing curricula and other programs for their schools. These suggestions were overlooked. Instead, two principals who had no working relationship with me were appointed.

The panel arrived on the day of the assessment with no written information about me, despite the fact that the Education Department had been given extensive supporting documentation.

Promotion to positions in secure businesses relies on telling interviewers what they want to hear. With the wisdom of age and hindsight, I now understand the stupidity of discussing in the interview all the problems of the Education Department and how to solve them. "Shouldn't the Education Department run schools that parents wish to choose for their own children?" I asked. Even the desirability of providing Christian schools within the Education Department was raised. My Grade 7 teacher would have recognised this as swimming against the tide.

The two unknown secondary school principals were probably Education Department true believers. They failed me. I was deemed ineligible for promotion because of a "lack of current knowledge and experience in the secondary schools' curriculum".

For them this should have been a safe bureaucratic checkmate. After all, I was not in a school. However, in the Salisbury Education Centre we were developing and publishing teaching materials for schools in technology, English, maths, art and history. Even the alcohol education course was by then in use across 450 high schools throughout Australia and had been commercially published by Rigby. Yet due to my "lack of experience in secondary schools' curriculum", I failed. There was no appeal process.

I was told that I would be eligible to apply again in two years. Against the rules, I appealed immediately. The reasoning the panel had given was demonstrably wrong. The curriculum was my strongest point. So that a precedent regarding appeals would not be set, a new bureaucratic process was designed to consider the matter. The department set up a new panel of just two: a Regional Director of Education from another region and the original chair. Through this process I gained eligibility with a straight-A review that was backdated by 12 months, giving an immediate three years of seniority. This was important because promotion was not by merit but by how many years you had been on the list of those eligible.

A system that needed changing

By this time I had a strong drive to seek change in the state education system.

Schooling in the 19th century had been designed to create a literate and numerate workforce. It then developed into training young people to be effective in the workplace. By the 1980s the aims had clearly become training children for life. However, values are caught, not taught. Children learn honesty, consideration of others and a sense of responsibility by example. What are the values worth living by? What is important? What is my role in society? What is the purpose and meaning of life? This was the hidden curriculum.

I was convinced that state schooling had developed a new hidden curriculum that was about 'me' in a godless universe. Secularism had become non-Christian, and new 'dreamtime stories' were to be told, even if they were nihilistic and existentialist. All truth in this philosophy is relative to the individual, and any meaning and purpose in the universe is an individual construct. Alternatives to this for parents seeking something else were non-existent in the state system and were solely the province of private schooling.

Just a generation earlier, the schooling Christian parents would choose for their own children was available in state schools. But 'secular' now meant a non-Christian, godless education. The individual child and their personal material success was the new god of the state system. I wanted all families to have a genuine choice of school. I believed that parents have the prime responsibility to educate their children. For many parents the Education Department did not offer a suitable choice, and at the time affordable alternatives were unavailable.

If I had wanted, as an 'educator', to design a school to de-Christianise Australian society in the 1980s, I do not think I could have invented a better structure than the state school system. It claimed to provide an education for all, yet the Bible was unacceptable, prayers at assemblies were unacceptable, and Christian stories and traditions were unacceptable. Things to do with God were an optional tack-on for those who wanted them outside the school environment.

State schools in South Australia introduced a religious education program that treated the Christianity on the same level as tribal religions, Buddhism, Islam etc. Indeed, the Christian story may not even have been taught. This was an important method of de-Christianising Australian society. It reduced Christianity to just another choice in the marketplace of religions. It gave no recognition to, or understanding of, the Judaeo-Christian foundations of Australian society.

Our own children were soon to start school, and there were no state schools that we would choose. In our local community the only Christian choice for schooling was the local Catholic school. Sixty per cent of its enrolment was Anglican. We understood that the school preferentially enrolled children from Catholic families, and with the population in the area growing, it would fill up and our grandchildren (if Anglican) would have no access. Nonetheless, given the options available, we gratefully enrolled Joanne, and subsequently Christopher, in St Catherine's Catholic Primary School in Stirling.

For Rosslyn our choice was ironic. As children growing up in Allenby Gardens, she and her friends would blow the 'bugs' off their fish-and-chips as they passed the Catholic school. But times had changed. The state school overtly founded on the Judaeo-Christian ethic and practice was no more.

Today Australians generally hold all things religious as akin to superstition and stupidity. But what were the 'dreamtime stories' we wanted for our children? Ros and I wanted them to know of a loving God who suffers with humanity. We wanted them to celebrate the birth of a baby at Christmas, rather than a Santa Claus who judged whether you were naughty or nice. In their education, we also wanted our children to grow up with a sense of the eternal, and a sense that their lives were a gift from God. We hoped our children would sense that life was not just for selfish ends, but was about showing God's love to all. We wanted a school that was about God and the greater sense, rather than just the individual. In my tradition, these were essential foundations for the abolition of slavery, for the growth of the democratic tradition and the rise of shared responsibility for all, unconditionally.

What my wife and I wanted was a Christian school, open to all, that supported families to educate their children.

Education by lowest common denominator

In 1982 I got another first-hand insight into the difficulties facing the state system. After seven years as director of Salisbury Education Centre, the Education Department allowed me to re-establish my connection within a school. I joined the staff at Daws Road High School.

No one was really in control there. The strongest power base was 'majority rule by teachers', and the whole staffroom was vying with the principal. The school council looked good on paper but was merely advisory. The teachers had competing interests and visions for the school. The school's educational content, philosophy and direction flip-flopped according to staffroom politics. The latest policy depended on which staff turned up to the meeting. The principal was a good man and an enthusiastic educationalist, and he had the support of the parent body; but the structure of the system meant he had influence rather than authority.

When you choose a school for your own children, education and schooling take on a different colour. Many Education Department teachers and people in the hierarchy worked happily in the state system for other people's children, but in the 1980s they were overwhelmingly sending their own children to private schools. Ros and I also wished to have our children in a school where the school's teachers and parents worked together with a shared philosophy of life. In that atmosphere results were outstanding. However, when school communities are changing their direction every six months, when the leadership is not clear, when the parents don't agree, then education by the lowest common denominator evolves.

Every teacher at Linden Junior Park Primary, where Ros worked, had their own children bar one in independent secondary schools. Most of the staff at Daws Road High did as well. The Education Department was no longer king. The tide had turned.

Tiger country

To enable the department to establish Christian state schools, three approaches seemed possible. My experience with the Principal Assessment Panel should have indicated the huge challenge and personal risk in trying to realise this change. However, all three options seemed worth trying.

1. Using the federal government's program "Choice and Diversity" to persuade the state government to institute change.
2. Establish local grassroots movements to open Christian state schools with the tacit support of the Education Department.
3. Involve the Anglican Church to seek this change in partnership with other denominations.

These were radical ideas.

As director of the Salisbury Education Centre, I had written a paper presenting the reasons for establishing some Christian state schools.[12]

The arguments, simply expressed, were:

1. Parents were the prime educators of children and needed a choice in schooling based on a school's philosophical foundations. This was needed because schooling had widened its mission from teaching the three Rs to 'training for life'.
2. State schools were beginning to lose enrolments and would become residual schools for the poor if parental needs were not met.
3. When parents, teachers and school worked together, a better result for children was achieved. All schools would be improved if parents, the teachers at a school and the school philosophy were in agreement.
4. State education was already committed to choice and the SA Education Department had even suggested that "a variety of schools is desirable".[13] The department also supported the belief that interaction between the teacher and the student was the most important single factor for children learning.
5. The federal government was promoting "Choice and diversity".[14]

This paper received surprisingly strong encouragement from the Director General of Education, Mr John Steinle, who wrote to me, "I am quite sure that what you are saying is a matter of immense significance to this country."[15] However, Mr Steinle also warned in a private meeting that the notion of a Christian school within the state system could lead to 'tiger country'. It could turn individual state schools into battlegrounds between competing religious interests.

Hills Christian Community School

In 1980, inter-church Lenten studies were held across our home suburb of Stirling. The study focused on how Christians changed the world. Ros and I hosted an interdenominational study group in our home. I shared the work I was doing at Salisbury with them and as a result an Adelaide Hills steering committee to work for such a school was formed.

As a multi-denominational group we were entering 'tiger country'.

The group worked hard through 1980 and registered the name "Hills Christian Community School". We called a public meeting for 1 December 1980. We knew we needed to state aims and guiding principles clearly, so we set ourselves the following questions:

- *What is 'Christian'?* Our answer: "the term 'Christian' implies a belief in God, a Supreme Being and Creator, together with an acceptance of the life and teachings of Jesus Christ as a guide to daily living".[16] This did not mean we wanted a literal, 'creation science' interpretation of the Bible. We just wanted our children to be taught that there is more to life than themselves, and we wanted them to understand the life and teachings of Jesus Christ.

- *Why a 'state school'?* An independent Christian school necessarily would have to charge tuition fees and therefore would restrict enrolments to those children whose parents could afford to pay. State schools, in contrast, were not elitist in this way. All children were accepted and schooling was basically free. The steering committee had a strong philosophical commitment to the concept of choice and diversity within the affordable state system of education.

- *Why a Christian school?* Schools were now claiming to train children for life. Christianity, we felt, should be part of life and not an optional tack-on. All state schools were seen as secular and provided Christian teaching only as part of their wider study of religious belief. A Christian school, on the other hand, would allow a Christian philosophy to permeate all aspects of school organisation and curriculum. Just as importantly, it would allow for a meaningful hidden curriculum. Secularism in state schooling was becoming existentialist: there was no intrinsic meaning in the universe and all philosophies were relative to the individual and therefore of equal merit. In contrast, our school would allow:

    1. Christian principles to influence all interpersonal

relationships: teacher/child, parent/teacher, child/child etc.
2. acts of worship and liturgy incorporated into the daily routine\
3. basic Christian teaching to be integrated as appropriate into all areas of the school curriculum
4. a specific Christian emphasis in the religious education curriculum
5. the various festivals of the Christian year to be celebrated.

- *Why a community school?* We wanted the school to be a focal point for the local community and hence to facilitate interaction between child, family, teachers, church and the wider community.

What else would characterise this school?
1. The school would be free of doctrinal and/or denominational emphases. It would stress the common elements of the Christian faith while accepting diversity of belief and interpretation. Instruction in particular denominational doctrines and practices would be the responsibility of families and churches.
2. As a state institution, the school would come under the discipline and curriculum responsibility of the Director General of Education in SA. The school program would be based on the curriculum guidelines of the SA Education Department.
3. The school would foster coherence between family life and the process of schooling, and so provide more effective training for life for each child.

The first committee was totally committed to the concept of public schools and public education. We believed that unless we provided a quality education for all children, we would all lose. We further believed it was in the interest of all that every child, including the most disadvantaged, receive an education with a good moral foundation and a good academic program. If the hidden curriculum of the school was right, then every child would learn to be a caring and loving individual ably participating in society as a whole.

There was extraordinary goodwill, with many private and some public backers. Our own children were attending St Catherine's Catholic School in Stirling and we received strong support from this community. By the end of 1980, we had commitments from 41 families to enrol 91 children.

The Education Department was faced with a campaign by a group of 30-year-old parents aiming to change the whole structure of state schooling. We produced papers and gained sympathetic audiences, including with the then Shadow Minister of Education in the Labor state opposition, Lynn Arnold.

Education Department officers suggested that we stack Crafers Primary School and stage a take-over from within. The principal was a Christian, and parents could send children to other nearby state schools if they did not like the change. We thought this approach would be divisive and unfair on those families who wanted a specifically non-Christian, secular education for their children. Moreover, the change could not be easily replicated across the state – it would only work in schools with vacancies due to declining enrolments, a sympathetic principal, and staff who were willing supporters of a Christian state education. The staff at Crafers Primary had not been appointed to a school with a Christian ethos.

Newsletters to parents throughout 1981 named many possible sites for the school in Stirling, Aldgate and Crafers. We always seemed to be on the edge of success. However, our efforts culminated in the Education Department, through its Director of Finance, indicating that all department properties were off limits. We clearly had some major opponents. Getting the department to accept responsibility for opening the school was not going to happen.

Despite his earlier encouragement, it was left to the Director General of Education, Mr Steinle, to announce why we were not going to be supported, for three reasons:

- The difficulty of establishing what was meant by 'Christian' because of denominational differences.
- Whether it was possible to run such a school and ensure non-Christian children were not discriminated against.
- The problems of 'testing' staff to ensure they were Christians.

To achieve our objective, then, we needed to show that Christians from different denominations could work together, could accept non-Christian children without discrimination, and could choose staff without using spurious testing criteria.

Despite all our hard work, it seemed progress was going to take many years, if it happened at all. I suggested that we consider going down the Para Christian Community Schools Association track, keeping as an option the opening of our own independent school using state government regulations and guidelines. It would be a model state school without actually *being* a state school. By December 1981 we were attempting to open the Hills Christian Community School as an independent model state school in a Uniting Church property. The committee lost some of its members who did not wish to proceed with an independent school.

We sent in the application for registration to open with 49 students in Reception to Year 5 for 1982 and 96 students from Reception to Year 6 in 1983. We held a public meeting and gained new enrolments, and the Uniting Church congregation voted to support us. Later, however, they decided not to proceed with the school because of the divisiveness it caused within their church.

The problem seemed insurmountable, but we did have quiet friends. As the school was now to be an independent undertaking, the Education Department began to support us, and during 1982 a school site at Verdun was suggested. It had originally been the old Verdun Primary School and then became the camp site for a state secondary school, but it had declining use. The politics within the department in allowing us access would be intriguing. However, as the site was not in the Stirling catchment area, some enrolments for a Stirling site were withdrawn. We would need a school bus to travel out to the nearby countryside.

The goodwill of those within the Education Department enabled our committee to gain a lease of the property for the purposes of establishing the Hills Christian Community School. We aimed for 70 students. We opened in 1983 with 66 in attendance, offering education from Reception to Year 7.

Taming the tigers

John Steinle had indicated that we would have difficulty with curriculum, staffing and discrimination against non-Christians. We didn't. Our planning and solutions were upfront and agreed to. Perhaps the Director General had done us a favour by making our application for a Christian state school so difficult. At the meeting on Monday 16 August 1982, the school council already had clear answers for parents considering the school. Parents who had filled out the enrolment form were to be invited to an interview where the following points were to be made:

1. It would be a Christian school.
2. It would not teach Christianity in the formal curriculum but through the life of the school and teachers.
3. Denominational teaching and formal Christian education were the responsibility of the family and their church.
4. Christianity would be integrated across the curriculum as a natural part of training for life. Prayer and worship were part of a natural Christianity – daily formal worship was not anticipated.

The Verdun site was neglected and unloved. I twitch as I remember the confidence with which we did up this wreck. What faith! What cheek! A small group of us walked all over the flaking roofs. We poured red paint from buckets and caught it with our corrugated rollers. A new playground was built alongside the main road, not just because it was a shady place for children to play but also because it was very good advertising. It cost $1800 and used our very precious financial resources.

We advertised for students and teachers, with two teachers already and myself as honorary principal. (My wife Rosslyn was the only one of these two to follow through.) The school was to open in four months and so we made new appointments to join the staff: Paul Martin (Baptist), David Woodroofe (Uniting Church) and Prue Goodes, a new teaching graduate (Anglican).

We invited Lynn Arnold, by now Minister of Education, to come to a school gathering of about 200 people. He stated that "the concept of a Christian state school was a serious issue needing full public debate".

We did gain some sense of the 'tiger' problem. Even before the school opened, the Anglicans at barbecues and picnics would set out their rugs with fine wines. Other families were non-drinkers. To our minds the teetotallers were somewhat Puritan while some of us must have seemed rather too cavalier to them. Our cultural traditions were clearly at odds. Yet we kept our sense of humour and managed to work together.

There was one key issue which, although covered in the constitution, we failed to deal with explicitly: who runs the school? The parents were always going to be the major voice in running the school. There were pressures from many of them to make the school parent-controlled on a day-to-day basis. I, and others, wished the school to be run by a professionally qualified principal, appointed by and answerable to a school council with parents in the majority. The principal was to have sole responsibility to recommend to the council the appointment of staff, to develop a curriculum to be approved by the council, and to look after the day-to-day running of the school. It was through the council that parents had an oversight and say in their school.

Director General John Steinle had been correct in predicting tensions, but we worked these through. His prediction of tension about the school's Christian curriculum was not a problem at Verdun. Parents understood and supported the statements in our prospectus. They were very happy that their children were going to receive a typical state school curriculum but with the Christian life of teachers and families infusing the teaching. Christian stories were to be told. Easter was about the death and resurrection of Jesus, not the Easter bunny – but there was still chocolate!

As honorary principal for the first year, my regular visits to the school for staff meetings were enjoyable and exciting. Ash Wednesday 1982 was memorable, with howling north winds and many out-of-control bushfires across the hills. Being in the path of the fire with candle-like pine trees waiting to explode, the school should have burnt down. It didn't, and the students were safe.

It was now a school which should be able to attract a Christian primary specialist principal. We considered applicants who were known and who would be acceptable as principals to the Education Department. Eventually we appointed Pat Derham, principal of one of the prestigious state primary schools, Highgate Junior Primary School. Pat was willing to share her authority with parents and the council and took up her position in 1984.

The third prong – the Anglican Church

Clearly the two schools at Salisbury and Verdun and a philosophical paper were not going to change the tide to allow for a Christian state school. To achieve further progress I thought I needed to persuade the Anglican Church to be involved.

At the same time as we were establishing Verdun, I was working in parallel to challenge the Anglican Church in South Australia to provide an education for the children of families that desired a Christian education. Being elected by our Stirling parish to the state-wide synod of the church as a lay representative was very helpful. Speaking to the hundreds at synod, I claimed that the education Anglican parents wanted for their own children was not available. I stated, "The clergy present have scholarships for their children at the high-fee Anglican colleges and are catered for. But how can the average family with three children afford this choice?" I told the Verdun story, complete with budgets, constitution and results. I asked: "Why don't we do our homework and investigate what our parents need in educating their children?"

Synod voted to support the establishment of a committee to prepare a report on Anglican needs in education. Dr A.J. Shinkfield, principal of St Peter's College, a former inspector and principal of state schools, was appointed as chair. Initially he believed that the needs of Anglican parents were catered for within the existing range of schools, including state schools for those who could not afford existing Christian schools. This was checkmate. The committee agreed to test this proposition by carrying out a full study of 1000 Anglican children attending church over two Sundays. We surveyed a section of parishes across a slice north of Adelaide, from the Port to the Hills. We added a large evangelical city church into the mix (Holy Trinity Adelaide) as well as one of the wealthiest congregations (St Michael's Mitcham).

The results were deafening. The influential laity could pay high fees and so were happy with the existing choices. But 99% of respondents wanted a Christian school for their own children and most could not afford the high fees. Only one respondent was happy with the existing state school offering. For the Anglican Church the report changed everything.

The report was released to the Education Department for comment. The statement in the report that state schools were a most effective tool for the de-Christianisation of society upset a number of senior people in the department. However, with the support of the Catholic Church, an enquiry was set up by the Minister of Education, with the support of the Education Department, and was announced on the front page of the *Advertiser*. What could go wrong? The change and diversification of state schools seemed imminent.

However, despite the proposal having cabinet support,[17] it was rolled by the Labor caucus. The Hills Christian Community School was on its own. By the end of 1984 a state school with a Christian ethos was off the agenda. Indeed, the chance to create a genuine philosophical diversity in public state education was lost.

The real tiger country proved not to be denominational or Christian differences, but rather who controls the hidden curriculum for other peoples' children.

Lessons learnt

1. Christian differences were not a problem but the issue of power and control can be.
2. When state schools are a monopoly business, they do not need to provide the schools that parents wish to choose.
3. The authority, responsibility and accountability of the principal is a key issue for a new school community to agree on in advance.
4. State schooling had developed a new hidden curriculum that was about 'me' in a godless universe. Alternative state schools for parents seeking something else were not allowed and were solely the province of private schooling.
5. Diversity in state schooling based on philosophical and religious differences was rejected and became the responsibility of private schooling.

4
Impossible tales
Learning what parents want

I believe the famous Russian writer Leo Tolstoy was right when he wrote that the man in the most dangerous position on earth is the man who believes in nothing, because then he will believe anything. My experiences with the Para Christian Community School in Salisbury and the Hills Christian Community School in Verdun convinced me that parents did not want a value-free education for their children. They wanted an education with discipline, values and a supportive peer group, and they accepted the Christian tradition.

This conviction was born out when I reluctantly became involved in a Christian schooling venture that I was convinced was doomed to fail.

An Old Testament story has Jonah eaten by a whale.[18] He spends three days in its belly and is then coughed up on a beach to take up an unwanted challenge. The following story describes a similar experience. Let's start at the beginning …

An easy choice – or was it?
It was 1984 and the choice should have been obvious. We were meeting as an Anglican Schools Commission to establish a new group of low-fee Anglican schools. We were about to vote to select the foundational flagship school. There were two contenders. One was full of promise; the other was barely open and, in fact, dying.

These schools were to follow a new vision. They were "to be open to all, and hence low fee". They were "to be Christian in the liberal educational tradition". They were to pursue academic excellence, led by a headmaster on five-year contracts accountable to a school board. The largest single group on the governing board of these schools was to be parental and the majority (though not all) were to be Anglican.[19]

One site in contention for flagship school was Pedare, to be built on the city's north-eastern outskirts in the new Tea Tree Gully suburb of Golden Grove. It was shaping up well. I had been a member of its founding committee for several years. With the Verdun school experience as the working model, Pedare's finances, educational philosophy and school uniform were soundly developed. The working party had members from two strong Anglican and Uniting parishes, and land for the school in the new middle-class 'prestige' Delfin development had been arranged.

We proposed co-locating three secondary schools, a state school, a Catholic college and Pedare (Uniting and Anglican), all of which would share some common resources. The opportunity to establish a new, high quality independent Christian school was obvious. The plan to open in 1986 was going well. This site, with the state and Catholic systems sharing facilities and students mixing with each other, was the closest achievable school to our original vision of state Christian schools.

The alternative to Pedare was a school called Trinity College in Gawler, further north. Trinity had just opened as a Reception to Year 7 primary school with 24 students in the church hall of St George's Anglican Church, Gawler. Its steering group had sought my help the year before (1983) and I had addressed a well-attended public meeting in the Gawler High School Library. They wanted me to tell the story of Verdun: "how to start a new school and how to fund it". I was asked to describe the Anglican Schools Commission's vision for new schools and how, as part of the vision, we were still hoping to see the establishment of Christian schools as part of the state Education Department.

At this stage, to maintain political pressure towards that goal, the commission was already doing contingency planning for new schools. In building communities to establish Christian state schools, we needed to ensure that parents had a school for their children regardless of the Education Department's actions. In 1983 Trinity was a year too early, and at the public meeting at Gawler High School I recommended they hold fire for 12 months because our first option was to achieve Christian state schools. I suspected this vision was not shared by the rector, Father John Kinsman, and people of St George's. Many had lost confidence in state schools.

Trinity's financial problems were well known to the commission. It was not receiving any government funding. Without reference to the Anglican Schools Commission, the committee had applied for government funding, but the application forms had been messed up. Wanting to show the government how strong they were, parishioners who were registered teachers and were voluntarily helping with the school were listed as staff members. Under 1983 federal government rules, however, this meant their school of just 24 students was highly resourced and therefore ineligible for funding. With government funding 85% of its budgeted income, the failure to secure that money meant that debts for 1984 would have to be paid out of hoped-for growth in enrolments. The cost was anyone's guess.

For the commission to support Trinity would be to assume that a new application for government funding in 1985 would be successful.

Just before Christmas 1983 I attended a committee meeting at the St George's rectory as final preparations were being made to open the school. As I was told the story of how the teachers were chosen, I had a sinking feeling. Tina and Peter Hatchett had apparently knocked on the door of the Gawler rectory to offer their services. They were members of the Anglican parish in Salisbury and Father John believed their unsolicited visit was a response to prayer. They were newly trained secondary school teachers, Tina in biology/science and Peter in physical education. With no primary school teaching experience, Tina was given the post of head teacher. Neither was a fully registered teacher.

At the meeting, Father John informed me that the school was to be an

Anglican parish school, with priority given to church-attending Anglicans. This and a number of other philosophical positions deviated greatly from our vision. When the rector left the meeting and silence descended, I queried whether the committee really wanted my help. "You are very clear about what you are after for a school, but I have a different vision," I said. "I can quietly leave, wishing you all the best for the future." Some committee members, however, informed me in very clear terms that they also had different positions and urged my continued involvement.

Trinity opened in 1984 in the parish hall with 24 children. During Term 1, the steering committee asked Ros and me to visit the school. We discovered an inadequate curriculum: the students in Years 5, 6 and 7 were being taught mathematics for Years 2, 3 and 4. The teachers were unaware that there were other units of study for Years 5–7. We were told parents went in and out of the classrooms to take over the teaching because the staff needed help. During one visit, Tina said to me, "Michael, we can't attract the educated and the people in Gawler to our school. You've got to get them in."

The school was a mixture of parent-controlled school and 18th-century English parish school under the control of the rector. In fact, the parish hall was the original church school building in Gawler (the first St George's Day School pre-dated the formation of the Education Department). Use of the hall was meant to be temporary – the vision presented the year before at the Gawler High School meeting was for a fairly traditional Reception to Year 12 school of around about 700 students, and we were told there was an option on land at the edge of town, on the corner of Alexander Avenue and Main North Road. But the school had already borrowed to fund an upgrade of the hall, the cost of which was to be the rent to the parish for 12 months' use, and this was a substantial liability. In addition, there was no common vision among parents. Some wanted a small, loving Christian school as an alternative to the state system. Others just wanted their children to receive a good quality education in Gawler and thought an independent school might have something to offer.

In short, the school was a disaster. It was going broke and the Gawler community at large was not interested. It was going to close. Its future hinged on the support of the Anglican Schools Commission, which, with just a few hundred dollars, was being asked to help. Trinity would then become our responsibility and the first school of the South Australian Anglican Schools Commission.

A reluctant response

The meeting to consider this choice – Pedare or Trinity – was chaired by the dynamic headmaster of St Peter's College, Dr A.J. (Tony) Shinkfield. With plans for two other schools already underway (including Pedare and another in the southern suburbs), I was opposed to the commission's taking on a school I thought was a dead duck. However, John Strange, the treasurer of Trinity, had been invited to be a member of the commission and he passionately presented Trinity's case. We voted: four votes in favour of taking on Trinity College and three (including mine) against.

Gawler was hardly virgin territory for non-state schools.[20] The Lutherans were taking over the original Gawler East Primary School site to open a primary school with good facilities. This would act as a feeder school to Faith Lutheran Secondary College opening in Tanunda. The Catholic Church had a primary school already running. But Trinity's proposed new site was out in the wheat fields, beyond the urban area – a region where the Catholic system had decided that opening a secondary school would be uneconomic because the need was so small. Added to this was the fact that the new Anglican parish school was failing and establishing a bad reputation in Gawler. The picture did not look rosy.

On the other hand, having met the people involved with Trinity, I knew they were committed and sincere supporters. They were parents who wished better for their children. Despite all their own misgivings, they were determined to support Trinity against the offerings of highly resourced Education Department schools. At the time I did not realise how poorly parents regarded the state school system in Gawler (drug problems at Gawler High School were yet to become public).

Following the vote, John Strange asked me to meet him for tea in a nearby restaurant. Over a bowl of pasta he asked, "Will you come and be the foundation headmaster of Trinity College?"

Previously I had no personal interest in the school and my immediate response was terror. However, I did agree to provide a copy of my CV "so that the school which we have just voted to support would at least be able to advertise for a school principal". I added, "You may find it helpful as a measure in assessing applications for the position."

A number of weeks later John arranged for the two of us to meet with the Tony Shinkfield over an early breakfast at St Peter's College. I was asked again, "Will you take on the role of foundation head of Trinity?" I had no peace to make an on-the-spot decision, even though from a Christian perspective I felt called to meet a need. I began to understand the truth of the impossible story of Jonah and the whale. You feel swallowed up even as you rationally reject the offer.

I told Ros about the offer and her response was surprisingly supportive. Against my inclination, the mealtime discussion with her and our four children was one of encouragement.

I indicated to Ros, "It's a lot further away than you think and we would have to move out there." She thought I would be able to travel from home, so we arranged a car trip out to Gawler with Ros in the driver's seat. She drove and drove, and our children started asking, "Are we were there yet?" Suddenly the truth dawned: if we were to take on this project we would have to move, leaving our house in the Adelaide Hills for a promised, but unbuilt, "log cabin in the prairie". The prairie was just continuous wheat stubble; the house was to be built by volunteers.

In the Christian world, this invitation to become headmaster of Trinity College is known as a calling. It was not one I wished to accept, but it was a call which left no peace until acceptance was given.

At that point the personal bargaining began. "Will Trinity be good enough for us to send our own children to?" We avoided making a final commitment by insisting we needed a school that was large enough to offer a quality education. "The school will need to be led by its headmaster, responsible to the board." In my opinion the headmaster could not be an employee of the rector. Tony nailed that one by negotiating a suitable five-year, renewable contract for the foundation principal. Some of the steering committee were expecting to make staff appointments, control student enrolment and be involved closely in the day-to-day running of the school, but Tony insisted the head be able to appoint staff, not just nominate them. The steering committee was also asked to adopt the Anglican Schools Commission's model constitution.

Finally, my conditional acceptance laid down the following: "For our family to run with the school next year, and for Trinity to be the school of excellence you hope for, we need to have two classes of Year 8 in 1985, and over 80 primary school students. We can then achieve a high quality primary education, not only for your children, but also for our own (Caroline would be in Reception–1, Angela in 2–4, Christopher and Joanne in 5–7). At Years 8–10, with 48 students divided into two groups for academic classes and three for practical subjects, we will be able to cater for children with different capacities and skills."

My knowledge of early childhood education had come from working with early childhood teachers and their curriculum. It was not based on actual hands-on teaching. I asked the steering committee to meet Rosslyn so she could be considered for appointment as the permanent head of Reception to Year 4. This was agreed to. To work as a husband and wife team, we decided who would have the say and when. If a matter was solely R–4, then it was to be totally delegated to Ros.

Following the adoption of the school's constitution during 1984, Geoff Gordon became the foundation chairman of the Trinity College school council, and preparations for opening in 1985 began to accelerate.

An impossible challenge

To achieve what we wanted to do, however, we had to overcome obstacles that many considered impossible. The 24 foundation students still at the school were way below the 130 needed for a good school. How were we to attract parents to a school they would have to build before their children could attend it?

Our only hope was to provide parents with a new vision – a vision that would be strong enough for them to take their children from established and financially secure schools. In the community's mind Trinity was failing. We were asking them to gamble with their children's lives and send them to this school. Indeed, the rector of Gawler, the effective chair of the steering committee, planned to send his own daughter to Trinity for Grade 7 only. In a year's time, like so many other children, Elizabeth would attend an established independent school elsewhere, in her case Woodlands Anglican Girls School. The rector's being so upfront about his plans was admirable, but the information was not encouraging for others. How was Trinity going to attract new enrolments when even the driving force on the founding committee was choosing elsewhere in advance?

To gain enrolments we needed to establish that the school could overcome socio-economic disadvantage. I asked the question, "Can the school beat the home as a spur for success?"[21]

Trinity was in a lower socio-economic region, covering the poorest part of Adelaide. In fact, the region was the poorest educational performer at Year 12 in South Australia. Most parents and teachers believed that a school's success or failure was largely determined by the socio-economic background of the parents. Hence the success or failure of students was basically predetermined. For us to gain enrolments from Reception to Year 12, parents would need to believe that their child would not be disadvantaged at Trinity. This belief also had to be instilled in and held by teachers.

To what degree is student success related to socio-economic background? Teachers in schools serving poorer areas will often cite this as the reason for low achievement, leading to even lower expectations and a downward spiral. It need not be true. Student background does predict 10% of the outcome, but the school and classroom 35%.[22] In other words, the school is three-and-a-half times more important than socio-economic background. I even wonder how much of the 10% weighting given for parental background is due to the self-fulfilling prejudice of both teachers and parents.

Ros and I shared our vision with prospective parents. We believed that a school in a region with poor academic achievement could break the mould. "Our own four children are enrolled until Year 12," we said. "This college must have academic excellence. We will use external measures of performance by age. You as parents will know, with honest reporting, the progress of your child. Students will be given standardised tests for literacy and numeracy. We consider the Australian average to be low. Trinity will exceed this. Trinity, like other Anglican colleges on the outskirts of major cities, can become the state's leading college."

To underline this commitment to excellence, we added, "We have measured our starting base and our Year 7 students are starting three years behind the Australian average. But we promise you honest reporting, the good and bad." Parents in 1984 could not know that seven years later, using the same measure, Trinity's Year 7 students would be two years *ahead* of the Australian average.

The key to attracting enrolments in R–4 was the support of Rosslyn, who had experience as an Education Department regional consultant, a teacher and a remedial specialist. This gave prospective parents confidence, and she visited the Gawler kindergartens and preschools throughout 1984.

Finding staff

We believed the key to a successful school was agreement between parents, teachers and the school about what the school was trying to achieve, because then we would all be working together. Trinity would seek to ensure harmony between the teachers employed, the school philosophy and the parents who were prepared to support this vision.

Gaining high quality staff was critical to that goal. "We will employ teachers to teach our own children," we told parents.

This was our second 'impossible' challenge. Tony Shinkfield was worried we would not be able to attract good staff applications. He asked to look over the pile that came in. It was quite high. To his amazement, half the applicants were of the calibre he would expect to apply to St Peter's. There were also many applicants who "would not bother to apply to 'Saints' ". On paper, the applicants were either excellent or non-interviewable – there was no middle ground.

We shortlisted 36 applicants and invited them to our house in Aldgate five months before the school was to open. I tried very hard to persuade them to pull out. "The school has no funding," I explained. "We are relying on voluntary parental labour to build it. All that I can promise is a food allowance – no salary. For teaching materials, I can only promise a tin of blackboard paint with a brush to paint it on a wall and a box of chalk. We will also offer you a hammer to help build the classroom you might be able to teach in."

I believed most applicants would withdraw under these conditions. Because of this, we delayed our staff selections for seven days. Over the next week, however, no one accepted my invitation to pull out. Just before the final interviews began, I added an extra interview because a Mr David Smith had applied with skills in teaching woodwork, cricket, computing and maths. This was a most unusual combination for an experienced Year 7 teacher.

My capacity to appoint staff was tested immediately. Some of the school council did not like my recommendation of Dr Michael Liddle, a colourful applicant who persuaded me that French should be taught despite the fact that we had intended to offer German. The German applicants were very sound and very serious; with hippy-length hair Dr Liddle was a lapsed Catholic who offered flair, passion and style. He was not sure if he wanted to continue in teaching and sought a very part-time position. The council wanted all staff to be practising Christians and questioned my recommendation. However, after much debate, Michael was appointed.

What parents were seeking

We had now achieved a high quality staff and a minimum starting number of 150 enrolments. With my weekly visits to Gawler to meet prospective parents the numbers continued to grow. I told the council, "We can squeeze 184 students into the log cabin we are building – and except at Year 8 we will be starting with waiting lists."

There was still no interest from the government bureaucracy in funding the school. They told me, "The professional wisdom is that Trinity will fail." However, this lack of enthusiasm was not matched among parents on the ground. We already knew the dedication of the families of the 24 children attending the parish school. Many of these parents, under the leadership of skilled tradesmen Brian Phillips and Lyn Wilson, gave up all of their weekends and many after-work hours to build the new school by hand.

Apart from these original parents, why would others be interested in a new school?

One father, Hank, was a professional roofer and was assigned to help build the eight-classroom school building. The summer of 1984 was hot and dry, but Hank continued to run around on the roof trusses with the headmaster crawling behind. (The roof span across the double classroom was very high, and to me a slip seemed like certain death.) Hank was an older parent whose youngest child would be joining Trinity at Year 8. I asked, "Why are you sending your son to Trinity?" Hank was not generally a talkative man and his answer was straightforward and sharp: "I want my son to grow up right." Then a long pause, a few bangs and another comment: "Not like the others."

Other parents may have expressed their reasons more eloquently, but not more accurately. They recognised the important role a school has in enabling their children to "grow up right". The most important gift a school can give a child is a value system. What is good? What is important in life? Does anything in the universe have purpose and meaning? How do you know right from wrong and have the courage to act on it? How do you give children emerging as adults the wisdom to survive and succeed?

Even those who did not personally share the school's Christian basis agreed in their desire for a values-based education. After another eight-hour-plus working bee, Bruce and Cathy Tuncks invited our family to a barbecue and swim. Their children, Robbie and Jennie, had already completed a primary year in the parish hall. I recognised Bruce as a mechanical engineering lecturer from Roseworthy Agricultural College who had been at the meeting a year earlier in the rectory. He was an overt atheist; we had both read Richard Dawkins' book *The Selfish Gene*. Both he and Cathy were working so they had many educational options open to them. Yet their family gave their heart and soul to the new school. With laconic and ironic humour, Bruce told me how Father John saw him and the others making vital contributions to the school as "angels sent by God in answer to prayer".

Bruce designed the sewerage system out in the wheat fields (the sewage had to be pumped over a mile to join up with the Gawler town system). Our two families got on well, and we were generously invited often as the building working bees became daily. Bruce argued coherently and passionately for an atheistic universe and clearly had no fundamentalist commitment to the motto on the Trinity school badge, "In God is my faith". However, he hoped that his children would be well served at Trinity, and many other parents felt the same.

I explained my perspective to him: "In *The Hitchhiker's Guide to the Galaxy* the meaning of life and the universe is said to be the number '42'. But the important things in life are more than just a number. You have no meaning and purpose when life is reduced to a genetic chemical sequence. A painting pulled apart into its constituent paint strokes loses meaning and purpose. Music as individual, separate notes has no soul. Our genes are the instruction book to make us, but like the paint strokes or notes of music, they do not describe our soul. It is the soul of a person that I believe holds eternity, hope and transcendence. For me, a universe with meaning, purpose and beauty is a universe that I wish to share with our children."

What did other parents seek for their children? PARENTS LAY VALUE SYSTEM ON THE LINE was the headline describing a federal government report.[23] The study[24] found that parents rated discipline and values ahead of tradition, prestige and religion as the most important social factors when choosing a school. At Trinity, parents clearly rated values as the most important. But there were other considerations. About 40% of the new enrolments were children of Education Department teachers. These parents, being teachers, would very carefully vet the staff we had selected. The school had no academic reputation, no facilities and a difficult location, but it offered high-quality staff. I held that parents enrol in a school where they believe their children will have good teachers.

Not all parents want the same thing for their children, as is shown in the graphs below.[25] The differences between what is important to parents of state school children and parents of non-government school children are small compared to the similarities. By 1984 religion in the Northern Region had already come to be regarded by most as a matter of believing the unbelievable. However, parents did not want a valueless education and welcomed the Christian environment of the school.

Whose school would it be?

The year 1984, with its classes held in the parish hall and its exhausting preparations for 1985, was challenging and interesting. The passion of the founding group of parents underlined their commitment. However, their vision, as diverse as it was, was not necessarily the vision that new enrolling parents would have. The parents of the 160 children joining the school for 1985 had no ownership of the original school.

Would the families of the original 24 students, enrolled before they had met me as foundation principal and Ros as head of the junior school, be happy with where we were going to take the school? Whose school would Trinity be?

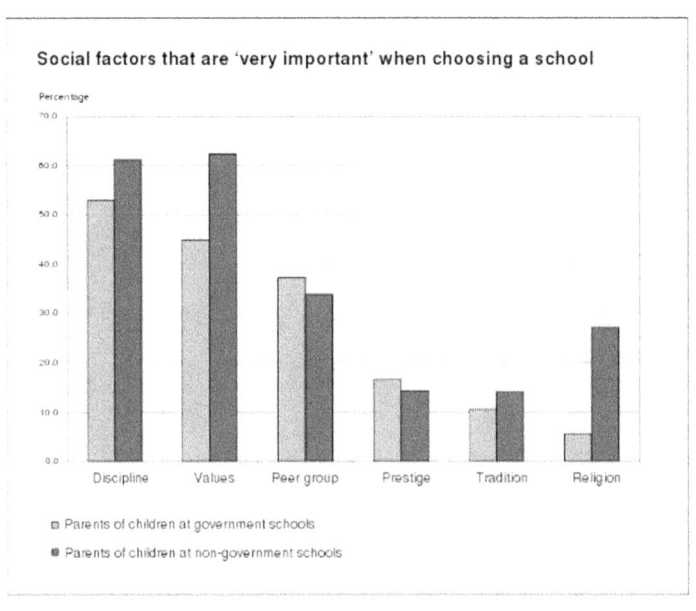

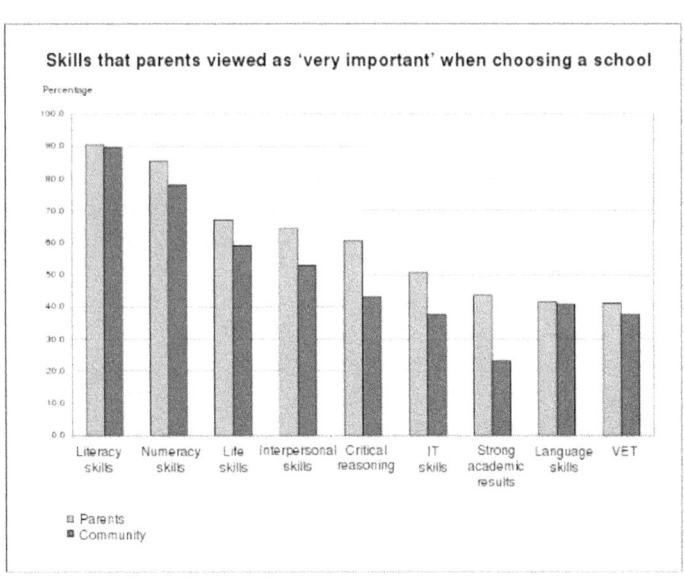

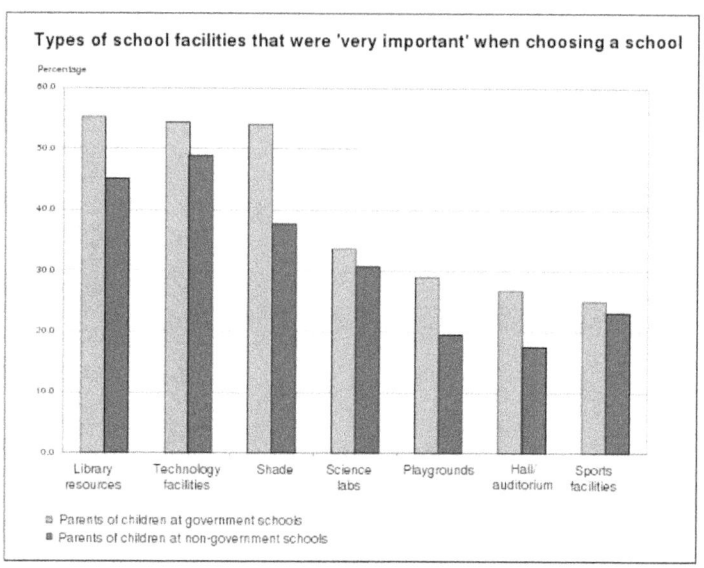

For the 16 founding families, the school was theirs. Some thought this new headmaster had big plans but could not achieve them. They believed the school would morph back into the vision they had for their family and their children. Some wished for a small, loving school run by parents. Some did not want any competition between students.

Troubles were looming. The original families controlled the school board. They controlled the future direction, ownership and leadership of the school.

Lessons learnt

1. The stand-out factors that parents wish to see in a school, according to research, are:
   a. Literacy (90%)
   b. Quality of teachers (81%)
   c. Secure safe environment (79%)
   d. Numeracy (78%)
   e. Life skills (67%)
   f. Values (62.3%)
   g. Discipline (60%)
2. In a region where schools are losing parental confidence with discipline problems, drugs and antisocial behaviour, values, life skills and discipline are more important.
3. The quality or reputation of the principal, the knowledge of authority (where the buck stops) and the quality of the staff are vital.
4. 'Without a vision the people perish.' Schools without transcendental values and visions of being human wither over time. They look inwards.

5
Teetering beginnings
The opening of Trinity College

A pile of rubbish was teetering on the back of an old lorry ahead. The sun blazed down on yet another dry, 42°C Adelaide summer's day. Parents, friends and volunteers were spending hours, days and weeks building an eight-classroom log cabin and a house. For some from the northern suburbs of Adelaide, the house for the headmaster and his family was a mansion. In reality, this 'mansion' was a small log cabin kit house. Wind and dust blew through the cracks between the logs. You could view the outside vista through the new walls.

The house was built with love and not much expertise. The expertise had been directed toward the main classroom block, which dwarfed the 'little house on the prairie'. The prairie was a field of stubble – the harvest had been taken in and then building on the site had started. Sal DePalma, owner of an earthmoving company, generously donated the cutting of the site for the new school. His boys were Trinity students.

To buy 25 acres of land, school treasurer John Strange, another founding parent, had signed documents to borrow everything from the bank. Building of the school started without any formal funding approval from the Anglican Church. The Anglican Diocese of Adelaide subsequently wrote a letter of comfort to the bank. This guaranteed that $100,000 would be paid to the bank should the college fail to meet its repayments. The school had no assets but did have the 1984 debt. Now, with two new buildings going up, the debts mounted. Beyond the low school fees charged, the school had no money, no capital and no income.

Indeed, with no government money the school was probably bankrupt and severely overdrawn.

Our family moved in January 1985, two weeks before school was due to start. We were arriving to build confidence that Trinity would open, ready or not, on the first day of the school year. There was no water, electricity or sewerage, and the days were long and fiery hot. There was an unfinished school building with no playgrounds, paths or parking. Yet for this venture my wife and four children had packed up our house.

The school building (right), seven days before opening. I am adding shelter to our log cabin (left) to protect the family from the western sun – over 40°C at 7.30 pm

As we now had no income, to keep costs down we moved on an open tray truck owned by one of the prospective parents. Ian Macarthur came with another volunteer to help load our furniture for the move to Gawler. By lunch the truck had pulled out and we were to follow shortly after.

Driving out, we spied in the distance a truck carrying a load of rubbish. As we drew closer it was obvious the truck was carrying junk furniture to the dump. As we came closer still we saw that the furniture was too diverse to be rubbish. We realised it must be some poor family moving house. Along the Main North Road we caught up to the truck and passed it. We were shocked. It was our furniture, our future, and we laughed.

This pile of rubbish teetering on the back of the truck seemed symbolic. Trinity was like the load on the truck, teetering. It was basic, tied on and there were no sides and no protection.

We had been told by the building committee that the school might not be ready for day one. Having insisted on a minimum of 80 primary school students and 40 Year 8s to guarantee a quality educational program, enrolments had kept growing. Many had put their faith in us and believed Trinity would open. We had already filled the planned R–1, 2–3, 4–5 and 6–7 classes, and after considerable debate in the school council, we had opened enrolments for an extra R–2 class. This extra class would have to be in the area planned for the front office. The library would now become the library, first aid room, front office and headmaster's office combined.

The headmaster's office had originally been planned as a storage pantry. There was no window.

With two Year 8 classes it was clear that we needed an extra teaching facility just to fit our students in. "What about a cheap all-steel garage?" I asked. The council debated. Were the enrolments real? We had no money and no space and so they made the realistic request, "Let's see the students first."

"But we need a shed to fit in 200," I continued. "A 24m-long steel home garage could fit in the music classes at one end and tech studies at the other."

The Year 8 numbers had grown to 48 students. I was yet to discover that Don Fraser, the principal of Gawler High School, had read with a great deal of interest that this new independent 'private church school' would be open to all and non-selective in its entry. He had met with the parents of the Gawler High students who had failed Year 8 and advised them to send their children to Trinity College to repeat that year. No wonder we had so many Year 9-aged students starting Year 8.

Why did we go?
Why did our family pack up and drive to Gawler to establish a new life in such perilous conditions? We were leaving our house at Aldgate, our Anglican Church community and the Hills Christian Community School at Verdun for a situation that lacked everything from basic services to security.

It is funny how in life you can head on an unknown journey. If we all knew the path ahead, we might not get out of bed in the morning. The vision of a final goal can mean that small steps are taken. At the time you think, "I can go back on this; I can retreat to safe ground." However, as each step is taken, new people join you and new commitments are made. There is no return, and you launch out into the unknown.

As the school's opening date drew near, there was still no commitment from the federal government to fund the school, yet the building work was rushing ahead. None of these teachers we had appointed had withdrawn. With commitment like that – from teachers, parents and children alike – our family was also committed to go.

The staff members appointed to open the school on the new site were an astonishing group. At their interviews in 1984 they had been confronted with the blunt reality. The school had no money. The existing primary school had been unable to attract parents to enrol. The plan was to build a school with volunteers. Teachers would have to bring their own teaching resources and their own furniture for the classroom. Until government funding arrived, all the school could offer was a living allowance to survive on. By January 1985, these prophecies of gloom would become real.

In addition, in coming to Trinity, each teacher would have a full teaching load, plus undertaking a minor and major co-curricular activity, a sport and a cultural activity. Trinity was planning for strong after-school programs. As an innovation, each teacher was to offer a co-curricular activity in an area of their personal interest. Mine was bagpipes.

On the positive side, Trinity offered an opportunity to present a new way of schooling. It had an air of excitement. The newly appointed teachers and their families attended social functions at our home in Aldgate – a core team spirit was building. Teachers could see that the other members of the staff team were quality professionals. As they mixed with committed parents at working bees, they could also see a school that was owned by its community. This community had a personal investment through building the school. Perhaps the teachers came because their new personal relationships and the chance to build a school with a new vision were worth more than money or security.

Further, teachers were to be given professional authority and freedom, including the ability to give honest reports to parents. This was in contrast to other schools where all reporting had to be positive. There was a belief across schooling that students only responded to positive stimuli and that those who were criticised would be repressed and their growth inhibited. The learning that can occur when the possibility of failure is part of the learning process was looked down upon by the educational establishment. However, positive reporting can easily become dishonest reporting. Trinity teachers were able and required to tell parents the truth in their reports, not covering it up with nice sounding words that obscured the real meaning. Bad news was to be given. At Trinity there was the belief in the power of truth.

The staff rollcall for 1985 was a rollcall of the committed:

Reception to Year 1. Jane Threadgold, fresh out of college, had been offered permanent employment in the south-east with the Education Department. She had an outstanding tertiary academic record. This was backed by exceptional reports from her teaching practice, including from her old school, Annesley College. She was an outstanding tennis player, athlete and musician with Grade 6 piano. She was to pair with an experienced Reception teacher in Rosslyn. She was appointed as the one beginning teacher, despite the proven experience of other applicants.

Throughout the holiday period her parents and siblings collected furniture. With their trailer hitched to the family car they unloaded it in the unfinished classrooms. With a new coat of paint the furniture looked loved. Living at home, Jane was to receive just pocket money.

Reception to Year 2. Rosslyn Hewitson.

Years 3–4. Paul Harris was a permanent primary school teacher in the Education Department. Young, with a major in drama and some experience in all areas of theatre, Paul's passion was the Christian mission of the school. He served with distinction during the school's first five hard years before entering theological college.

Years 5–6. Tina and Peter Hatchett pioneered the school in the parish hall.

Years 6–7. David Smith, being the late pick for an interview, surprised us with his understated skills and competence, and continued to impress by 'winning' the position of Years 6–7 teacher. He had a major in mathematics and postgraduate studies in computing, an unusual quality in 1984. He was also an Indonesian specialist and would be the Year 8 technical studies teacher because he had excellent woodwork skills.

David was married and had the support of his wife Carol, a medical practitioner. He required just a small allowance. In the following years he would become head of Years 5–8 and finally deputy principal of the whole college.

Year 8 Humanities. Shelda Rathmann was a young but experienced and dynamic humanities teacher. She would be a role model for young girls and was an outstanding organiser, meticulous in her planning.

Language (French). To complete the staff making this extraordinary commitment, I had to nominate either a German or French teacher. Dr

Michael Liddle had certain advantages in broadening the background of the staff. He had taught as a volunteer in a Catholic mission in Papua and had eight years of teaching in the SA Education Department. He was also employed on a part-time basis by the Gawler TAFE (Technical and Further Education) College as a teacher of life skills. He played guitar professionally and was an old scholar of a Catholic College in NSW, where he won their senior French prize.

Why does such a group of highly expert teachers commit to a project that seems so unlikely to succeed? For all the negatives, Trinity's teachers aspired to make a difference. Teaching is about the transcendental rather than the material. It is about the future – teachers develop the young people who will determine what sort of society we become. It is a humbling experience.

The teachers would be backed up by some other very part-time staff who were already involved in the parish school. Grandparent Eric Strange, whilst not a registered teacher, was an organist and musician. Sue Atkinson was a qualified art teacher. With extra enrolments the team was widened, adding people such as Verle Wood, who would teach commerce, and Sister Juliana from the Church of the Holy Cross in Elizabeth, who would teach a couple of classes in religious education. Gail Hudson, a friend of the rector of Gawler, had taught in Victorian state schools and would also teach a couple of Christian education classes.

All this and more, such as the size of the school's land, provided positives that counterbalanced the negatives. But there was one more potential stumbling block to success.

Teachers hope that their beliefs and values will be supported by the parents who choose the school. With a common vision between staff, parents and school philosophy, great things can happen. But the founding families of Trinity had not enrolled for the new vision for the school. They had enrolled for different reasons. Their common vision was that state education was not the answer for their children. They were used to a school where parents could walk into the classroom and assert their own control. They had a say in what happened in the learning in that classroom. There had even been shouting matches between parents and teachers in front of the children. These families had very different aspirations for Trinity.

Moreover, the two founding teachers at the original parish primary school, Peter and Tina Hatchett, were now to be given direction and a vision they had not chosen. They would be expected to teach a prescribed curriculum backed up with testing. They would be professionally accountable for the delivery of that curriculum.

As 'distant landlords', the new foundation headmaster and his wife had taken over the curriculum eight months ago. In those eight months the school had changed totally. In the transition from parish hall to the paddocks of Evanston South, it had grown eightfold. How would the families who controlled the parish school blend with newcomers? Could this volatile mix even work?

The truck alongside with the teetering load was indeed symbolic.

We arrived to the sound of a chainsaw going through the wall of the kitchen. On this 42° day the sight of an air conditioner being installed was most welcome. With no electricity it could not work, but its installation showed care and hope. A caravan had been towed alongside the log cabin so that we could prepare meals at home – an important cost saving as home meals are much cheaper, especially rice meals. Our family would be living off our savings. We would wash and shower at Elsie and John Unstead's house next door, about a kilometre away.

With no power, no water and no toilets other than a porta-loo, I faced a great deal of pressure to delay the start of school. However, I believed any delay would undermine our children's education. We had come so that parents would know we intended the school to open on the first day of term regardless.

Opening day

It was still dark, and torches were shining outside the classroom block. The sun was yet to rise. It promised to be another scorcher. Our students were due to arrive in three hours' time. At home there was an air of tension. The school was going to open on the first day of term. Would it to be successful or disastrous?

The classroom block looked almost finished to us, but anybody familiar with building knows that 'almost finished' means the bulk of the building is up but a lot still needs to be done. The finishing touches included connecting electricity, water and sewerage. Other finishing touches included putting in fittings and architraves, painting and other time-consuming work.

I had nobody to blame but myself. As headmaster I believed we had to show confidence as a staff that Trinity would open. If we delayed a week there would be less pressure, but still no guarantee the school would be usable. We needed to set the tone from day one and open the school on time.

In the dark, torches were darting around the end of the log cabin classrooms. It looked like burglars. I intended to walk the site to pick up any sharp objects. I joined the light-bearers. The chairman of college council, Geoff Gordon, who had an electrician's licence, and the owner of the Smithfield second-hand store (whose children were not even coming to Trinity) were hard at work. Many others whose children were not coming had also been helping to build the school. The two men were connecting power to the building. It was certainly going to be a close call.

The dawn light began to appear across the eastern hill-line. The wheat stubble began to show and then glow. The black, empty classroom block became a tiny log cabin in a field of stubble flattened by cars. The tension gave way to partial relief as each classroom was checked and the lights came on. It was now 6.30 am.

To enable us to open the school, the water was also switched on – and worked. Toilets looked like they could be flushed. However, the sewerage was still unconnected and so a temporary storage tank had been brought in. It had to be pumped out as it filled up. All of this ate into the precious bank loan.

The playground was only rocky wheat stubble but there was also a dry creek bed cutting through the school's land. The creek was more accurately an erosion gully. Occasionally this gully carried flowing water from the adjacent hills towards real creeks. Also breaking the wheat field was a dry dam that had been used as a rubbish dump. Half of it had been cleared, and an enormous old rusty slippery-dip, steadied by three railway sleepers, had been installed. The sleepers weighed down the climbing end below the 14 steps to the top. Some disused swings had also been found and relocated. There was still a lot of probably dangerous material left in the dam.

It was with both foreboding and excitement that we ate our breakfast at home. It was a significant day. Students and anxious parents would no doubt arrive early, in about an hour. To fill the time we took a photograph of our four children in school uniform in our backyard. With no back fences, the backyard was really the school.

7.00 am, with school to start in two hours. Our children – Joanne, Angela, Chris and Caroline – show off their new school uniform. The school is really an unprotected building site.

At 8.55 a student ran cautiously around the school ringing a cow bell. The students went to class. Punctually at 9.00 am the roll was taken, notices given and a Bible reading and prayer said. One hundred and eighty-four students were present and correct. Trinity College Gawler Incorporated was open.

School uniforms were worn proudly. Uniforms in state schools were losing ground and in some places were even seen as optional. Misbehaviour outside school was able to be hidden because nobody knew which school the offenders were attending. At Trinity we bought the left-over uniform stock of Murray Bridge High School because the colours of their tie were similar to the colours of Trinity College. We had white shirts and grey Milan trousers from Coles, along with grey socks. All items of the uniform were cheap. However, there was one item which, as headmaster, I insisted we consider because it could be handed down, and that was a school blazer. A school blazer stood out. It was the one item of the uniform that was designed to match the quality of city colleges.

The classrooms in the school were large, purposely built to be 50% bigger than the usual classroom. This was to make up for the lack of other resources, because teachers were encouraged to have art and craft materials, musical instruments, displays, library resources and their own office within their classroom. Personally I believed that with good teachers this was desirable. The teachers could improvise with everything on hand.

The crowd of parents looked on anxiously. Questions, problems and issues came from all directions. There was a sense of disbelief that the school had actually opened on time, but now that the focus was on actual schooling rather than building, parents were asking new questions. They slowly moved away from the crowded front office. The school could not afford paid professional support staff, so all our non-teaching support people were part-time volunteers. The front office had two voluntary staff. We just fitted – the combined library, first aid room, reception, office and storeroom doubling as my office was now a reality. Every space in the school had people.

The school could not afford a full-time head so I was also scheduled to teach Year 8 science. As the sun rose higher and the temperature climbed with it, it was a relief to move out of my windowless cupboard-office and into the adjacent science laboratory. How exciting it was to be in a new school with students to teach! Looking through the classroom windows across the bright wheat fields, I also had a temporary sense of relief. We had brand-new science textbooks and an extraordinarily well-equipped science laboratory. Daws Road High School had written off microscopes and fortunately kept them in storage. They were senior microscopes with excellent definition, high magnification and quality resolution, though they required expertise and delicacy to use. Moreover, during the last year I had approval to bid for science equipment that had been ordered by an Aboriginal secondary school but never used. There was a geared model of the sun, the moon and the earth (on turning a handle the moon rotated, showing its phases, whilst the earth revolved around the sun). We had equipment with lenses and lights that would be the envy of most junior science laboratories. We bought the whole 6 x 4 trailer-load for a song.

The students lined up and then came into the classroom and stood behind their desks. There could be no slouching or leaning. "Good morning ladies and gentlemen; please be seated" – and so the lessons began. We started with hands-on problem-solving tasks. I asked, "How does light bend? Why are there rainbows? Is the red in the rainbow on the inside or outside? Why?" Science is fun. I was glad we were devoting 20% more time to science maths, English, history and geography than was normal. I believed that children from some families – often but not always disadvantaged or lower socio-economic ones –do need extra time on the basics.

It was to prove very fortuitous that I had taught in one of the most difficult schools in South Australia. Even so, the children from across this northern region included some of the most difficult and disaffected students I had ever taught.

From Reception, reading was taught phonetically. This method was very much out of fashion. The popular approach was the 'whole word method' in which students simply absorbed reading. This succeeded with students from high socio-economic settings because they had already learnt how to read for interest at home. We had many students from homes without reading. The phonics method teaches word groups, with lists of similarly spelt and sounding words taught each week. Spelling programs were put in place and the lists taught in every class from Reception to Year 10 were tested weekly. In the primary classes, the formal curriculum with testing meant that for the first two lessons each day, all parents and I knew what our children were learning.

There was a time in the Education Department when the Director General could look at his watch and know what was being taught in each class across the state. To the untrained eye, Trinity would look like this because half of the curriculum was to be structured, tested and ensured. The other half was to be up to the teachers – open learning, unstructured, hands on.

Recess was approaching.

Lessons learnt

1. Teachers who aspire to make a difference are indeed committed. Teaching is about transcendental values and vision.
2. Building personal relationships and trust is vital for the success of pioneering ventures.
3. Teachers care about the difference they are able to make with and for their students.
4. A core curriculum that is clear and available to parents is valued.

6

Survival or extinction?

Trinity College, 1985

Why are independent school principals generally overly conservative and cautious? At the Australian Headmasters' Conference in August 2000 we were informed that the survival time for half of all foundation principals of independent schools was less than two years, while the median time for all non-government school heads was just five years. But those whose five-yearly contracts were renewed continued for much longer, taking the average life expectancy of a principal to over 10 years. We were told the length of tenure of the chair of the school board is a good predictor of the length of time a principal serves.[26] Worldwide, rapidly changing school council chairs correlated with a rapid turnover of principals.

I was about to find out why foundation principals of new schools generally last less than two years.

Snake!

Mr Harris ran vigorously around the building ringing the cow bell to announce recess. Students poured out of their classrooms to explore their new environment. They drank water brought from home. With a cricket bat and ball in hand, they had many hectares to play on. They selected a patch of ground, cleared the loose stones to form a cricket wicket, and the game began. The soil quickly turned to dust and the ground boiled as the ball bounced. There were no fences and the wheat stubble rolled over the horizon.

Other attractions were the dam half-filled with rubbish and the long grass and weeds lining the slopes of the dry creek.

Shade, so important in schools, was only to be found under the verandahs. On the dam wall a row of four elderly gums struggled for survival. Brian Fischer, a farmer and parent, had dropped off some hay bales to go under the verandahs and they provided some welcome seats.

The clean concrete under the verandahs accumulated yellow-red dust. The boys' white shirts and some of the girls' light dresses were changing colour.

The boys from Gawler High who were repeating Year 8 showed the way and looked for snakes. The bell rang to end recess and none had been caught. The disappointment soon changed at lunchtime with delighted squeals of success. Whilst I was concerned that the venomous brown snakes might not only injure but kill one of our students, the children were fearless. I thought I had better go and check it out. It was for real.

"Don't touch! " I ordered. "Jason, go and get the rake from the back verandah of our house."

With the snake killed, a large following of students and a concerned yard duty teacher set off to the staffroom with the snake-entwined rake. The danger was real and the staff needed to know. It was also time for a classroom biology lesson on snakes. The snake-capturing exercise was not just limited to the students. Over the year Mrs Hewitson was told off not once but twice for killing brown snakes just outside her classroom with a brick. "Ros, Snakes can jump quickly. Using just a brick in your hand is too close."

Other lunchtime activities proved popular. Groups of girls gathered in the creek bed to yack. (This would soon prove more dangerous than snake catching.) Picking through the rubbish dump, some boys found corrugated iron sheets with sharp corners. These made wonderful sleds to slide down the creek banks. It was dangerous and I was soon under pressure to stop it. In a school with no obvious playground, students

Survival or extinction?

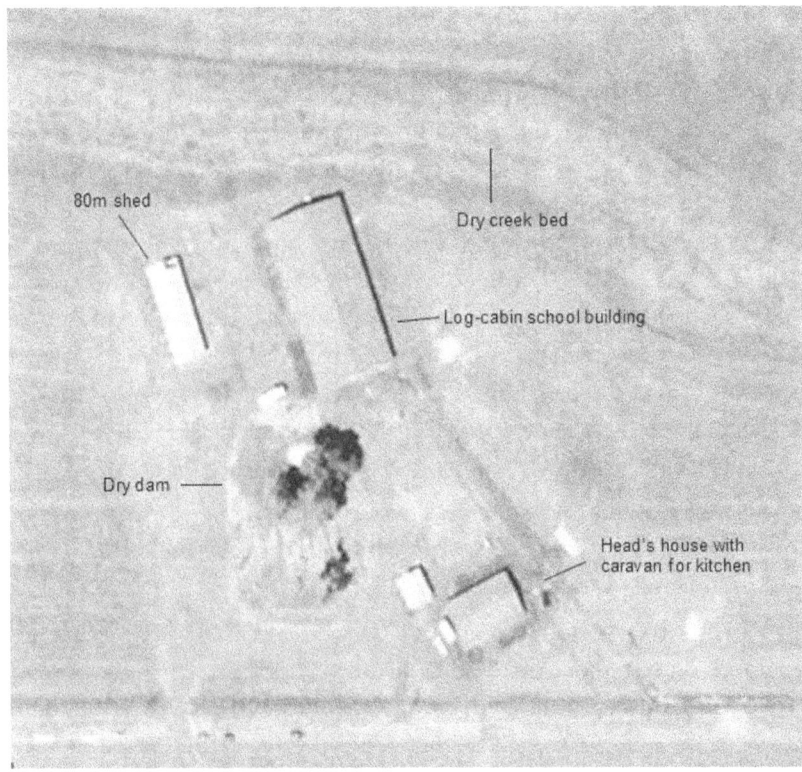

Aerial photograph of Trinity College campus, 1985

needed outlets, but they also needed to be safe. We limited the age group allowed to slide down the banks and told them, "It will stop for all classes and ages if someone is hurt." The slope was so dry the sledding was slow, and for now interest quickly waned. One day it would rain, soursobs would come up and sledding would be fast and fun.

Every afternoon and weekend there were more working bees to finish building the classroom block. We picked over the dam floor continually, clearing the rest of the rubbish until eventually it was clean. One Saturday morning I was finally able to visit the main street of Gawler for the first time – 13 weeks after moving.

From the early days parents tut-tutted about the danger of the rocky slippery-dip, which swayed as students climbed 10 feet up and slid down. After adding a few more railway sleepers to anchor the base, the secretary, Christopher Hebart, and the chair of the grounds committee, Bill Wormald, declared it safe. It was a reprieve for several years. One day, though, worried parents would successfully push for it to be cut down. The slippery-dip would then be mounted into the bank of the dam so it was just over a foot (40 cm) higher than the ground all the way down the slope. The tall, wobbly slippery-dip had been in constant use with no student accidents. When it was made 'safe', students now had no sense that it was dangerous, so they invented games to make it more challenging and fun. They would run along the top of dam wall and jump onto the slippery-dip. We had two broken arms in two months.

However, at this early time the physical safety of our students was not the greatest danger. The yacking of girls in the creek was reported home, and trouble followed.

Parents at any school eagerly ask, "How was school today? What did you do?" With so much invested in the new school, some parents pushed students for information. Sometimes the stories students related at home grew in the telling. One day Father John, the rector of Gawler, spoke with the chair of the college council, Geoff Gordon, because he was concerned about the girls fornicating in the creek. "This 'moral evil' must be stamped out and dealt with," he declared. I asked Shelda Rathmann, the Year 8 humanities teacher, to investigate the 'fornicating girls'. A tricky task. Both Shelda and I were surprised by what we considered an overreaction to an exaggerated retelling of schoolgirl gossip.

However, the complaint was made into a council issue, and the question was asked, "Is the headmaster able to give adequate moral leadership and provide effective discipline at our school?" The matter became a tool to fight the battle for control of the school. Father John believed he should be (in his words) "the spiritual dictator of the headmaster of Trinity College". He expected me to confide in him the deepest secrets of the school; to submit to his authority and take his advice. Appalled at the prospect of the headmaster effectively being the puppet of the rector, and believing it would be a break in trust between the headmaster and the students, parents and staff of the school, I declined his demand.

Then one day a student, Debbie (not her real name), disappeared. "She is not in class and cannot be found at school," her teacher reported. It was suggested to me that she might have left in "Mrs Hudson's car". Later I learnt that Father John had one of his parishioners pick a student up from school without the staff or head knowing. He had believed it was within his power and authority to have Debbie driven about five kilometres from the school to his office in the middle of Gawler. He wanted to find out for himself about the 'fornication in the creek'.

The teachers wondered why he was so seriously concerned with something they assumed his daughter Elizabeth must have told him. However, by removing a student from the school without the knowledge or approval of staff, he was exercising authority beyond that of a concerned parent seeking support for his daughter. Rather, he seemed to be trying to establish the need for the rector to exercise authority in the school beyond that of the headmaster. The creek chatter could have been used to establish a wider concern among his parishioners about the tone and moral education at the school, thereby establishing doubts about the headmaster's adequacy in dealing with this.

Winning the right to discipline

This was not the only bone of contention we had to deal with. Some parents of the original 24 students from 1984 were unhappy with the discipline their children received from their teachers.

They had hoped Trinity would be a small, intimate and caring Christian school with an always positive, encouraging word for their child. In a new school with hopes so high, some parents considered their own child to be deserving of love *without* discipline. They saw discipline as necessary for other children, just not their own. Many students who had come to Trinity had also never experienced a teacher actually disciplining children and maintaining an ordered and respectful classroom. The state school system had effectively reduced teachers' authority by making the disciplining of students so difficult, stressful and time-consuming that it was easier not to bother. The cane and corporal punishment were still legal but on the way out. Any detention became a time-consuming argument and a draining paper war, because students and their parents claimed they were not at fault. It was the teachers who had got it wrong!

The capacity of the staff to effectively discipline students needed to be won, and this against the odds. We instigated a formal council-approved discipline policy with a range of after-school detention options.[27] The system was tested at all year levels. I received various complaints from parents: "What right does the classroom teacher have to give my child a detention?" "The teacher didn't listen to my child's version of the events; it was the other children who were guilty." In the debate between the child's version and the teacher's, I often had to point out to parents, "Neither of us can really know what happened – we weren't there!"

I continued to reassure parents and students. "After the detention is done, it is our policy to listen to the child's version, and if the teacher is wrong, to take appropriate action. I will listen, and if the teacher has made a mistake, the student will receive an apology." As headmaster I stood firmly behind my staff and said to the few parents who were still dissatisfied, "If you wish your child to attend a school where the teacher giving a one-hour Friday detention cannot make a mistake, then please consider moving them to a school where the teachers do not have that authority." I was able to add, "As a parent of four children at the school, I want my children's teachers to have defined, limited but real authority."

This approach, whilst hard fought for, worked very well. Once students had completed a detention, their sense of righteous indignation, supported by their parents, tended to evaporate.

Of course, this was not always the case. I recall three instances in 17 years where a teacher did indeed apologise meaningfully and genuinely to a student. The policy may have caused the withdrawal of one or two students over the years, but parents generally understood that it was important for their children to attend a school where a teacher could make the call to take disciplinary action without entering into a complicated and difficult process.

Teachers at Trinity were flat out coping with the demands of their teaching loads and co-curricular expectations. They were also flat out meeting their own high expectations of what they wished to achieve with the children. Having made such extraordinary sacrifices to come to Trinity, they were not inclined to settle for second best. They needed support to be able to apply discipline quickly and effectively, and were given it.

A devastating accusation

Not all students and parents were happy, so personal attacks on the integrity of the head should not have been a surprise. My morality and suitability to be a headmaster were about to be seriously questioned by a new issue which dominated the recess time talk of the Year 8 girls: "Does the new headmaster fiddle with Year 8 girls' bra straps? Is he a seducer when disciplining?" Being innocent on these questions did not count; the onus of proof was on the accused.

To understand how such a situation came about, some background is required.

At Tony Shinkfield's instigation we applied to join the Inter Collegiate Co-Ed Sports Day run by the prestigious independent schools. A successful application to participate was far from guaranteed. Did the prestigious high-fee schools want to associate with a low-fee school fighting at all levels to survive? The northern suburbs were removed from Adelaide, a separate low-prestige world across Grand Junction Road. In fact, 'low prestige' was above the actual perceived reality. Giving the underdog a break was part of Australian culture, but when their children would be mixing and meeting with ours, would the high-fee schools still find it acceptable to give this underdog approval?

After much debate we were eventually invited to compete in the Inter Collegiate Co-Ed Sports Day at the Olympic Sports Field in Kensington. The invitation to participate was a conditional trial for one year only.

This chance and privilege was communicated to the student body. "We must prove ourselves to be worthy of the invitation. When you leave Trinity to apply for jobs, the reputation of our school will be important to you." We were still only a few weeks old. Our students were not used to discipline let alone self-discipline, and many had low self-esteem and displayed a loud, challenging façade to disguise this. They were used to being in control: "Nobody tells us what to do." Even as headmaster in controlled classroom lessons, I was finding our Year 8 students the most difficult I had ever taught. Some were so rebellious that later generations of teachers would probably have called for psychiatric assessments. For some, we were their parents' school of last resort. Yet most families did have other schooling choices, and their trust in sending their secondary child to Trinity was humbling.

The day arrived and our 14-strong team of Year 8s travelled by bus to Kensington. We had some good athletes, and some of our top students already had a great attitude and would give their best. That night, however, I received a report via the staff of other schools that some of our girls had been smoking behind the stadium grandstand. As headmaster of a young school in such a volatile setting, I knew Trinity was extremely exposed, and I was mortified.

The next morning I interviewed the girls who had attended the athletics' carnival to establish who had been smoking. Because my 'office' had no windows and a solid door, I interviewed the girls with the door ajar. Our volunteer secretary, Christina Short, was sitting three metres away just outside the door and in my line of sight. Inside, and on the other side of my converted storeroom office behind the open door, was a cedar miner's couch on loan from home. The girls were interviewed one at a time and sat on the couch opposite me about a metre-and-a-half away. Some told me the truth with consistent stories of what had occurred. Others told stories that did not agree with anyone else's. These girls blatantly obfuscated and lied.

After teaching my classes and following lunch, I called the smokers back. "Smoking on its own is worth a Friday detention," I said. "However, despite being given a clear understanding of the importance of the event to Trinity, you have broken the school's trust by doing it on the sports day and lying about it. You have brought humiliation to other students. I must give you a Saturday detention and phone the other schools' headmasters to apologise." Then the phone calls to other heads were made. They were given a personal apology and a report of the actions I had taken. Eventually, with other paperwork and calls made, I was able to make my way across the playground to our log cabin home.

That evening the chair of the college council, Geoff Gordon, advised me that an extraordinary council meeting might be needed. A new issue questioning my disciplinary actions had arisen. Geoff was a straight talker. "Michael," he said, "I have been asked if you fiddle with Year 8 girls' bra straps when disciplining them." It was devastating to hear, but I was grateful to have such an honest and transparent council chair.

It was fortunate that I had many years of experience and was able to describe the open office door and the presence, both visually and within earshot, of our volunteer secretary Christina Short and another volunteer, Jennie Evans. However, the discussion went badly. Geoff must have been under severe pressure. He spoke of the "cumulative bandwagon of challenges" I was facing and stated firmly, "Even though the door was open, it was not impossible for you to have 'touched the girls' backs and fiddled with their bras' out of the direct line of sight." I told my family. A formal crisis council meeting was called so I could address the accusation.

At recess next day I shared the problem with staff. It was now the word of two Year 8 girls against their headmaster's. David Smith, our

Year 6–7 teacher, heard the news later that day from other teachers and thought it was a joke. He told Jane Threadgold he had overheard the girls plotting to get out of the Saturday detention. Jane passed this rumour on to me and I immediately resolved to find out what David actually knew. First thing the next morning he came to see me. "Michael, I was in my classroom after school and overheard a group of four girls plotting to get out of the Saturday detention by making up some accusations. I've already told some of the other teachers."

The situation was affecting my family. Our Year 7 daughter was exposed to sideway glances and barbs from other students. She knew that both Dad and Mum were very worried. Her stomach cramped and she became very ill. We drove her to Gawler Hospital and she was admitted with this stress-induced illness.

David Smith's evidence was checked out by the council, together with the information from Christina and, to a lesser extent, Jennie. Both Christina and Jennie were core parishioners at St George's Church and were well aware that their rector was unhappy with my leadership. Christina's husband, Chris Short, was on the college council. I presented my case knowing my leadership of Trinity was on the line. If I was not supported there was no way I could continue. After I left the council meeting so they could discuss the matter in private, the council decided to "give permission" for the Saturday detention to proceed. The girls were told that if they did not attend they would be expelled.

Saturday arrived with another working bee to finish the building (there were still no paths, car access roads or plantings). Council treasurer John Strange decided he would come to the front office to work on the school's books, helpfully ensuring he would be nearby during the detention. Neither he nor I were sure the girls would come. I was worried at the prospect of having to expel them; school enrolments are an almost universal pressure on independent school heads. But the students arrived, and, with the door open between the front office and the laboratory (where the detention was held), Trinity's first-ever Saturday detention began.

The girl who organised the complaint against me was later withdrawn from the school to attend Gawler High School. A year later I received a phone call from Gawler High saying that an accusation of sexual impropriety had been made by her against a member of Gawler High's staff. "What happened at Trinity?" I was asked.

The right of staff to discipline had been closely fought and only just won.

Testing provides a shock

We decided to test the reading age and mathematical ability of our students, and our staff were shocked by their low academic levels. Our Year 8 intake had an average score appropriate for Year 4. Our 12 to 13-year-old students were, on average, four years behind, having the reading and arithmetic skills of eight-year-olds.

We had, through our open enrolment policy, unknowingly taken in the failed Year 8 students of Gawler High. I discussed the problem with Don Fraser, head of Gawler, who was giving me professional help during this year and acted as a valued mentor. Don told me he had encouraged parents to send their children to Trinity to test the open enrolment policy. Some could barely read.

We provided students with beginner readers designed for Grade 2 students. They would have to read the story to the R–2 class, but first they had to learn how to read it themselves. Self-esteem was the most important ingredient in this strategy. What 13-year-old is happy to read a Year 2 reader if they cannot read? It is an admission of failure and a source of ridicule. But reading a story to a younger class is different. The pictures and the story need to be simple. By the end of Term 1, Rosslyn's R–2 class had two Year 8s learning to read.

I reminded myself of Jesus' story of the stone that the builders rejected which became the cornerstone, the most critical stone. These disaffected students had learnt to reject education, yet they might well become the future foundations of our society. In my Headmaster's Report of 1985 I wrote:

We expect discipline, care and academic excellence in a Christian environment. This is not an easy task we set our teachers. Many [students] do not remember their teachers with good favour; Mark Twain wrote: 'Soap and education are not as sudden as massacre, but they are more deadly in the long run.' In many schools, teachers can be equally unappreciative of the efforts of their students. Irvine Edmund, a teacher in America, sadly disillusioned by the cruel ingratitude of his students, complained that "Education is the process of casting false pearls before real swine." At Trinity after we had a year together, I believe we can thank God for much more. Our teachers had a high regard for our students as individuals and for the progress they were making. This high regard did not mean we were yet impressed by their academic excellence!

This policy of taking account of students' varying abilities was not universally welcomed. Some parents who had invested time and personal resources and done favours to enable the school to open believed this gave them power and rights within the school. Some required favours to be repaid. As we started to discover what a wide range of academic capacities our students had, I initially proceeded fairly carefully as this was a struggling school with limited resources. Even so, I began to have battles on many fronts.

I made plans to group the maths and science classes by ability so that the more able students could be extended whilst extra support could be given to the struggling students. This proposal became another battle ground with a board member's family. Both parents were very close to Ros and me but were totally opposed to academic streaming. They believed that their son would do better in a mixed-ability class.

I did not agree. The humanities subjects such as English and history benefitted from a wide range of student experiences in a mixed class. Able students were helped by working with others, and those receiving extra help from able students also benefitted. On the other hand, my experience with mixed-ability classes in maths and science was that lessons tended to be pitched to students making slow progress. This often resulted in both the able students losing interest and those who really needed extra help missing out.

But the college owed this family so much. The decision to set science and maths into ability groups would have to wait.

The curriculum and the co-curriculum

Against the trend in most schools, the formal curriculum at Trinity was rigorous. At Year 8 we had mathematics for 250 minutes, English 250, science 200, history/geography 200 and French 200. Schools often reduced teaching time with timetable quirks – shortened days, longer assemblies, sports and cultural activities. The claim that Trinity offered 20% more time than usual on its core curriculum was in reality understated because interruptions to teaching time were not allowed.

To ensure a broad, balanced curriculum from the first day of school we ran a 3.15 pm to 4.20 pm lesson. This would have been regarded as after-school in most schools. To enable increased emphasis on core academic subjects there were only 100 minutes of physical education in normal school hours, 50 minutes of art, 50 minutes of music and 100 minutes of tech studies. The balance of the week was made up of current affairs/religious education (50 minutes) and a school assembly (50 minutes).

The Year 8s were expected to undertake something cultural and something physical. The co-curricular program was seen as the key for them to develop skills in physical and cultural activities, given that Trinity provided less class time on these pursuits than other schools. The co-curriculum was planned to involve both staff and parents and was to be a time of fun that allowed students to see their teachers differently in shared relaxation.

Trinity's identity is clarified

Easter was coming and I wanted our school community to be able to celebrate the Easter Story on Maundy Thursday evening so that parents could join in. (This was another after-hours commitment the staff prepared for willingly. The drama group, the choir, the art group and the music group all required staff preparation and effort.) Only about 20% of our school families were churchgoers and quite a number were atheists. Many of our children had never heard the Christian account. When asked to draw a picture about the Easter story, some drew anything from whales to pretty flowers.

Father John refused to be involved in a service at the school and sought to stop it. He seemed to believe such services should be in the parish church and be a parish affair. He advised all the other clergy in surrounding parishes that Trinity was in his parish and they would not be welcome without his approval. Despite this, Father Ben Jones from a neighbouring Barossa Valley parish agreed to come. Father John saw this as a foreign priest entering his parish without his permission. The stress made Father Ben ill, and a few days beforehand he phoned sadly to advise he could not come, though he still felt he should.

For me to have led the service would have been seen politically as exceeding my authority as headmaster. Council member Chris Short was a licensed lay preacher at St Georges and indicated his willingness to help.

Our school community was invited to attend on Thursday evening for a washing of the feet service to represent Jesus' action as a servant to his twelve disciples at the Last Supper. The shed overflowed, with more than 300 attending. It was very pleasing to learn on the night that Father John had allowed his daughter Elizabeth to come and play the flute. The school orchestra – more correctly, the music ensemble – gave its first major public performance. They could manage a couple of hymns and some incidental music. The contemporary music and the service were a success.

But clearly the headmaster, faced with a critical board member in the rector of Gawler, and other unhappy members of the parish, was putting his own position at risk.

I wrote to the Archbishop of Adelaide, the Most Reverend Dr Keith

Rayner, to seek help and advice on whether Trinity was a parish school under the spiritual directorship of the rector of Gawler or a diocesan school. Compared with the Roman Catholic Church, the constitution of the Australian Anglican Church takes away some power from the diocesan bishops and gives it to parish clergy. Rome has its Pope; the Anglican Church has its parish priest. So long as a parish was financially viable, the local priest, called a 'rector', had life tenure. To remove a rector required proof of extreme misbehaviour before a church court. The archbishop could not command from on high, yet he did come from a tradition of command and authority. We would need to wait for his response.

During the months we waited it was dry, but eventually, for the first time in the year, it rained. There was neither track nor road nor footpaths from Alexander Avenue to the school. Dust turned to thick clay, then slushy clay. After lunch our classroom carpets were covered in a layer of mud. We had to learn that shoes must be left outside under the verandahs when it rained. How could parents collect their children? We had an extra impromptu parental working bee spreading truckloads of dolomite to provide access.

On 10 May 1985 Archbishop Rayner issued some 'principles for the administration of religious life of the school' (Trinity College Gawler). He outlined ten carefully drafted principles. The archbishop declared that, unless the decision was challenged by synod, Trinity College was now a diocesan school with a new constitution, new staff and new recognition by the Commonwealth Schools Commission.

The archbishop was aware there had often been problems in other schools between headmasters and their chaplains, and hence he wrote, "The relationship between a Headmaster and a Chaplain is always potentially difficult. The Headmaster has total responsibility of the school and the spiritual life of the school cannot be divorced from this overall responsibility." The Archbishop continued: "The entry of a Parish Priest into the life of the school was a matter of invitation, not a right."

The archbishop's letter, coming from an independent authority and backed up with legal advice and sensitive pastoral care, helped Trinity by clarifying relationships between its headmaster and others. Trinity was an independent school with parish clergy participating at the school by invitation. The authority of the school was underlined and its careful relationships with parishes described. The authority and responsibility of the headmaster was resolved.

What was not resolved in the minds of some was whether, holding such authority, I should remain as headmaster.

Resignations – and it is still Term 1

While teaching a science class one day, I had an urgent knock on the door. "Mr Hewitson, our teacher, Mrs Hatchett, is going off at the class. She's walked out!"

I was completely in the dark about what had prompted this. I had hoped to support Tina and Peter because they had put so much into the school in their first year of teaching, with so little knowledge of primary education and almost no teaching experience. I believed we owed them and should bring them with us by developing their capacities as teachers. But the school was not the same school they started at. We were now all demonstrably accountable for the effective delivery of a formal curriculum. This was a major challenge for teachers who believed in students learning when they were ready, with learning focused on the individual student rather than the external constraints of a curriculum of study.

The management of negative and bitter attitudes will always be a potential problem in any changed school. Progress was being made, and Peter, with his sunny disposition, was working well. Both teachers and parents can sometimes lose it in front of children, but this seemed different. That day Tina resigned, and the following day Peter reluctantly followed suit. He had been offered a full-time position at Trinity and had seemed very keen to accept it. He explained his deeply personal reasons and I gave him my full though sad support, wishing him well for the future.

Only much later did I learn that there were health issues involved that helped explain what happened that day. This incident demonstrates how headmasters operate without full facts and must make calls on the evidence in front of them.

For some parents from the parish hall days, this development was a real blow to their confidence. At the time, with no medical knowledge, it was another damaging blow to my relationship with those on the board who believed that, unless my authority was curtailed, I should go.

I now had to find a Burton House housemaster as well as a Year 5–6 teacher (Tina and Peter together made up a 1.2 staff load, so a little adjusting of other part-time staff meant we needed just one replacement teacher). At the end of term 1 we had no money and still no response from the federal government. We would need to be very lucky to find a proven primary teacher who could teach Years 5–6, run a co-curricular activity, be housemaster of Burton and support the Christian life of the school.

Michael Burvill-Holmes applied, newly arrived in Australia. He had been both a student and a teacher in an elite, very high-fee, private primary boarding school in England. How could he cope at Trinity? As the sole breadwinner for his family, he needed to be paid. He joined Trinity as our highest-paid, but still not fully paid, staff member. Students can be very good judges of teachers. Burton House had always been bottom, but Richard Greig, a Year 8 House Senior, wrote, "After a slow start in the first term, Mr Burvill-Holmes, our present housemaster, arrived and we have made quite a large step forward since then. One of our major achievements was a marvellous Term 2 assembly with several plays, skits and musical performances."

The House, class and school lifted.

Pastoral care – and funding at last

My experience of the House system at St Peter's College had been extremely positive. Houses have children of different ages with siblings generally being in the same House. There was strong student leadership in

Houses with eventually 60–80 students in each House. At St Peter's we had House-time twice a week, with classroom teacher time three times weekly and formal chapel for the whole school before class time. Pastoral care was shared between a form master (class teacher) and the House. For Trinity I decided the House would be the care group. The House met daily.

Houses were communities of children from Year 5 to Year 8 who prayed and played together. Competitions were established as recess and lunch-time entertainments. School assemblies were led by a different House each week. The three prep school classes also each took a turn.

By mid-year a school operating for 18 months with no government funding needed political and financial help. St Peter's College, through the efforts of Tony Shinkfield, announced a grant to Trinity of $22,500 per annum for three years. Spirits were raised – this would cover the salary of one teacher for three years! Pulteney Grammar School sent out some students with their technical studies teacher and they erected a small bike shelter with a seat halfway between the road and the classrooms.

At the end of Term 1 we again turned to Archbishop Rayner for help. He phoned Prime Minister Bob Hawke to advise him that unless Trinity received notification of funding, the school would have to close. The school's original faulty application had been resubmitted correctly during 1984 for the 1985 school year, but twelve months later there had been no response. The Anglican Church had effectively underwritten $100,000 of the school's bank loan by providing a letter of comfort. It had accepted 100% of the risk whilst putting no money into the school to enable it to survive. Moreover, despite the church's holding the risk, assets such as land were in the school's name. The archbishop was clearly serious in telling the Prime Minister that unless Trinity College received notification that it was to receive federal government funding, then he would make the federal government's lack of action public. This was backed up in writing in a letter dated 4 June 1985.

The Anglican Church in South Australia was founded as a diocese in a colony of dissenters. In one country town, there were 19 Methodist churches and also a number of Baptist churches. These tended to be committed to state schooling. However, Trinity was becoming a significant political asset for the diocese and other high-fee schools. The established independent schools were under attack by Senator Susan Ryan, the federal Minister of Education, who categorised independent schools as either Catholic or "silver spooned and privileged", thereby justifying granting less money to non-Catholic schools. The privileged status of high fee Anglican schools made their government funding an easy target. Senator Ryan was reportedly warning that any initiative by wealthy private schools to generate independent income to replace lost government subsidies would further jeopardise their funding levels.

The archbishop was able to write:

> As an example at the other end of the scale, we have recently opened a new school in the outer suburbs of Adelaide. Its enrolment is 190 students with a projected growth to approximately 500. The school was built in three months using voluntary labour of parents, and without the benefit of people, capital, and grants. Whilst the recurrent grants for 1984 were eventually forthcoming, no grants for 1985 have yet been received. The top fee is a modest $240 per term and there are substantial family concessions.

As Archbishop Rayner's words imply, after 18 months we finally received the first indication that the federal government would change its decision. They agreed to pay the funds owed for 1984. These funds eventually arrived in the last half of 1985 and we were too exhausted and indignant to celebrate. However, we could now pay teachers their salaries and avoid bankruptcy.

1985 draws to a close

Some students from our 1984 families gave notice that they would leave and attend other schools in 1986. A Year 8 student from a family with a father whose engineering skills had been vital for Trinity's foundation was going to attend Faith. Some Year 7s also indicated they would leave for city schools. However, the families who began in 1985 overwhelmingly spoke well of the school, and enrolments for 1986 were 387 strong.

Some things were working well. The relationship with Gawler High was supportive, strong and very healthy. Our first sports day was held on the Gawler High ovals. Don Fraser, the Gawler High headmaster, had now enrolled his own son to attend Trinity College in 1986.

Our growing school required more classrooms and the building committee subcontracted this work. The school was receiving no capital funding and would have to pay for building another eight classrooms by increasing its debt and diverting daily operating funds to capital.

Archbishop Rayner asked me to reflect on my first year at Trinity College "to provide effective development for the whole community involved in the school". We were heavily in debt and running on a financial shoestring. There was no paid support staff though the school did have the benefit of volunteers. The teachers were watching every cent. The management of the school's finances was also being undertaken by volunteers and had a large degree of ambiguity about it. However, whilst we did not actually know our financial position, we were very likely to be running in the black and our growing debt was because of our building program.

In my letter of 4 December 1985 responding to the archbishop, I discussed the importance of the new non-Anglican Christian congregations springing up throughout the northern region. I hoped the school could meet the spiritual need of those not involved in existing congregations. I continued: "For the Headmaster of Trinity College, these are treacherous waters and I will be well advised to stay out of them. Against this, as a dedicated Anglican, I see that our church has a mission that could be fulfilled."

The school had finished 1984 with 27 students, yet by the end of 1985 it had 189 students and 387 enrolled for the next year, with a growing waiting list at every year level. We had a staff/student ratio of 25 students to one teacher. A surprising feature was that the number of Year 8s going to Year 9 had grown from 48 to 56. Yet by the end of 1986,

12 of the original 24 students enrolled in 1984 had been withdrawn. The school had still received no government capital grants (as opposed to recurrent or day-to-day funding) and was reliant on its running funds not only to service high interest payments for 100% debt on assets, but also to provide some capital funds to attract even more borrowings.

We eventually discovered that in 1985 we had finished the year with a 25% surplus as a percentage of total income. Whilst this was extraordinary, the position of the headmaster of Trinity College was still not secure. I had made strong enemies within the leadership of the school on very core educational principles of religion, power and money.

Christmas arrived with more building, more enrolling and our family determined that we would continue the following year. But I sought a formal vote of support from the college council or I would resign. This was treacherous; the 1984 families and the Gawler parish were strongly represented on the board.

Lessons learnt

1. Teachers need to be able to exercise clear and easy authority whilst having the responsibility to ensure good discipline amongst students.
2. Co-curricular after-school classes have a different tone and discipline to formal classrooms and are a shared experience where special pupil/teacher relationships are developed.
3. Governing school boards benefit greatly by having an external visitor or umpire with reserve powers.
4. A school board needs members in touch with parents and future parents, and some with legal, financial and educational expertise.

7
"Burn the lot!"
Shaping the character of a school

Geoff Nairn, the architect of Faith Lutheran School, asked to be shown around the school and joined one of our parental tours. With the growing interest in enrolling at Trinity, I ran tours three times a week for up to four families at a time. Parents wished to meet the headmaster and ask him questions. They wanted to see the school, meet students and understand how their child might benefit from attending.

It was vital to the school that parents learnt what we were doing. If they then enrolled, they supported the education we offered their children, ensuring partnership between parents, teachers and the school. A second benefit of these tours was that I learnt what was being taught across the school and was able to talk with individual students about their work.

I always liked to start with what parents knew. One of the families in this tour had a student in Year 5, so a visit to the Year 5 class was included. With my signature 'rat-a-tat-tat' on the door, our group entered the classroom. The students stood up quickly with broad smiles on their faces.

"Good morning, Mr Burvill-Holmes, and good morning, boys and girls," I said. "Our visitors today are —— and one of them has a student in Year 5 at another school."

The students resumed their work and the parents and I looked through the students' workbooks. The class of 28 was hard at work, and as we looked through their books, their pride in their work was obvious.

Already our students were making significant academic progress and were a year ahead of many schools in the region. This was not saying much because our students were still below the Australian average, yet our visiting families often showed strong approval and were very keen to follow through with their enrolment.

As I was squatting and chatting to students about their work, Geoff tapped me on the shoulder. Although he had politely but cursorily looked through some books, the education of our students was not what he was there for. He took me outside to comment privately on the furniture and classrooms.

"This is a disgrace," he said after an angry pause. "Burn the lot!"

This shocked me since we were very proud of our achievements. We had worked hard with many parents over the Christmas 'holidays' and had restored unwanted classroom furniture from a western suburbs state high school. We had acquired desks and chairs for a school of 380 for a cost of $1500 – just $4 per student. The graffiti of previous decades had been sanded out and the timber beautifully polished. It was true the wire chairs had metal fatigue and kept breaking at the edge, exposing an upright wire that tore occasional holes in an unwary student's or teacher's clothes. But at least we had desks and chairs.

Our pride in having log-cabin classrooms and a school at all did not deter Mr Nairn. "I would put a match to it all," he continued. "A school with such shabby facilities, such poor grounds and such unusable resources and furniture should not be allowed to operate."

After the shock, I realised on reflection that Geoff was correct. The school's facilities *were* poor. The existence of the school was indeed a minor miracle; it should not have survived 1985. Was it true that it should have been banned and a match put to the lot?

Faith Lutheran School and its architect had certainly done things right. It had received government funding from day one and enjoyed a huge federal government capital grant. It had designed and built a long-term, double-storey, solid masonry school building. Faith also had a master plan and vision. Geoff Nairn knew me as a board member of Pedare Christian College and had been appointed as Pedare's architect. With correct government funding applications and approvals in place, Pedare had a coherent vision with the financial means to achieve it. We lacked a master plan for our buildings and grounds.

Despite the careful and strong leadership of our college council chair, Geoff Gordon, Trinity also lacked a coherent governing body. Throughout 1985, council meetings were trials, both mentally and literally. Any parent in the school with a problem who knew a council member would share their concerns. Happy parents did not take the trouble to make demands on council members, so council members could very easily have believed that almost every parent was unhappy. Many 1984 parents were especially dissatisfied with the school's direction. Council members had mainly been appointed in the parish primary school days and had understandably strong connections with the rector of Gawler, who was now an ex-officio council member. The chair and the treasurer of the council were both core members of St George's Church, and the People's Warden was also on the council.

During 1985 you only had to attend one of these tense, attacking, angry council meetings to know trouble was brewing. A new constitution had been put in place, but we were yet to have the 1986 Annual General Meeting which might enable a variety of new council members to be elected. Even viewed in advance, Term 1 of 1986 was going to be traumatic. In hindsight the trauma was even greater than anticipated.

The father of the first of our core families to leave the school had provided a key balance on council, having strongly supported the separation of the role of the rector of Gawler and the daily running of the school. He, with his engineering knowledge, and his wife, with expertise in education, had provided months of physical labour, love and passion. They had survived the difficult 1984 year and were after a school they could be part of and share in, despite its being a Christian school. Yet when I raised again the prospect of grouping students in mathematics and science by ability, and insisted on it for 1986, this was the final straw for them, and their son left to attend Faith in the Barossa and their daughter to attend a high-fee girls' college in the city.

To make matters even worse, a top teacher, Shelda Rathmann, another close family friend, decided to leave the staff, although she would need to work at the school throughout 1986 while seeking a position elsewhere. The impending departure at the end 1986 of such a valued teacher and housemaster affected one-third of the school's parents, and it was a major destabilising influence within the staff as well as the parental body.

The college council problems and the demands made on our family were such that I determined to resolve the future direction of the school by offering my resignation in February for the end of 1986. With the position and authority of the headmaster remaining fragile, the school would remain divided because every decision taken would be open to immediate challenge. The traumatic loss of such core parents and students to Trinity's competitors, and the traumatic loss of friends who had worked so hard for the school, was only going to be the beginning.

The determination to ask council for a vote of confidence was fully supported by Ros, who had to cope with the difficulties we had in resourcing the school. During 1985 our family had used our own savings to finish off the headmaster's house, which we were required to rent, and to purchase basics such as an oven, sinks, carpets and vinyl for the floors. The internal doors of the house were only put up six months after we moved in. I knew the role was a mission and a calling and I had been on call 18 hours a day, seven days a week for 18 months. Should my resignation be accepted, our family was at peace about my returning to the Education Department. It was pointless to continue at Trinity without strong support.

The council knew that if I was given a two-thirds vote of support with a contract that offered greater security and authority for leadership, I would stay. I asked for a further five-year contract, to be subject to a review before 1989 by council that would also require a vote of two-thirds to terminate my appointment in 1989.

The 1985–86 council met behind closed doors. Finally I was told I was being asked to stay with the terms of a review agreed to. On 4 March 1986 I wrote to the Archbishop of Adelaide, advising him that the college council had given me substantial and continued support and had extended my contract. I explained I was able to be removed at any time by a vote of two-thirds of the council, conditional on the support of the Anglican Schools Commission, but that "such a dismissal must have its foundation on an act or acts of a substantiated lack of professionalism by the Principal".

New council elections were held and some new members joined. The resolution of the headmaster's appointment made for workable, if still stressful, council meetings.

Although the position of the headmaster had been resolved, this did not mean the school would necessarily flourish or survive. We were still fighting to get our first government capital grant, and with just a secretary keeping paper records for an honorary treasurer, our bookkeeping was inadequate. We had no audited record of our capital expenditures until 1987 and by then our capital expenses totalled $1.73 million. The recurrent day-to-day financial records were all historic; we had no real idea where we were going financially. We were cash-strapped and faced with strong competing schools. And, according to Geoff Nairn, the facilities we had borrowed for from funds intended to pay teachers and run the school on a day-to-day basis were a disgrace and should be burnt.

Trial and trauma

Nineteen eighty-six did not start well. Our visiting school chaplains, Father David Williams and Father Alan Courtney (of Elizabeth Downs and Parafield Gardens parishes respectively), made a formal request to the parish of Gawler for a service of dedication on the first Monday of school term. The wardens of St George's Church agreed, but the rector refused. In fact, Father John asked me to leave St George's and take our family to another parish. We joined the parish at Elizabeth where we were welcomed by both the people and the rector, Father Donald Grey-Smith.

Later that term we did have a service in St George's, but it was a student's funeral service. Year 8 boys believe they are immortal.

"Mr Hewitson! Come quickly! There has been an accident on the Main North Road, and I think one of our students has been hit!"

I ran across the wheat stubble, across the new unlevelled oval space that some of our farmer-parents had dug out and over the rock fill. And there was Anthony with a mangled bike lying on the gravel. His skull had been cracked open, but his heart was beating. The ambulance had not arrived. The driver of the car had swerved to miss him. Anthony thought he could cross Main North Road ahead of the car travelling at 110 kph and had done so. However, the driver did not believe Anthony would cross in time and so swerved up onto the gravel median strip. The car hit Anthony on the median strip.

Anthony's parents were phoned and I went to the hospital with the ambulance, cradling Anthony and talking to him. When the parents arrived, his father was totally distraught. He told me he had been given instructions by his wife to drop Anthony up at school, but with Anthony's encouragement had dropped him at a closer point on Main North Road instead.

On returning to school, I called an assembly. We moved the furniture from two classrooms and sat on the floor to squeeze our 400 children and teachers in, as we did for our weekly assemblies. I and other teachers said prayers for Anthony and his family.

How do you share a loving and caring God when bad things happen even to children? I feared that Anthony would die.

The children were told the facts. I read out the words from one of our assembly hymns. It had been written by the Jesuits[28] and, being a modern hymn, was well sung by the school. The students knew it was about facing danger and having courage to act:

> Be not afraid. I go before you always.
> Come follow me,
> And I will give you rest.
>
> You shall cross the barren desert, but you shall not die of thirst.
> You shall wander far in safety though you do not know the way.
> You shall speak your words in foreign lands and all will understand.
> You shall see the face of God and live.
>
> If you pass through raging waters in the sea, you shall not drown.
> If you walk amidst the burning flames, you shall not be harmed.
> If you stand before the power of hell and death is at your side,
> Know that I am with you through it all.
>
> Blessed are your poor, for the Kingdom shall be theirs.
> Blest are you that weep and mourn, for one day you shall laugh.
> And if wicked tongues insult and hate you all because of me,
> Blessed, blessed are you!

The news from the hospital was not hopeful. The world slowed down and time seemed to stop. Anthony died that day. We told the whole school and said a prayer for him and for all of us who knew him.

Driving out onto the plains west of Gawler, my attention was drawn to the tall triangular augers that mixed grains to make chicken pellets; they towered above Anthony's family home. This day, they were stationary and silent. I wished to support the parents and offer the inadequate condolences of our school community. The vacuum, loss and grief were palpable. I gave them the words of the hymn "Be Not Afraid" and told them how we had shared this with Anthony's fellow students. Some days later, his dad asked me whether we could have this hymn at Anthony's funeral. It would become part of the soul of those early students. Many years later, I attended old scholars' weddings where this hymn was sung.

Father David and Father Alan were known and trusted by the students. Over the following days they provided loving pastoral care that gave students a vision of the transcendent in our lives. I was determined to try to include all the students in the funeral as part of their grieving for a student who had been with us for a few short weeks.

Having a God who loves and suffers with us does not mean that bad things are not part of life. Suffering can enable us to grow in love.

Enrolment pressures – and bribery

It is hard to imagine a time before computers. We were taking enrolment deposits from everyone applying and organising our enrolment lists by hand. By 1986 I was receiving offers that might have been too good to refuse. Not only were personal inducements – bribes – offered for children to jump the queue to gain a place, but specific business deals were offered which tested the will of council.

A major Gawler businessman asked me, after I explained the school was full and we did not have the capital to grow any faster, "Mr Hewitson, how much does it cost to build a classroom?" I answered, "Each complete classroom costs us $25,000." He replied, "I will donate $25,000 to build another classroom to enable my daughter to come to the school."

Because this offer was beyond the bailiwick of a headmaster, I put it up to the college council for a decision. The council considered the offer seriously. To accept would create an exception to our 'first enrolled, first in' policy. Yet the money would build another classroom and enable another 27 students to attend next year. We had established a vision for the college that it would be open to all, regardless of religious or socio-economic background, yet we were desperately short of finance and capital and had long waiting lists.

(Being a public school financed by the government did not mean that Trinity was a state school. However, as with a state school, both federal and state governments exercised considerable control over Trinity and its curriculum. The state and federal governments controlled both the registration of non-government schools and, for Trinity, 85% of our budgeted income.[29])

After some discussion, the offer was refused because, by applying the 'first enrolled, first in' policy, the businessman's daughter would still not have been enrolled, even with another 30 additional places.

By the end of 1987, no more bribes or inducements were being offered to take students into the school, yet enrolment pressures continued to grow. We were even receiving enrolments prior to birth, and since June 1986, the places in Reception were already taken five years ahead. Was it fair to exclude all families whose children were born in the second half of the year?

The chicken shed

Our family was invited to visit the Copeland family at Kangaroo Flat, just north of Gawler, where they grew hundreds of thousands of chickens each year. Looking inside the massive air-conditioned chook sheds and seeing 20,000 chooks in each shed gave me cause to think. We needed an assembly hall, and with our 387 students set to rise to 557 in 1987, we needed more teaching spaces. We still had no government capital funds, so why not build a very large chicken shed?

The college council narrowly agreed to cost what was effectively an enormous prefabricated agricultural shed. The cost was very low – only $80,000. Looking at the figures, council asked me if I knew anyone who might build it. "Who better than a chicken farmer?" I replied.

Tony Copeland was approached and, within budget and on time, negotiated not only the building of the shed, but also a concrete floor and a concrete path around it. The shed featured a temporary stage and basketball court with an electric wire strung across the creek to power it.

To cope with an annual growth of 200 new students, the 'chook shed' provided space for four temporary classrooms, one in each corner. This formed the nucleus for rapid growth, even though the classes it held had to be very conscious that the noise they made might interrupt the learning of three other classes. We were also delighted because we could now meet together as a whole school.

Finally, during 1987, with nearly 700 students coming the next year and with Year 11 being offered for the first time, we had the promise of government capital funds to help build some laboratories and a small technical studies centre. The original 1985 household car shed which had acted as our tech studies classroom was about to be superseded. It became a new classroom for agricultural studies. Great progress was made with an architect, a building master plan and government grants.

However, because bureaucratic wheels turned a little slower, the building was delayed. To cover the gap of eight classes without a classroom, two transportable tin classrooms, each divided into two very small, cramped teaching spaces, were brought in. Being so small and confined, they had the luxury of air-conditioning. We now had four classes planned for the chook shed, and four further classes jammed into the two divided transportables.

Despite our family's living on the campus, the air-conditioners from the transportables were stolen overnight. Insurance replaced them, but they were stolen again. Our chair, Geoff Gordon, had had enough. "We will not be able to afford insurance," he said. So, very publicly, he slept in one of the transportables in his swag. The word went out. The thieving stopped.

Hunting for more teachers

As I've already said, I believed the reason so many students were enrolled in such a poorly resourced school was that the teachers were good – very good. It was my first responsibility as headmaster to recruit the very best staff. I could not do everything, but I had to ensure I was totally focused on ensuring we thoroughly researched every promising applicant. My benchmark was that each and every teacher selected would be a person I would want to teach my own children.

In the 1980s few teachers lived in the Gawler and northern Adelaide region. The professional pool was reduced further because for most teaching at Trinity would involve two hours' driving each day. Additionally, Trinity was clearly a hard work school. We advertised nationally even though in 1986 we could not afford to fly applicants over to be interviewed and see the school.

The Fischer family was a core school family and were holidaying in Queensland when I asked them to meet an applicant, Kevin Butler, in a Queensland country town. Brian Fischer changed his holiday plans and visited the town to find out from the parents at the school where Kevin was teaching whether he was a teacher Brian would want for his three children. What he heard impressed him. Kevin had resigned as a priest in the Catholic Church and was now a mathematics teacher with a passion for athletics. He was duly appointed to Trinity to teach maths and develop athletics.

On arriving in Gawler with his family, he discovered the roughly turfed oval carved out by farm tractors and declared it unsafe for serious athletics. To clear the rocks, our students formed up, class by class, behind trailers pulled by cars driven by parents. Each class had just 30 minutes of rock picking and the race was on to fill a six-by-four trailer ahead of the other classes. A competitive short burst for each class meant it was still fun for the students and they took just two days to clear the oval. Grass seeds were sown, sprinklers carted by volunteers and the rough grass grew. Slashers behind tractors were used to mow the oval, but the grass was still too rough for a running track. Without complaining or being asked, Kevin brought his lawnmower from home. I was embarrassed and grateful.

Other teachers were found by pure chance, or at least serendipity. On a family camping trip we visited the Burra Area School and there, on the beautiful school oval, was a man manicuring the running track with his lawn mower. I have found that the grounds staff can tell you what a school is really like, so I went over and introduced myself. Richard Bednall, however, was not the groundsman; he was a physical education and health education teacher. I gave him my card and invited him to apply to teach at Trinity. No application came, but two years later, when Richard did apply, I knew his commitment to teaching and students was real. He joined us in 1990.

I believed strongly that the team of staff working with a new member needed to also own the appointment and hence work hard to enable that appointment to succeed. The positions for the following year were generally filled by May because other schools did not staff so early; we believed our early selection enabled us to meet the best. We were also able to keep on file staff we wanted to appoint but did not have an immediate position for. Some teachers waited two to three years for the vacancy that fitted them.

Why good teachers continued to come

There were three key factors that attracted good teachers to Trinity: curriculum, freedom and discipline.

First, curriculum. Whilst teaching at Trinity was known to be hard work, teachers were supported by our clear, sequential core curriculum. We had a planned spelling program from Reception to Year 10, along with sequential reading, writing and maths programs. Teachers knew how much progress their students were making as this was quantified when their students were tested against international standards.

On the other hand, teachers were also given great freedom in non-core teaching areas. A new teacher fresh from training had to spend a lot of time on the core curriculum because it was new and they were inexperienced, but experienced teachers could easily teach the core curriculum in half their allotted classroom time. They were then free to explore, to share their love of learning with the students.

Third, discipline. By 1987 teachers were well supported by a good school discipline policy. They had the authority to give a Friday detention without an argument until after the detention was done. Once the detention was completed, few students remembered why they were upset, but those who were still upset were listened to and respected.

We made mistakes. With retrospective wisdom, I would have given more time to humanities teachers, who incur large marking loads if they do their job well. With classes of 28+ students the marking load was heavy. Some attempt to share the workload fairly was made. We eventually timetabled teacher loads with extra time off for those with classes of more than 28 students, and teachers taking both a major summer and winter co-curriculum class received either an extra 5% in salary or extra non-contact time. Older teachers with families, often from the Education Department, frequently chose to have either 5% less salary or extra lessons with no co-curricular expectation. The school's program needed an average of one major co-curricular commitment per teacher, and those wanting more co-curricular involvement balanced those seeking none.

With the school growing so quickly to nearly 1000 students within five years, we had to recruit about 12 new teachers a year to cope with growth. Ros and I placed our children in the classes of the new teachers so that parents would also have confidence in them. To parents, the number of new staff sometimes seemed to mean the school must be losing lots of teachers. And indeed, we did lose some teachers (mainly to the priesthood in both Anglican and Uniting Churches), and one in 12 new teachers did not serve beyond their probationary contract. When a new appointment did not work out, I always felt I had failed both the school and the teacher as I had the sole responsibility to appoint staff. However, of the three in a hundred who resigned, over half re-applied to return within two years. The work was hard, but the professional rewards were also high. Staff morale, trust and friendships were strong.

Another attraction for newly appointed staff members was that their children would, as a matter of policy, be offered a place at the school when they took up their teaching role. If they wished to delay, they would have to join the queue.

And the enrolments kept on coming

With no money spent on marketing, parents found out about the school by word of mouth. Our students were well dressed and had pride in their uniform, both in and out of school. The students were making observable academic progress against a core curriculum and external measurement. School reports were honest and jargon was removed. Some parents were, of course, upset by this direct approach and shocked when their child received a poor report. But on the whole parents developed confidence in reporting that was 'as the teachers saw it', without garnish. Despite any unhappiness, they saw that their children were happy at school. Most parents wanted to see their child challenged, develop self-confidence, make academic progress and be positive about school. With this, the word of mouth spreads.

We had zero money for advertising but I promised our senior students that we would write a prospectus before they left school. Indeed, when we computerised our enrolment list, we discovered we had over half the student population from the extended northern Adelaide and Barossa region on the waiting list. Clearly, many had no hope of a place. To prevent looming bad publicity about taking money under false pretences, we began a policy of informing parents who wanted to pay a deposit for enrolment that there was no real chance of being able to gain a place. By 1990 this enabled one in three of those choosing to pay to actually be offered a place. This was better than one in four, and those on the list were now able to be shown exactly where they stood on the list.

Student politics and power

With limited resources I believed we needed to maximise the capacity of our students to lead and to provide supervision and co-curriculum leadership. I wanted them to be able to run the school so that when they left, they would be able to run the country. I thought Australian business and government needed leaders with developed practical experience in handling authority and responsibility. In my view, student representative councils cheated students as they did not exercise authority or responsibility, only representation. I hoped our students would be involved in policy setting and writing.

In Years 8 and 9 students had leadership roles akin to those given to students on student representative councils. These roles were valuable and involved public exposure and speaking, but did not carry the exercise of power and authority. Year 10 students were appointed as College Seniors and were the first group of leaders across the whole college who were given real authority. They learnt a lot about the responsibility that goes with it; they wrote in the 1987 school magazine:

> The five College Seniors who began the year, did so with nervous anticipation. It took some time before we ceased marching around the grounds on yard duty looking for trouble, to strolling down to the oval and back to the canteen area, hoping for no trouble.

The reports written by students in the school magazine clearly indicated growing maturity beyond their experience as a senior within their particular House. The 1987 College Senior's report went on:

> Yard duty is only one of many responsibilities held by College Seniors. A general position is to delegate and practise authority throughout the College, ensuring that everything runs smoothly ... The College Seniors have also enjoyed holding dinners. We have been treated to Chinese and seafood among other things. Miss Gates has kindly allowed us the use of her flat several times so we can attempt to poison our beloved staff with the famous or

infamous College Seniors' cuisine. The video night organised by the College Seniors for the Junior Primary School, was mainly to the advantage of relieved parents who very bravely entrusted us with the care of their children whilst they went late night shopping. This was most successful and we have intentions of holding another in the near future.

The author, Megan Poore, continued, "College Seniors aren't simply ogres with red stripes who pull out check tickets from their top pockets and book naughty little vegemites who run in the breezeway. We are there to help people (and the teachers, I am sure you would agree!)."

I wanted students from Trinity College to be well trained in the art of leadership, with the capacity to exert authority, discipline and care with responsibility and accountability. This vision was initiated over time with students being appointed as House Leaders, House Seniors, Campus Seniors, Campus Prefects and finally School College Prefects.

The Houses were purposely too large for housemasters to run on their own. To enable them to carry out their full duties of care, they had to develop student leaders who they could entrust with responsibility. The school's seniors were chosen by students making a full, written job application and then meeting with an interview panel. All students applying were given interviews as part of their real-life experience and were given feedback on the interview process. Their housemaster was their primary referee and they could nominate two others. Within the House, House Seniors learnt to handle their limited authority, exercising it if needed by the imposition of 25 lines for offences against standards of the House. Such offences might include wearing the school uniform incorrectly, dropping paper in the yard, not attending yard clean-up on time and being late for morning assembly. House Seniors could only exercise authority with students of their own House.

In exchange for being given this authority, House Seniors were provided with a model of leadership where the leader serves by example. The concept of leadership in the school was that of the "Servant King".

It was modelled on the life and the teachings of Jesus Christ, who said that "the first shall be last and the last first". Good leaders make sacrifices and serve those they lead. In Jesus' time, washing the dirty feet of guests before a banquet was the job of the lowest servant, yet Jesus washed his disciples' feet before the Last Supper. When running a function for the students or for the House community – say, a barbecue – the leader would be expected to be the last to receive their food; you made sure that you first provided for those in your care.

Housemasters could nominate their House Seniors to become College Seniors. These students continued their House responsibilities but could exercise their authority across the whole student body. They supervised the behaviour of students travelling to and from school on public transport. They maintained an area of the schoolyard and carried out yard duty. The College Seniors were officially backed up by a teacher on duty, based in the staffroom. They knew they could call on help.

Year 12 College Prefects met weekly with the headmaster. They provided leadership at both the executive and management level across the whole student body. They assisted in supervision and leadership preparation of the College Seniors. They exercised their own formal, independent detention system, leading to, if necessary, a one-hour detention on a Friday afternoon after school. Parents were given notice, and returned the signed notice to the Prefect Room so they knew their student would be attending a prefect detention.

The Prefects were on sub-committees of the college council; they were on the curriculum committee, the uniform committee and other policy-making bodies. It was a shock for new teachers who came to Trinity with a great belief in a student representative council model to find that students at Trinity did not just represent opinion but exercised leadership to the extent that even curriculum changes they proposed were put up to a formal college curriculum committee.

Whilst student leaders were a very effective support, the housemaster had to start again each year and develop the skills of a new student group. It would have been easier to have a paid teacher as an assistant because the training would not have been required every year. However, student leaders did certainly reduce the load on staff, benefitting the bottom line as well as the students themselves.

By 1992 the prefects totally organised Trinity's 1268 students in order for the whole college photograph to be completed within 50 minutes. The photographer took just as long to seat the staff. The photographer had asked for half a day to complete the photo, but with students running the show, we were back in class within two lessons. In 1997 we allowed two lessons, and again the students, without any staff, organised 2505 students within 50 minutes.

It remains to be seen whether the vision of a body of students capable of running the country and contributing to the world environment will be realised. It was my hope and vision that the students, before they left Trinity, would be able to recognise the limits of leadership, yet have the capacity and confidence to lead a large complex community with vision and purpose. I hoped our students would gain wisdom, courage and the capacity to lead.

Lessons learnt

1. "Where there is no vision, people perish."[30] School communities need clear vision for a future that matters and can deliver. Master planning, even for school buildings and grounds, provides physical form for a vision.
2. When bad things happen, such as the unnecessary and untimely death of a student, a school with vision, purpose, and a sense of the transcendent enables students to grow.
3. Death and its finality are part of education, if education is training for life.
4. Co-curricular sport, music, drama etc. should be recognised in teachers' salaries and loads, with flexibility given.
5. Parents value honest reporting.
6. Student leadership can provide great expertise in a school, as well as in society later.

8
Demand grows, but obstruction wins
How parents' wishes are frustrated

Public schooling in lower socio-economic areas was clearly failing.[31] Parental demand for a different type of school was not limited to Gawler and the northern region of Adelaide. One reason only parents of low-income families sought a different type of school was highlighted in a 1989 federal parliamentary inquiry. A newspaper report[32] stated:

> Coming from the "right side of town" is a major factor in student performance and achievement in SA schools.
>
> A parliamentary inquiry into Year 12 retention rates in schooling and training has identified huge disadvantages for students in SA's poorer suburbs.

This chapter describes how, for all the talk of doing something, when lower-income parents in these regions sought en-masse to solve their children's schooling needs, they were stopped.

A school at Port Adelaide?

Our log-cabin house was right at the front of the school on a treeless public road misnamed "Alexander Avenue". At 7.30 am one Saturday, after another full-on week at school, the front door rattled with loud knocking. It was a mother with her son in tow. Seeing us in our pyjamas, she said, "Sorry to trouble you. My son has left his cricket togs in the classroom. Could you unlock it for us because the match starts at eight?"

Fifteen minutes later our lie-in was again interrupted. This time it was a young man with a carload of cricketers dressed in white. "Our kids are playing yours and we can't find the cricket oval. We're from Adelaide and don't know the area. Can you direct us?" In 1986 we were playing on any park with a concrete wicket. I directed the group to the small triangular public park in Evanston South.

The second interruption before 8 o'clock did it. We needed to look for a retreat.

The north-eastern region of Adelaide around the port was not one of Adelaide's expensive suburbs. We purchased a weekender in the suburban beachside suburb of Semaphore, a low-cost area to buy into and only 50 minutes away by car. We found a little post-war, cream-brick cottage only 18 lots from the beach. It seemed an ideal retreat.

By 1987 Trinity's waiting list had gradually grown to include cousins of existing students who lived across the northern and north-eastern suburbs of Adelaide, including the port. Residents of Semaphore I did not know struck up conversations with me that confirmed I was indeed the headmaster at Trinity. They asked, "Can we have a school like Trinity in Port Adelaide?" On one of my walks around the area, I noticed vacant waste land on the Port River, opposite the original landing site for the colony of South Australia known as "Port Misery". We planted the idea and invited a few people to our house. From this a committee was formed.

I was very pleased when the Council of Port Adelaide became involved in formulating the constitution and establishing the school. At the time, the idea that local government would be involved in setting up new non-government schools was novel. The gulf between the state system of public schools and local communities was highlighted when two other local councils made written requests to Trinity to establish new schools in their council areas. Local government councillors generally lived in their communities and understood that poor schools were not going to improve the liveability and viability of their regions.

The Semaphore committee was joined by Horst Lucke, president of the Semaphore Residents' Association and Professor Emeritus of

Law at the University of Adelaide. Given my workload at Trinity, I only reluctantly agreed to chair the proposed school, in exchange for Trinity having access to two rowing boats for an eight and a four on the Port River. Although this demand was made half in jest, it was an important story to relate to the parents at Trinity. The exchange was duly minuted and Trinity's access to two rowing boats was agreed to. All new schools need actual parents who intend to send their own children to the school, and it was pleasing that Deidre Calvert and Belinda Rosser, who both had young families, were elected school secretary and registrar. The Anglican Schools Commission agreed to become strongly involved.

The concept of a school owned by its local community, unashamedly seeking the maximum government grants available to enable very low fees and hence provide access to all, was gaining ground. We called a meeting in the library of the local state school, Le Fevre High, to test demand.[33] At 7.30 pm on 22 October 1987, the mayor of Port Adelaide was among 300 people who heard Dr Tony Shinkfield outline the history of low-fee schools. I introduced the committee and explained the draft prospectus.

Given such a large turnout, we knew we had to be very serious, and we ensured that those wishing to start the school could decide its name. Parents were given the choice of two names suggested by the committee, as well as a third option to reject both names and continue the search. This process alone made it clear to parents that this school would be different. It would be theirs. By a vote of three to one the name of St Nicholas, the patron saint of seafarers, was happily chosen ahead of St Vincent, the name of the Gulf the port was on. A uniform committee and a curriculum sub-committee were established and we released our prospectus. An astonishing 996 paid-up enrolments were quickly received.

The committees reported back to a public meeting of parents, which was attended by well over 600 people, filling the Port Adelaide Town Hall with many people standing. Chinese was voted the foreign language to be taught, and the school uniform designed and displayed by the uniform sub-committee was adopted. In 1987 we formally applied for the school to open in 1990.

Opposition and obstruction

Then the opposition began. To its credit, the Catholic school system was openly opposed. Others were covert. With the closest Lutheran college 17 kilometres away, we made an agreement to decline enrolments closer to their school. But privately we had opposition from just about everyone, including other Anglican colleges.

The federal Labor government decided to refuse the school's application because of new rules brought in to ensure a "planned provision" of schools. Under the guise of order and the efficient use of resources, new schools could only be established if they did not have any significant impact on surrounding schools. The region's state schools had many vacancies, and the Catholic system was concerned that a new school would also create vacancies in Catholic schools.

The people in the region found they could not opt for a school of their choice. Without competition, standards in this lower socio-economic region continued to drop.

Then the Education Department held a review of state schools in the region and closed West Lakes High School. This was a near-new school with outstanding facilities which had been very expensively built. The argument that St Nicholas would cause unnecessary duplication of school buildings had now been removed. A collection of brilliant, near-new, publicly funded buildings was empty and could immediately accommodate 1000 students.

A "letter to the editor" by a Mr P.A. Patterson, whom I did not know, made two important points.[34] First, he stated that the Education Department "has for too long treated Port Adelaide as 'only a working class area'." Then he quoted Aristotle to emphasise that the future of our state "depends on the education of our youth". So many parents in the region sent their children elsewhere for their education.

The committee continued to work hard to win approval and asked Trinity College to purchase the now vacant West Lakes High School. The Trinity council agreed to pay $4.1 million to buy the property. Clearly the council had no fear that the purchase was a risk should the school be given permission to open. The signed sale had a clause to ensure it was subject to the federal government giving approval to provide recurrent grants. Given the growth pressures on Trinity and with redevelopments for another 1000 students planned at Gawler and a new campus planned at Blakeview to the south (see chapter 9), the decision to sign up to purchase West Lakes High School was remarkable.

Enrolment numbers for St Nicholas grew to 1200 and the retiring heads of St Peter's College, Dr Shinkfield, and Walford Anglican Girls' School, Helen Reid, agreed to become the principal and deputy principal for three years to ensure a college of excellence. The St Nicholas council would then be on its own to appoint the next principal. The state government signed the sale documents with Trinity and Professor Lucke flew to Canberra to argue the case for St Nicholas' approval. There would be no duplication or oversupply of buildings; they were there, bought and ready to use. The area had a growth rate of 1.9% and strong local and state government support, and it only missed the required population growth rate to approve a new school by 0.1%.

But St Nicholas still had some covert enemies, including one from among those who should have given strong support: the chair of the SA Anglican Schools Commission (which was officially backing the school). Many years later, as chair of the commission myself, I read a letter from a previous chair, the then head of Pulteney Grammar School, who wrote on Anglican Schools Commission letterhead to oppose the opening of St Nicholas. The demand for schools like Trinity and St Nicholas, it seems, was too great and too threatening.

The poor academic performance in the Port Adelaide region was not quite as bad as the catchment area of Trinity, but it was also clear that these suburbs, with their existing schools, were not delivering the required educational outcomes. Despite this, the people of Port Adelaide were not going to be allowed the new type of school parents had hoped for. Even though Professor Lucke argued that 80% of state school parents in Victoria in 1989 backed Christian religious instruction in state schools,[35] the demand for St Nicholas College in a state without such a provision had a number of strong opponents. St Nicholas did not open.

How long will Australia accept recurring reports that our poorer regions are underachieving in education? Public education was and is no longer delivering. Even when an empty school built at public expense is allowed to go to wrack and ruin, the blocking of new schools that have too much parental demand highlights the need to change the system.

There is no doubt that non-government schools can also fail to deliver. When they fail, however, they either change direction to meet parental aspirations, try to prevent and remove competition, or go bankrupt. Both the Catholic and state systems are large enough to try to prevent new competition, and certainly, in the case of St Nicholas, other independent schools tried. As a result of the federal government's actions, West Lakes High School facilities decayed through under-use.

Woodcroft wobbles, Lindisfarne goes under

Woodcroft Anglican High School was planned for the southern suburbs of Adelaide and opened in 1989 with Dean Barker appointed as principal. The chair of the Woodcroft council, Barbara Neilson, was the principal of another new low-fee Anglican primary school, Lindisfarne, in the City of Unley.

The ability of educational leaders to provide schools to which parents wish to send their children depends on the aspirations of the school council and principal they appoint. Woodcroft seemed to be offering a loving Christian school with an academic program typical of state schools in the southern suburbs of Adelaide, albeit with some interesting group-learning innovations. The Anglican Schools Commission had founded the school and Dr Shinkfield had been a driving force in its beginnings. However, providing a Christian school with qualified teachers was not enough for parents to choose this school, and Woodcroft was rapidly going bankrupt.

I was invited to carry out a review and make recommendations for Woodcroft's future. My first recommendation was to change the philosophical direction of the school, a shift embodied in a new name: Woodcroft College. A change in the culture of the school to become academically rigorous and financially tighter was undertaken, and following the resignation of its founding principal, I recommended that the board consider appointing the deputy principal of Woomera Area School as the new head. To be just a Christian school charging fees but offering a state school-type of education did not cut it; academic rigour and discipline were also important.

With the original chair of Woodcroft as its principal and a small band of loyal supporters, Lindisfarne also struggled. Each year the school was running at a small financial loss, and while it met some people's needs, it did not have enough parents wishing to choose the school to support its spending. Like Woodcroft, it did not offer a rigorous and tested core curriculum that was sequentially arranged, but rather taught a curriculum based on the individual child and their interests. Again I was invited to carry out a review and offer advice, but unlike the case of Woodcroft, my recommendations were ignored. The school continued to bleed.

Eventually, following requests from the chair of Lindisfarne council, Trinity offered to take over the school and run it as an Adelaide primary school campus. This may well have been a stunning success because by now we were used to offering efficient low-cost schooling which attracted higher government funding. We had staff who could deliver the curriculum and who would expect to assess students using our common tests prepared by other teachers. Even though Unley was in an inner region of Adelaide which was variably wealthy, there were many families that were not well off. The state government had a policy of mixing in public housing in areas such as Unley, and there were also many families who had lived in inherited property in the area for generations who could not afford high-fee schools.

State primary schooling in Unley and wealthier suburbs was more successful than in the north, with fewer disruptive and difficult children. Teachers would send their own children to these schools. The Lutheran Church with St John's at Highgate, however, had demonstrated there was a demand for lower-fee Christian-based education in an area where the best state schools, such as Highgate Primary, were run almost next door. Such schools still need a principal who will bite the bullet if a staff member is not delivering, who will protect staff from unfair parental pressure, and who will support teachers in their discipline of children. If either the principal or board of the school allows things to just flow, the non-government school, unlike a state school, will eventually close.

While this handover of Lindisfarne had the support of its school board, Barbara Neilson was totally committed to her original vision and decided to persuade the council to approach another Anglican school, St John's Grammar at Belair. What Trinity offered in terms of academic rigour was unacceptable. This new direction may also have worked given that St John's was a success, but with its fee structure, St John's was moving quickly into the upper middle-class, and the facilities and resources in Unley were not competitive at that price. With the school still losing money, they raised the fees – and within two years St John's closed Lindisfarne down.

Once again just being a Christian school, with an independent board providing an alternative educational offering, was not in itself sufficient. Parents wanted a school with values, academic rigour, exciting challenges and a caring environment.

Lessons learnt

1. Schools that a majority of the population seek for their children are very threatening to existing educational providers, and government policy is used to restrict parental choice.
2. When independent schools are able to oppose new schools that they consider parents will find more desirable than their own, they will oppose the opening of a new school rather than change their own offering.
3. Neither government nor existing independent schools seek to really meet the needs of the poor in lower socio-economic regions.
4. Being both non-government and Christian are not sufficient qualities for a school to be chosen by parents for their own children.
5. Parents want a school with values, academic rigour, exciting challenges and a caring environment.

9
Pressure grows at home
Trinity expands southwards

With the demands of a young and growing school at Gawler, it may seem surprising that I spent so much effort on new schools at Port Adelaide and elsewhere. My role at the new schools differed from the pressures at Gawler. Elsewhere, everyone involved was keen and pleased to accept my leadership. At home, the founding parents, who generally wanted a small community school of about 600 students from Reception to Year 12, were not so enthusiastic. At the annual general meetings of Trinity and in the college council there was continuous pressure to restrict growth. The oft-repeated wish for Trinity was "the need to consolidate".

Why did I push to grow the school and thereby disappoint so many of the founding parents? At first my aim was to grow to the smallest number of students possible to allow for a financially efficient use of resources, enabling Trinity to become a high-quality academic school. If this growth was not achieved, Trinity would not be able to remain low fee and still pursue excellence.

My hope and dream was to have a secondary school with at least four classes of 28 in Year 8, which would ensure the school could economically offer a range of subjects in Year 12. This growth policy was hard fought, with voting at the school's annual general meetings drawing hundreds of parents to vote one way or the other. Teachers voted for growth. With the policy won during 1986, we were able to enrol four classes of Year 8 students in 1987 to start in 1988.

But demand for places was still outstripping supply. As already mentioned, even enrolling a child at birth no longer ensured them a place at Trinity. By 1989 only children born before July, and who had been enrolled at birth, could be offered a place. When enrolling their future child as 'Baby X' after a first positive pregnancy test, many parents asked us to keep the enrolment confidential for a month. Most outside the Trinity community thought this was just propaganda.

In 1989 we had 3500 students on our waiting list and 826 at the school, with 957 to attend the following year. We faced a dual tension: we needed capital to build facilities for a Year 11–12 College at Gawler, and yet we had to cope with the demand for more places in both primary and middle-school years. This would require still more capital expenditure to build new classrooms for more primary places. Clearly the enrolment pressures suggested we needed an extra primary feeder school as well. However, whilst drama productions in a tin shed had a certain charm, for the college to put off finishing the existing school to build a new campus would be crazy. It would divide the Trinity community and potentially destroy it. It would be political suicide for the principal.

Fortunately, back in 1987, John Duncan, a grandparent of children at the school, had forcibly persuaded me, albeit reluctantly, to spend precious money to employ an architect and develop a master plan for the Trinity campus. With our limited resources, these architect's drawings were used on photocopied publicity handouts because we had no prospectus and no actual buildings to show. Having a master plan enabled our community to picture the future educational resources that would provide for a senior secondary college.

The centrepiece was to be a chapel, a building that was more than basic and would be a future heritage site. It had to earn its way, however, so it was planned to seat 300 and be used for lectures, music concerts, drama productions and meetings as well as worship. We called the proposed building the Performing Arts Centre/Chapel. It would symbolise the transcendental nature of Trinity's foundation. The rest of the school would be utilitarian, functional and built at the lowest cost to meet the needs.

A new development

Driving to Adelaide one day in 1989, I noticed a bold, sparkling new billboard in the suburb of Craigmore advertising a subdivision called 'Springvale Estate'. I took down the phone number and rang to see if the developers were interested in a primary feeder campus to Trinity College as part of their development. They were.

Already the rules to establish schools in Australia had been tightened so that a new school could not open without three years of planning. It would obviously be a very delicate project to have a new school built for the next year. The school council would need to be persuaded, the school community would need to be won over, and financially the project would have to be totally separate from any support for the existing college.

"Here we go again," I thought, "starting a school with nothing and against considerable opposition!"

However, we did have a supportive Anglican Schools Commission, still chaired by Tony Shinkfield. Executive officer Charlie Williams, a retired state school principal, moved quietly among the planning authorities to explain the problems and the need. He was well known to them from pushing for the St Nicholas project in Port Adelaide, but in this case no one could argue there was no growth in the region.

The Trinity council put a toe in the water, and being prepared to see how the plan would progress, called a public meeting in Trinity's audio visual room for 12 March 1990. The situation was explained to the existing school community in the school's weekly newsletter. They were told that only a quarter of those applying for a place at Trinity actually

Master plan sketch for future Trinity development, 1987

achieved one. Half of the waiting list wanted to enrol for Reception, and two-thirds of these came from Gawler and areas to the north. Those who were enrolled for a secondary school only came from areas at least eight kilometres *south* of Trinity. Sadly, students joining Trinity in Year 8 were academically two to three years behind our own Year 7 students. The newsletter stated how, by opening a new R–7 campus in this area (which included Craigmore), we would improve our secondary school's academic capacity, with more of our own students entering Year 8 from a Trinity primary school.

Trinity could not afford to lose its diversity of enrolment. The areas south of the school were the most socially deprived in South Australia. A third of the school's parents were unemployed and were eligible for free books under a government program. On the other hand, the parental leadership of the school was drawn, by and large, from the 20% of parents whose children could have attended schools in the city. These were using Trinity as a primary school with a view to probably transferring at Year 8. Maintaining the confidence of the highly educated and well resourced, as well as the aspiring middle-class, was important.

Although we called the public meeting about a new school because of our overwhelming waiting list, this fact was not universally believed. Rumours abounded. Was the waiting list real? Those interested in sending their children to the new campus had been invited to attend, and council members were keen to see what the interest level might be.

Strangers kept coming. By 7.10 pm, 20 minutes before the meeting was due to open, the audio visual room holding 240 people was packed. Keys had to be found to open the big chook shed, which we ambitiously called 'the gym'. We were clearly unprepared. Ten minutes later we asked people to carry their chairs across the two asphalt basketball courts which were doubling as a car park for the night. The vast shed was full.

Palpable fear was in the air. We had planned to see if there was the demand for just a single-stream primary school of just 220 students, so those attending realised that their children might not get in. Their questions reinforced this: "If the new school is only going to offer 220 places, how are you going to meet the demand? There are many more than 220 here at the meeting." Some of the 800 present already had children at Trinity and were considering transferring to a campus closer to home, but this information failed to reduce the sense of panic.

To the council members present, other rather more important questions should have been asked such as "Do you have government approval?" and "How can you open a school next year?" The answers would have been honest: "We have to give two years' notice and the school may not be allowed to open until 1993. However, given the huge demand shown tonight, we will try for next year. Yes, 1991. We will ask the authorities to invite our application for next year."

Also in the mix were the local government council and the Education Department, as they were planning to establish a state school in Blakeview, a new suburb adjacent to Craigmore. We had already agreed to shift from the site I had arranged in the Springvale Estate to a new site so we could co-locate with the new Blakeview Primary School. Although we had made this change to be adjacent to the primary school at a site allocated by the local council and planners, the state school was on paper only and was years away.

The hearts and minds battle was truly on. The rumours needed squashing. In the school newsletter following the meeting, I wrote, "The Craigmore Campus is enjoying very strong enrolment guarantee payments." These payments were equivalent to one term's fees, yet we had no refusals. For those on unemployment and other benefits, a term's fees might be only $65, but for these families it was real money required within 30 days.

I continued: "This campus is financially self-sufficient. All stories that the Chapel Foundation money is being used to fund Craigmore ARE WRONG! ... Craigmore will not drain resources from Gawler if it opens. It will strengthen the Year 8–12 program and the financial viability of the whole school."

In the same newsletter we reported that on Thursday evening, John Duncan, on behalf of the Chapel Foundation committee, had presented the college council with a cheque for $119,000 in promised donations. This was above and outside normal school funding and enabled the chapel to be planned with a bell tower (minus the bell). It enabled a functional building to become a long-term symbol. Rumours of the Chapel Foundation money being used to fund the new school ended.

With so many on the waiting list missing out on a place at the existing Trinity campus, we obviously had to explain to them, as well as to existing parents, that building a second campus altered nothing for their enrolment except that their children would enter Year 8 (on the existing Trinity campus) via the Craigmore campus. Those students entering Craigmore from the enrolment list wanted a primary education but had been unable to secure one due to the lack of places on the existing campus. How could we claim to be open to all when parents were clearly wanting an R–12 education but we said, "No, you can't come until Year 8"?

Built 1990-1 Trinity College chapel

We opened the new campus within 10 months and renamed it Blakeview in line with the shift to the new suburb. We were full, with classes of 30 and not 28 because every single enrolment from the year before followed through.

Finding a principal

The key to any new school is its founding principal. We had to find an excellent one to ensure Blakeview succeeded.

All outside senior appointments to a school involve real risk. Following a formal review by Trinity College culminating in my confirmation as principal for another five years, I was given a new contract and the college had a new constitution which gave me the right to actually select staff to be appointed by council. This now meant that if the appointment of this new campus principal went pear-shaped, it would be totally my responsibility.

Kevin Whittington was among the applicants. He was principal of the state school at Hamley Bridge. I was pleased to receive his application because in the Year 8 entrance tests, Hamley Bridge Primary was the only feeder school to Trinity whose students academically matched ours.

Kevin, as an Education Department principal, was finding the department had changed. Pressure was being applied for him to turn Hamley Bridge into a typical state school of the day. The changes meant the curriculum would have less content and would lack a strong planned and sequential build-up of knowledge from Reception to Year 7. The strong secular bias in state schools was underscored by the removal of the celebration of Christian festivals, and there was an expectation that all students had to win a prize. By this stage formal testing was also under review and becoming unfashionable. Reporting to parents was becoming generalised and jargon laden. Kevin was tiring of fighting to keep teaching the curriculum he wanted. He felt he was slowly losing the battle with the bureaucracy and the new staff being appointed to the school.

In 1990, however, to appoint a non-Anglican head with no experience in independent schools was unlikely. Kevin was a Baptist attending a Uniting Church. How would he handle the pressure of running a school operating with fewer resources than a state school? And how would a non-Anglican leader work with the Anglican parish (Elizabeth Downs) that was strongly supporting the new school?

A selection panel was set up to advise me on my nomination. We had four great applicants. Kevin was brilliant, relaxed and experienced; but underneath he was paddling furiously. He preferred the curriculum offered at Trinity and was keen to facilitate common testing between the two campuses. He was selected.

Blakeview opens

Before Blakeview was built, all-day working bees were held to plant trees. Kevin proved to be a superb leader – with a great appetite at the lunch time sausage sizzles, he ensured all were welcome. Camaraderie was

Blakeview opens day one

being established. I proudly planted tree number 167 and informed the whole Blakeview community that, come next February, my tree would no doubt be the tallest on the block. To ensure this, I said, I would visit over the summer period before the school was opened to water the tree and nurture it. The opportunity for the parent body to meet each other as well as Father Bart O'Donovan of St Catherine's Elizabeth Downs and members of the parish had a huge unifying effect.

Kevin and Father Bart became part of the new school community and were embraced by them. Father Bart was appointed as the visiting chaplain and Kevin was clearly the man in charge. He had a passion for gardens and a passion that the school would be a wonderful environment for children. The programs were child-focused, and as always a playground was part of the early provision. The community elected its own advisory committee, with similar authority to a state school council (in other words, effectively advisory). It brought together a great group of people, including some who became outstanding future members of the college council. One was Brian Carr, CEO of one of Adelaide's large councils, Tea Tree Gully. An entrepreneurial go-getter, he was quickly nominated and elected to the Trinity college council where his vision, skills and drive made me as headmaster seem moderate.

Blakeview opened enrolled to capacity from day one, with 237 students. Karen Mitson, an outstanding teacher from the Gawler campus, became the R–3 curriculum co-ordinator and provided continuity of knowledge of the curriculum. Together with other proven Trinity teachers, Wendy Stimson and Julie Bruce, she formed a core within the school who knew the curriculum standards. Wendy's husband, John Stimson, donated the master site plan for the building, and John McDonald, whose price was about half that of other builders, built the log-cabin classrooms. These were becoming a sign of quality education to the parents of this northern Adelaide region. Gawler had log-cabin classrooms and the Blakeview parents wanted them as well.

The core curriculum was exactly the same as Gawler's. Term tests were exactly the same. Teachers from the year below set the term tests for the mid-year exams, and teachers from the year above set the tests for the end of the year. Rosslyn was the overall head of R–4 and she vetted all the early learning tests. David Smith had oversight of Years 5–8 and vetted the primary tests. Our claims that all students would receive honest reports with meaningful marks and that the testing would be the same across the whole college were important selling points, as well as being promises made to the parents of children at Blakeview.

Without any government capital grants, the cost of the land and buildings meant the new campus slowly lost money. Sums had been carefully added up to show the cost of the land, library and other overheads would be the same for 500 students as for 200, so in 1991 the decision was made to double stream the Blakeview campus. This meant there would be two classes at each year level from Year 1 onwards. This was an important learning experience for the Trinity council because it taught us that a low-cost, quality education required maximum efficiency, and to achieve this required a two-stream primary school of around 500 students. Within a few years, Blakeview began running a budget surplus.

But the pressure of enrolments did not ease. With the opening of the new campus, enrolments on the waiting list surged across the whole college. We had added 500 more primary places and 60 extra Reception places at Blakeview, yet the enrolment list jumped by the same number. We were beginning to learn that demand for the kind of school we were running was measured by the availability of places. As word got out that people were gaining places at Trinity College, more enrolments followed.

With so much pressure on places, what should we do? In my statement to the college council in 1989, two years before, I had noted the demand for enrolments and for a period of consolidation during the next five years: "This period will include planning and completing our existing resources. During this time, plans for the 20-year development of the school are to be developed ... A period of consolidation will be necessary to establish control of the administrative procedures ... We need to think carefully and quietly before launching ahead with the major new developments."

In 1992 I made good on this commitment and stopped any growth of enrolments. We were full and "consolidating". With the school remaining unchanged in 1992, I took long service leave and visited some leading educational institutions in the United Kingdom. But the consolidation of this one year in the first eight years of Trinity's history was to be short-lived.

Lessons learnt

1. Parents value common testing and honest reporting. Accurate academic reports based on valid measured benchmarks enable parents to understand their child's actual progress.

2. The key to a new school is its principal. He or she must enjoy the support of the school community and be keen to strengthen and support the philosophical foundations of the school.

3. A core curriculum with a disciplined yet caring Christian school environment, as modelled by the school at Gawler, was successfully transferrable to a new school.

4. Working together as a school community for a new school builds friendships, enthusiasm and ownership of the school in its foundation year.

10
Drugs and sex
What's a headmaster to do?

It wasn't even Friday the 13th and I got it wrong, causing a blow-up outside a staff celebration for my birthday.

In the small staffroom there was a very happy, relaxed gathering of teachers. It was Friday afternoon, 23 October 1987, and the party, which had started at 4.30 pm, was in full swing. Rosslyn had prepared food and our family supplied both soft and alcoholic drinks. The staff of the school worked ridiculously hard, and the party was one of the many ways we were able to recognise their effort and say thanks.

Striding up the path at about 5.15 pm was a parent on the warpath. She insisted on speaking to the headmaster and I reluctantly left the party to have a word. She was furious.

"I hear you are planning to expel my son," she declared.

'Richard'[36] and his sister had been in the school a matter of weeks. They had attended one of the House camps. For a young teenager transferred from a state school in the south-east of South Australia, it was a chance to impress his new peers, and taking marijuana to the camp seemed to Richard a sure thing. But it backfired when he was reported to the housemaster by another student. His previous school, in common with all other schools, had a 'no drugs' policy, and so did Trinity. Drugs in the school meant expulsion.

I explained this to Richard's mum. Mum replied, "But the marijuana he took was to a camp, not to school, and this was just common practice at his last school."

Richard had shown in a very short time that he was an able student with leadership qualities. I understood that the family shift had been one of great stress. He had made a mistake, and as his mother pointed out, "Other schools won't take on a drug student." One of Trinity's chaplains backed Richard and undertook to look after his future. However, our policy gave me no leeway, so I expelled him. I also contacted and recommended him to Blackfriars (a Catholic boys' school). Because Richard had been open and honest with me, I was able to tell the Blackfriar's headmaster, "I believe Richard would be an asset to your school and deserves another chance."

I had acted according to Trinity's policy, recommended by me and endorsed by the school council, yet the decision to expel Richard disturbed me. I couldn't help feeling that something about our approach was wrong.[37]

Ros and I were invited to dinner the next Saturday evening by the president of the Parents' and Friends' Association of Trinity. Another couple from one of Adelaide's socially elite co-ed schools was also there. Their son was in a psychiatric hospital. "Michael, do you know he is in a psychiatric ward full of 24-year-old males, all of whom have smoked dope?" I was both shocked and heartbroken for them. He continued, "As a young student, my son started smoking marijuana at school. The old scholars would drop the drugs over the school fence at recess time." I shared my story about Richard and he responded, "The drugs were a problem at our elite school too and they have the same policy: caught with drugs at school and you are expelled."

Even in the 1980s it was known that marijuana for many young people was the trigger to switch on schizophrenia.[38] In 1987, marijuana use by teenagers was a rapidly growing phenomenon, with studies showing about 12% of Year 9 students (13-year-olds) and 26% of Year 11 students trying it. By 1996, over 55% of Year 11 students throughout Australia had used marijuana.[39, 40] Publicly, we could not be seen to be soft on drugs.

However, I was not happy. Expelling Richard meant that the student who reported the drug use would not see justice done, but injustice. The message was: "If you report your friends, they will be expelled with no hope of getting it right." Reporting meant they were letting their friends down. With our 'no drugs' policy we were effectively teaching our students to remain silent and not report drugs. Yet a student code of silence is just what drug dealers need to expand their trade and we were creating that code. Teenagers make mistakes as they advance from childhood to adulthood, and they need to be able to make mistakes, with consequences, to enable learning and growth as independent adults.

We knew we would inevitably have more students come to Trinity who were in the habit of using and even abusing drugs and who saw this as normal. Young people believed smoking marijuana was not as bad as drinking – in fact healthier, and with no hangover! We needed a policy that enabled the drug pusher to be exposed and not protected by student secrecy; one by which students who reported felt empowered and in control. The student reporting needed to see that the student they reported was being helped, not damned. The school needed to teach students to accept responsibility for developing a healthy, caring environment.

We could not condone illegal drugs in the school, so we developed a policy that clearly gave our students the chance to initiate the reporting of their peers, and by so doing control the outcome. Our policy guaranteed that if students reported illegal drug use to their housemaster or principal, their friends would not be expelled. We raised the bar even higher by making an additional commitment that if they did not report their friends, and their friends were found out by staff or parents, then we would report them to the police and expel them from the school. Because the stimulus for this policy change occurred at a school camp and not in school, we made the following wider statement: "Any illegal drug use by students of the college which affects the life of the college, in the opinion of the principal, shall be acted on by the principal in the same manner as if it occurred at school."

The policy was soon tested by a long-standing, well-established family in the school who used marijuana at home as part of their family lifestyle.

A nervous Year 7 boy came to see me. The boy had obviously had long talks with others, including a school chaplain. The words tumbled out in a rush: "Sir, we were invited … with my friends from our class at school … to visit Alvin's house to play … and we smoked marijuana."

By talking to each of the students involved individually I was able to piece together their story. Over the school holidays, a group of Year 7 boys had smoked marijuana at the host boy's home. The marijuana was rolled into cigarettes and kept above the stove in the kitchen.

I set out to apply our new policy. The chaplains had become deeply involved in the situation and the housemaster had a vague idea something was wrong, so clearly it was affecting the life of the school. On the other hand, to smoke marijuana was socially accepted in Alvin's household and extended family.

Not wishing to expel Alvin – given that the information about his supplying marijuana had come from a student – I met him before lessons began on the next school day. I explained the school's policy and told him I believed he had been smoking marijuana with other students at home. I had no doubt about the facts when I first met with him. "Alvin, you must think about your position," I said. "You will be expelled unless you tell me the full truth, as is required by school policy. I can't have a student supplying another student with illegal drugs and then lie about it."

I could see Alvin believed I was trying to trick him into a confession. He did not believe that I already had corroborated reports from three independent sources. He denied the accusation and I became very worried.

To give him time I ensured that he had a discussion with one of the chaplains and his housemaster. Just before lunch he stuck to his guns and again said nothing had happened. "Alvin," I said, "I'll see you at the end of the day, straight after school, and if I do not have the truth you will be expelled." After school he once again said: "I didn't supply marijuana. It's not true, sir, and I won't admit to anything." I told him he was expelled.

I was devastated. This was the first time a student had not owned up. He then broke down and said: "My Mum and Dad made me promise never ever to tell anybody we smoke marijuana at home." They ran a highly regarded, elite business in Gawler.

Alvin's admission created a dilemma. Should I break with our policy and allow an admission of guilt after his expulsion?

At about 3.45 pm Alvin's mother stormed into my office. She took me to task: "How can you prove any of this? You can't! You have no evidence as you can't know definitely. My son is innocent." She continued her rapid-fire arguments, but I had already understood the foundation of the defence. Thanks to Alvin I was able to say: "I will give Alvin a good reference to another school as he actually admitted to supplying other students with marijuana after I expelled him." I gave a good reference for Alvin to attend Faith Lutheran College.

With a heavy heart I reported this incident to the school council. Alvin had obeyed his parents' wishes. Families like his across Australia were supplying their children with marijuana. Clearly our school could not be an island, and our students were compromised by the failure of our community to control the supply of marijuana.[41]

It is very difficult for principals to know what is actually happening in their schools. One principal of a leading Adelaide college told me he had no drug problem at his school. Yet in conversation with one of our family's previous rectors, we learnt that his son attending the school had joined with a group of other boys at lunchtime and crossed into the Adelaide parklands for a few joints of marijuana. I had tried to persuade other independent school heads to try to change our state marijuana laws because of the evidence that our current approach was failing and we were actually developing a climate that enticed more teenagers to smoke dope as well as rewarding the criminals who supplied them. Privately about half the heads agreed, but they said they could not go public because their school community would not support them. One head actually mentioned that the pressure to maintain enrolments was too great to make a public stand.

Alcohol, the legal drug

In order to save the school the cost of a salary, I taught maths and science classes, even though the workload was a struggle. However, I discovered that teaching enabled me to get to know each student well. Even more important was the rapport I built with teachers because I shared their experience of teaching some very difficult students. This established an invaluable collegial relationship with the other staff.

After the first few years, we were financially stronger and I taught every Year 8 class in the school for just a two-to-three-week block of science lessons using the textbook *Your Shout*, the alcohol education program described in chapter 3.[42] With tongue in cheek I informed the Year 8s that Jesus' first miracle was his best. Although we could not turn water into the best wine like the wedding feast in Cana, we could at least attempt to win a trophy for winemaking. We planted a small vineyard in the middle of the School with a special strain of Cabernet Sauvignon grapes. Students could undertake the Year 9 viticulture and Year 11 winemaking[43] classes in agricultural science.

My concern was that the major drug of abuse in the 1980s was in fact alcohol. The students were taught the physiology of the body and how alcohol alters this. They were taught the best ways to become an alcoholic and how this disease destroyed families and weakened Australia's economy. I had one in seven students stand up in class and informed them that this was how many of them in the Australian context would statistically become alcoholics. I hoped that the old scholars of Trinity would have perhaps only two alcoholics per class compared with the four students standing.

But classes alone weren't enough. To effectively teach students about the careful consumption of alcohol and the reasonableness of abstinence, students had to see this modelled. Each year the college's Presentation Ball provided the opportunity for this.

The Presentation Ball was one of the rites of passage for Year 11 students. The girls, now young ladies, wore long white dresses and the boys wore dinner suits. To teach responsible consumption of alcohol, we allowed those over 18 to purchase alcoholic drinks from the bar. We wanted the ball to give our 16- and 17-year-old boys and girls the opportunity to experience formal ballroom dancing and to learn the skills of formally mixing with the opposite sex. I believed young people needed milestones that signified their gradual coming of age. Mixing with the opposite sex and consuming alcohol can develop an environment where they make mistakes they later regret. The ball was about both.

The rule was clear. As headmaster I could not run a function that allowed underage alcohol consumption. In our community, people over 18 can legally drink, and so when any student of Trinity or old scholar attended, if 18 they could legally be offered alcohol for sale. I hoped that these older students and former students would drink moderately and provide responsible role modelling for the younger students. Reports to me from other schools of student parties indicated that many teenagers believed the purpose of drinking was to get drunk, preferably quickly. However, during the school balls, the older students, old scholars and parents were impeccable, and over many years I was not disappointed.

We only had trouble with underage drinking once – on the first year we held the ball. Max Smith, being a Year 10 student, had to wear school uniform to the ball, but he was determined to test the system. He put rum into a Coke bottle and brought it with him. David Smith was now the head of the middle school and had the job of ensuring there was no underage drinking. The students were warned that Mr Smith would be going around smelling students' drinks. Max was discovered, and the discipline policy had to be followed. It was well established: no student was permitted to consume alcohol or smoke cigarettes at school, in school uniform or at school functions. Students who did so were to be given at least a Saturday detention and then suspended for one week for the offence. Three Saturday detentions in one year and you were to leave until the end of the year.

Max had already accumulated a number of detentions, and with this third Saturday detention he was expelled. Years later he wrote to me: "I am in prison at the moment and I had a drug habit for some nine months, [but] I have kicked my habit and I am now completing my Year 11 education … I am proud to say I have not received a mark lower than a B. Things have come a long way for me and after I am released I will be coming to visit you and Trinity College." He remembered many happy times at the school yet also railed at the school's discipline structure. He believed our expectation of students was too high.

We may have sometimes failed, but I was pleased a person expelled in Year 10, about to be released from prison, was able to write to me to say that he had had many happy times at Trinity. He was also coming to tell me what was wrong with the school. I looked forward to it. Tragically, on leaving prison Max became a courier and was knocked off his bike and killed.

The fight for better drug laws
By 1989 the college council was becoming a real sounding board for me as principal. Eventually I was able to share ideas and concerns with them honestly as colleagues. One day I informed them, "This morning, the parents of two girls visited to enrol their children. They told me that their daughter in Year 8 is under enormous pressure to smoke tobacco and marijuana at her current school." After this meeting, a teacher applicant travelling up by train noted the drug dealing among primary school students, but notably added, "Not amongst the Trinity College students."

The pressure on students to be part of the drug trade was immense. Two senior staff members reported that a Uniting Church youth worker had contacted them and told them that "drug sellers are unhappy with sales at Trinity, and are considering placing some plants in Trinity uniforms on buses and trains to offer drugs". Our teachers knew from my confidential reports to them that I now favoured changing the state's laws to gain control over the supply of marijuana for young people. In the fight against drugs I felt as effective as King Canute commanding the rising tide to stop. Marijuana was freely available and pushed at our students in many social settings. I suggested to the council a plan to change the law while indicating I believed it would be bad for our school's image and enrolments to make it public. But at least I got to let off some steam.

Two years passed without returning to the issue. Articles were published in the newspapers describing similar problems in other schools. Then in early 1997, to my astonishment, the vice-chair of Trinity council, John Ragless, raised the idea in general business that perhaps the council should encourage the headmaster to go public with his ideas to encourage discussion. I suggested we could hold a public and open parental evening with a debate on two motions approved by council to be put to a parental vote. Basically I believed we had better control of nicotine than marijuana because cigarettes were legal and criminals were not making fortunes. They needed to protect and promote marijuana sales because they made so much profit from them.

My idea was straightforward. Governments tax cigarettes and use the money in general revenue to advertise the truth about the damage done through smoking. The state government could also license and tax the growing of marijuana and control its sale through chemist shops. Negative advertising telling the truth would then protect our children by changing the attitude of the whole community.

The college council approved the following two motions to be put before a special meeting of parents:

> Motion 1. "The Trinity College community endorses the drug policy of the college and encourages the state to produce tighter

and effective laws regarding the availability of marijuana in our society."

Motion 2. "The Trinity College community encourages the leadership of the college to promote the headmaster's plan for discussion as a basis for a change to our marijuana laws, namely:

1. Banning private production of marijuana.
2. Effective tight control by government supply.
3. Stiff penalties for supply to under 18s or for trading with adults.
4. Strong anti-marijuana publicity on TV, radio and in schools (e.g. Quit Program).
5. Zero blood (THC) level when driving.
6. No smoking of marijuana in public places.
7. Taxes raised on marijuana sales would pay for police, education and health programs."

The press gave us bad headlines: LEGALISE POT, SAYS COLLEGE HEADMASTER.[44] My reputation was on the line and the reputation of the school with it. We were attacked not only by those who believed we best 'protect' our community by prohibition but by the pro-legalisation of marijuana lobby group as well.[45]

I fully expected a hit on enrolments, but I was able to report to the council that we had yet another wave of new enrolments and were already telling applicants they would probably have no chance of a place. However, we were still unsure whether the publicity would cause a walkout of our existing parents. We invited the most senior political figures from both major parties, representatives of the police and all our parents and college community to a meeting. Our college council chair, Dr Rupert Thorne, a local GP, presented both his professional perspective and the view of the council. This time I was very happy with the press reporting: I was no longer going to "pot" but calling for drug law changes.[46]

Annette Hurley, the MP for Napier (the state electorate just south of Trinity), spoke clearly about the need for change. Many parents who were opposed came to the meeting, but most changed their minds and voted to support a campaign to change the laws. Other speakers at the meeting were cautious and extremely surprised that after the discussions and questions there was an overwhelming vote of support from the hundreds of parents present for their school to pursue a change.

Did our policies succeed?
We failed to change any laws. We did succeed in raising the issue and exposing the growing role of cannabis in motor car accidents. Our students were still endangered. Back in 1997 Dr Thorne had travelled with me by train to meet the Minister for Health, Dr Michael Armitage. We talked with another passenger, a young man on his way to court for sentencing. He told us, "I've had just a few joints to calm my nerves." Rupert very kindly said that this was probably not a great idea. He replied, surprised by the suggestion, "But I might have to go to prison."

The minister gave us a sympathetic hearing and described our proposal as having "merit". But he wrote to another local MP saying, "In any event, as a government we remain committed to the enforcement of laws relating to the commercial cultivation and supply of cannabis."[47]

I still feel a sense of failure when any student or old scholar is entrapped by drugs or their effects. Attending one funeral of an old scholar rammed home the deep loss and grief. He had become schizophrenic, yet despite this he was a wonderful, hard-working young man. He committed suicide. The bright spot at the funeral was the very large presence of old scholars, some with their young families.

Knowing that too many headmasters did not know what was really happening in their schools, I welcomed the chance in 2000 to be part of a national study of student drug-taking to find out what was happening at Trinity.[48] A federal government agency surveyed our students about all drugs, alcohol and smoking. Did we achieve any change in behaviour through our programs of drug education and openness? Yes. But honestly, not as much as I expected or would have liked. With students who had never tried cannabis we had about 4% more students. Those claiming to use cannabis more than six times in the last four weeks was 5.5% across all the Trinity schools, compared with 7.7% in the national sample. Overall we had reduced the problem by around 20% compared with schools across the nation.

Clearly we had made a difference. However, it was still a great surprise to learn that this survey came across about 10% of our students who had at some stage smoked cannabis, and even worse, around 3% who were 'training' to be regular users.

In retrospect, our policy of openness in dealing with a problem that was going to continually recur in the school had some merit. Even the small reduction of 2.2% in students using cannabis regularly meant that about seven of the 300 old scholars graduating from Trinity each year were safe, even though 15 were still at risk. However, student behaviour away from school was strongly influenced by the surrounding community, and this reinforced the need to change community attitudes and behaviour.

Sex education

Sex rates pretty highly during puberty and adolescence, so it followed that we should teach about relationships with others in our Christian Living classes, as well as overtly in science lessons. The biology of sex and procreation does not necessarily enable value judgments, love and purpose to be explored fully, yet in science many questions overlapping these issues are asked, and with changing bodies these lessons are important. Science does not address questions such as "How should you as a young man or young woman treat those of the same or opposite sex?" School chaplain Father Alan Courtney, happily married with a young family of his own, prepared a program to cover this. His wife Cherryll was also involved.

There were frank and open discussions of the issues, with separate classes for boys and girls. The single-sex classes met with GPs, both male and female, and students were able to ask the bluntest questions. Parents were invited to the school to be given background on what was being taught and were also invited to ask questions. In the first year of the program, nearly every parent attended. We told them students would be able to ask sensitive questions and outlined the content of the course.

An information night like this for parents was planned every year before their children were about to enter the program. When the parent night was on in the second year, only Sue and Tony Copeland turned up. Sue was on the college council and felt duty bound to come. The sex education program must have gained the trust of parents.

Practical skills in relating

Two adjacent classrooms were crowded with Year 11 students waiting with expectant and excited chatter. Girls and boys had been separated. In each room the young men and ladies were lined up by height with the tallest closest to the door. As the two lines came through the door they were partnered by height. To ensure the numbers were even, a few experienced older students were included.

They were preparing for Trinity's first Presentation Ball. Actions speak louder than words, so we established these balls for our Year 11s to develop some social skills and respect.

Young girls grow up to be young ladies, and we believed this transition needed to be celebrated in the wider community in a formal way. We borrowed and changed the traditions of the very old-fashioned Debutante Ball. Unchanged were the ballroom dances – waltzes, the Military Two Step, the Gay Gordon, the Pride of Erin and, after supper, the Progressive Jive. Both boys and girls were presented, the girls in white and boys in dinner suits. Our family bought second-hand wedding dresses to ensure that those families who struggled to pay Trinity's low fees could be part of the occasion; our own three daughters' dresses (bought second-hand for $80) were lent out discreetly to others. In contrast, some families paid hundreds of dollars for exquisite tailored dresses that I thought would be suitable for the grandest weddings.

Because nearly all our parents and students lacked any experience with ballroom dancing, there were dancing lessons for both. Students were taught four formal ballroom dances and one presentation dance. For the presentation, students crossed the dance floor and presented themselves to the guest of honour as their life highlights were read out. The five steps up and then down needed practice because many of the girls chose to wear high heels for the first time. The Queen's Waltz was the presentation dance, which the 150 presentees danced as a demonstration of their poise and new-found skills. Parents were then asked to join them in a second bracket of the dance while the students noticeably and proudly relaxed.

Part of the etiquette taught to both boys and girls was the acceptance of the other sex as a friend. Partnering a person of the opposite sex did not imply either lifetime commitment or sexual obligation. We wanted to develop relationships characterised by charity, concern and compassion, mixed with a sense of joy, love and freedom. Learning to hold and move with a person of the opposite sex in a cooperative and formal way in front of parents, family and friends was very much part of a balanced sexual education for young people.

Fortunately we had a core of parents and grandparents who could dance and pass on a lost culture from at least a generation-and-a-half before. Nonetheless, the situation was like a ticking time-bomb. Slowly post-ball parties grew in number, and while they had nothing officially to do with the school, they began to impact negatively on us. Teenagers were put at risk, with free grog lowering inhibitions and degrading the dignity of relationships developed through the school.

We published guidelines for parties in the student diary which were actually meant to be instructions to parents. We held parents responsible as hosts for other people's sons or daughters. We encouraged them to be responsible for the transport of their sons and daughters to and from social occasions. We expected host parents to exercise direct control over alcohol and moral conduct. We regarded parties and social functions as worthwhile activities that should be enjoyable and believed they offered families the opportunity for cooperation between family members. However, students observed varying standards of social behaviour at parties, and we insisted adults make it clear which standards were acceptable and which were not. This provided students with a basis on which to build their own ideas.

An unfolding nightmare

The behaviour of teachers is another way students learn. If staff are sexually lax, this is noticed and talked about. If teachers abuse the trust of their position, then hypocrisy is learnt, and often lives are damaged way beyond school.

It was a matter of instinct. While walking around the school I was not comfortable with the interaction between the Witt House housemaster and students during lesson time. It seemed a bit strange to me that one housemaster would need to counsel students quite so often, even when it was out in the open in the schoolyard, sitting on the raised garden bed surrounds. We had no rooms for student counselling and normally the classroom would be used. We had glass panels in the doors, but even with this I strongly advised any teachers on their own with a student to ensure their door was open. I did not know what was actually wrong, but the relationships between 'Mr X' and students seemed too intense.

However, Mr X was one of our most effective teachers and was highly regarded by staff, students and parents. He was also married to another staff member who had other extended family members in the school, both as students and staff.

At Friday night staff drinks, Michael Burvill-Holmes casually had a quiet word with me about concerns raised by one of his parents. I asked him to speak with the father and ensure that either he or his son came and spoke with me. The following Monday the matter quickly became very serious. As a result of meeting 'Chris', I understood that improper suggestions of a sexual kind might have been made by Mr X. After two discussions I decided to meet with a number of other students who Chris thought might be able to help. My separate interviews with 'Evan' and 'David' confirmed the need to treat Chris seriously.

I now had the word of two Year 11 students, supported by a third. (David, who was a cousin of Mr X's wife, could only tell me to believe the other two because Mr X had made him feel uncomfortable during an extended family holiday.) Being out on a limb, I decided that I needed the students to put their information in writing. I asked them to meet separately with the college bursar in his office and to write out a statement in front of him. Horrie Shilcock, a respected retired bursar from Pulteney Grammar School, was helping on a part-time basis to bring order into our accounts. He witnessed their statements. When I read them, I found they were graphic descriptions far beyond the careful suggestions and allusions the students had made in their discussions with me.

I was now suspecting that other students might be involved. I asked some senior staff to try and find out. After two days of discreet enquiries, nothing further came to light. With only the statements from three students outlining improper, unprofessional and graphic invitations to sex parties, there was no indication any other student had suffered similar abuse.

What had been claimed, I believed, needed to be acted on. I consciously decided to back the students, even if I was faced with denials from Mr X. With what I knew, his position at Trinity was untenable. To find out what help I could get, I contacted the Department of Community Welfare and informed them confidentially of the state of play. I advised them that I would contact them on Friday after I had spoken to Mr X. In the 1980s, government departments were unable to offer any real support, but at least I could discuss the matter with them. I also sought the advice of Tony Shinkfield and the college council chair, Geoff Gordon. I then contacted Mr X on the Thursday to ask him to meet with me the following day.

To keep a record of our meeting I asked another senior staff member, who knew nothing of the developing crisis, to be an independent witness. Dr Michael Slocombe, head of our senior school, attended and took minutes. Michael, Mr X and I met on Friday afternoon, 24 November 1989, in the headmaster's house as my office was very visible and open and not soundproof.

I explained to Mr X that this would be a difficult meeting and that Michael (who knew nothing about the situation) would be taking minutes for us both to sign, with a copy to be given to us both. I then said to Mr X, "I have written statements from two students stating that you were trying to arrange a sex party with them and another statement backing their claim." Mr X denied the allegation and asked, "How can I prove my innocence?" It was a very good question because I had no direct proof of guilt.

Michael was stunned by the accusations but continued to minute the meeting as an independent observer. I said, "X, here in my hands I have three independent written statements from students witnessed by Mr Horrie Shilcock. I do not think you can prove your innocence. You and I are in an impossible situation, and I can only offer to suspend you on pay and ask the police vice squad to carry out a full investigation. Given these three student statements, your reputation in the school is ruined, whether you are innocent or not. The only other option is for you to resign on condition that you do not teach under-age children again."

Mr X was in a lose-lose position. He resigned, maintaining his innocence, and the minutes of our meeting which registered his agreement not to teach children were signed.

I was on very thin ice and knew it because I feared a wrongful dismissal charge. Our fragile young school would be devastated by a long, drawn-out battle and a split community. Hence I made sure my files and homework were fully documented and reported to the college council.

After school, I rang the Department of Community Welfare again and asked them to come in the following week to meet with students and double check my work. They were grateful for the update but said they were too overloaded with cases to commit the resources to help and were happy with the outcome achieved. I explained it would be very helpful to both me and the school to have an independent investigation to ensure justice was done. However, the more I requested their help and the more I underlined how this would be valued, the more reluctant they became to investigate. Mandatory reporting was yet to come in.

I was determined to go public with the police, staff, students and parents as I believed the bright light of exposure was needed to protect our students in the future. Generally schools at this time took the opposite approach and kept such matters confidential. I could not even get Mr X deregistered as a teacher as there was no legally tested crime involved. However, with an additional informal approach to the CEO of the Independent Schools Board, who was also a member of the Registration Board, I was assured no renewal of his teacher registration would be made when required.

Rosslyn had already agreed to meet Mr X's wife, along with Mrs X's father, to brief them. At the following Monday's staff meeting, the information that Mr X resigned on the condition that he was not to teach children again was received badly. There was disbelief that he would have acted improperly with students, let alone groomed or solicited them for sex. I then called a school assembly for the Wednesday to tell all the students from Years 6 to 11. I can still see their faces and where they were sitting or standing at this assembly 23 years ago. I told them that Mr X had been dismissed for making improper sexual suggestions and invitations to students. (Due to the sensitive nature of the allegations, I didn't go into too much detail as there still was only the suggestion of impropriety.) Students were given the opportunity to come forward privately with any further information or concerns.

All parents were advised. I also consulted those Elizabeth police who were parents of children at Trinity. I was advised 'off the record' that a police investigation was no sure resolution. It was likely to end in limbo, student silence, ruined reputations and no proof. Given the available evidence, I could be left with a dysfunctional and distrusted staff member able to shift to another school and successfully corrupt other children.

No new information was forthcoming from either students or parents, and many of our staff had a crisis of confidence in me. Eventually the fact that Mr X had chosen to resign, along with quiet discussions between staff who thought I was wrong and staff who felt I had no choice, enabled some trust to return. I would have very much valued more evidence.

Around 2000 I received a telephone call from New South Wales asking about Mr X and his suitability to teach. The caller claimed to be from the NSW Teachers' Registration Board. To confirm their identity, I asked my secretary to return the call via the NSW Department of Education's official office phone number. I was then able to speak honestly with them about my concerns. They sent me papers by post to be filled in confidentially. My commitment from Mr X – that should he resign from Trinity College he would not work with children again – was emphasised in the paperwork I sent back. I checked that his registration in South Australia had lapsed.

Despite the legal changes before 2000 requiring mandatory reporting of such incidents, I was told in writing to keep no records and to destroy the NSW board's letters to me. Clearly the large state educational bureaucracies were also still skating on thin ice when refusing teacher registrations or denying applications for employment by people with suspect pasts.

In 2004, when making a statement to police after new information came to their attention, I found they already knew the names of those I thought were involved. Another student from Trinity had accused Mr

X of abuse and had given the police a written statement. My statement was going to be used in court. Eventually, with the weight of the extra evidence, including a letter Mr X had written to another staff member some time after his departure, Mr X pleaded guilty and was sent to prison.

I was proud of the students who came forward. I was proud of the way we had handled the matter. It was common and normal for schools of the time to hide the dirty linen.

You do not expect to employ a wolf in sheep's clothing, a trusted person in the staff who abuses his trust in the worst possible way. But with my experience in schools, I understood that sometimes I needed to know what was happening below the surface. It was not fear of a sexual parasite within the staff that drove me as a young headmaster of a young school to ensure that we had a good sex education program in place; however, the awareness of what had happened among the students became vital. The reason I believed sex education was important was because it so often occurred mainly by the modelling of staff, parents and others in the community, including those on television and in the media.

The above story highlights the value of mandatory reporting for school principals. However, it does have downsides. With so many people, including all teachers, being required to report any suspicion to a state welfare agency, even without evidence, parents and children may see their teachers as legally backed 'spies' of the state. To whom, then, can a child with internal family abuse turn for advice? With mandatory reporting, would the courageous students involved in the case of Mr X reported him? I would hope so, but they would have had good reason not to open up to me.

Certainly the principal is better protected today. Men, however, feel under suspicion. With the onus of proof having swung in favour of the accuser and men seemingly more vulnerable to false accusation and innuendo, it is not surprising that teaching has lost its appeal to men.[49] Primary school male classroom teachers are now rare.[50]

The pendulum seems to have swung too far. Government departments are so overloaded with reports that investigations and support for students is once again not there for many.

Lessons learnt

1. Schools are part of a total society when educating young people. Drug education is both a societal and school responsibility and the laws of the land are part of this education.
2. Schools can make a difference in behaviour away from school, but they are not the major influence. Trinity reduced marijuana abuse by only 33%.
3. Bad things happen when students are implicitly encouraged to be secretive about problems.
4. Parents have an important role in social education and should be involved and supported in the sex and drug education of their children.
5. Mandatory reporting has strengths and weaknesses, but denies children an adult to talk to about a really serious problem without the full force of the state being involved.
6. When children have been endangered, an open and public response protects children.

11
Academic failure
Change takes time

WHERE EDUCATION FAILS screamed the banner headline across page one of Adelaide's only city newspaper, *The Advertiser*. The date was 15 January 1997. Below the newspaper's masthead proclaiming 559,000 readers each weekday were the words: "Achievement gap shows lower-income suburbs need help."

Education writer Nicole Lloyd told readers that the state's education system was under pressure. A major report on Year 12 results compiled by the SA Health Commission showed that the lowest average subject scores were recorded in a band across northern Adelaide from the port to Smithfield and Evanston. This region covered about a third of Adelaide's population.

The report revealed that students from northern and outer southern suburbs were overwhelmingly outscored in Year 12. The article blamed living in particular postcodes for the bad results: "The report's co-author, Mr John Glover, said there was a direct link between below-average scores and low socio-economic belts which had high unemployment, low-income families, unskilled workers and Housing Trust dwellings." However, according to the University of SA's Dean of Education, Professor Kym Adey, the low achievement results "should in no way be seen as a measure of the student's raw ability". The article stated:

> Professor Adey said the majority of students living in Adelaide's higher socio-economic areas came from homes with an "extensive history of education".

And they were surrounded by the "positive benefits" of an education.

"Unless children present themselves at school with an attitude that says 'I value this stuff' they will not tap into it,' Professor Adey said.

He said he did not believe there was anything "inherently wrong with our schools".

I believed then – as I do now – that there was and is something inherently wrong with our schools. These results meant that a student living in our region had just a one-sixteenth chance of attending university compared with a student in Adelaide's eastern suburbs. But some schools, such as Trinity College and Salisbury High School, refused to accept the status quo.

The *Advertiser* article stated that the state government had "vowed to tackle the problem by ensuring cash grants for disadvantaged schools this year are spent on literacy programs and special measures to tackle individual learning problems". This focus sounded educationally right. It was what we were already doing at Trinity, focusing on core basic skills at primary school level. But throwing more money at a non-performing school system would not increase student access to quality schooling.

Wrong suburb, low results

Trinity was right in the middle of the region where education had failed. In the 1980s Trinity was barely any different. We failed too.

The reality of preparing students for Year 12 in our region was not surprising, but it hit us like a steam train. Our results in the first five years were appalling. The number of our students in the top 5% cent of the state, from 1989 until 1992, was zero. (See table below.)

Schools often massage results. They play with As, Bs, Cs, Ds and Es, which do not take into account the academic difficulty of the subjects taken. "We want to get lots of As. Let's counsel our students to do

Trinity College Year 12 results, 1989–1993

Trinity student results (% of total year cohort)

State scores (TER)	1989	1990	1991	1992	1993
95+	0	0	0	0	1
90+	2	0	0	1	5
80+	≅4	5	2	19	26
70+	≅12	19	43	59	67
Subject merit awards	1	3	2	8	11
Total Year 12 cohort	57	63	84	97	99

the easiest subjects." In subjects that have been developed for the least-able students there is less competition for an A. The measure that really matters for students wishing to win a place in university is their tertiary entrance score (the TER score, now known as ATAR).[51] This measure includes a comparison between subjects that allows for the difficulty of a subject and is a total score out of 100 rather than just five separate subject grades. I have quoted the TER scores to enable state- and Australia-wide comparisons to be made.

Our daughter Joanne (1990) and son Christopher (1991) were Year 12 graduates. We had no one in the top 10% of the state in those years. Yet at university both achieved first class honours degrees with academic prizes in engineering from Adelaide University. Other Trinity old scholars from these early years also gained first class honours degrees and doctorates. Clearly we were living in the wrong suburb.

Our academic performance in those early years was so woeful we invited advisers from the Senior Secondary Assessment Board of SA (SSABSA) to coach our staff in how our students could achieve excellent results. SSABSA's Warwick Souter ran Monday afternoon staff workshops. We worked through the system to see why our able students were not gaining the TER scores we believed they could. We had experienced Year 12 subject teachers and some very able students, yet all our grades were bad.

Many schools accept that they are serving lower socio-economic students and dumb down their offerings to keep their clientele (teachers, students and parents) happy. I could not believe students from poor areas would inevitably achieve low outcomes. Our teachers attended their subject conferences to ensure they knew, along with those from elite schools, what the chief examiners of each subject were looking for.

Even so, some of our teachers voiced concern that we were trying to achieve the impossible.

We knew that the woeful primary school academic level our students started with overall meant that in these early years Trinity had a very long tail. Actually, in most schools in our region there was a long tail. At Trinity we had a *very* long tail, with a bottom group of students who struggled to almost pass their Year 12 subjects. We learnt that by giving this group of students passing grades in our internal assessments, we were in fact lowering the scores of our top students. The public examination provided only half of the marks for the TER. The other half were internal. If the average public examination score for the school was lower than its average internal score, its internal scores were marked down, including those of its top students.

Teachers worked so hard to enable the strugglers to achieve because they believed they were making a real difference for them. In fact, I had to try to persuade our passionate teachers to mark the bottom students hard, in line with a state-wide score. It was meaningless to give top students a 95/100 that was valid state-wide unless the student who was worth 40/100 state-wide actually was graded at 40.

In the 1990s it was harder to gain entrance to university. Only the top 30% were accepted. I had to persuade our staff that a student going from a TER of 40 to one of 55 was actually achieving very little because they still would not be eligible for university. Certainly students going from a TER of 65 to 80 had some university courses open to them. However, many 'elite' courses needed a mark above 90. To raise the bottom students to the middle could actually cost able students their choice of career.

To achieve academic success for our students, we would have to raise the bar knowing that some would 'fail'. I never considered a student aiming for a career requiring high achievement and missing the required score as failing. I regarded failure as not having the courage to go for it.

The long road to academic excellence

Academic excellence is a long, hard grind in lower socio-economic areas. I have already described how, on average, our founding students were three years behind in their reading, writing and arithmetic skills. With our core curriculum, good teaching and common testing of these core skills, we made sound academic progress. By 1989 our own Year 7s were about one year ahead of the state average. At the same time, we were enrolling Year 8s from around our region who were, on average, three years behind our primary students.

For this drive towards real academic excellence to be sustained, the support of the college council was politically essential. Yet the support of the council depended on who was on it. I encouraged a number of parents with skills and a commitment to academic achievement to run for office. This sounds simple and obvious, but their election heralded a new problem for a headmaster with my philosophy of education. These new members were financially secure and had outstanding personal academic careers. They had sent their children to a poorly resourced school and wanted it to be well resourced. Reasonably, they saw that the safe path to academic excellence was to raise school fees, which would increase income and improve educational resources.

With higher fees, standards would have risen automatically, not just because the school would have been better resourced, but also because poorer families, whose children often had less educational input at home, would have been priced out. The college could so easily become another elite school accessed by the middle-class and some local rich.

College council meetings were tense and muddy. We had kept our fees lower than even the surrounding Catholic schools, and, with additional discounts for 28% of our enrolments, this ensured Trinity was open to all. Even though we were in the poorest third of Adelaide, our large catchment area meant that a small, high-fee college was a real possibility. Some of Adelaide's highest fee schools started off with low fees.[52] With these families recruiting like-minded families to run for council, we had very large and vigorous AGMs.

With teachers also being members of the school community, I suspected they also voted for council candidates they believed would maintain the vision of providing an education for all. Debate was heated and the school divided. In the end the low-fee policy was retained. This ensured a continued financial struggle, but it was a struggle the teachers at Trinity owned and were proud of.

To ensure the success of their own children, it was no wonder that two academic families who were elected to the college council later removed their children to city colleges, one for Year 7 and the other for Year 9. Some other families with the financial resources to make a similar move visited these colleges to look around, yet tentatively renewed their commitment to keep their children at Trinity. Years later these families found out the Year 12 results of those who had left and compared them with those of their own children to check whether their faith in Trinity had been justified. Those who remained outperformed their friends, even though their friends also had good results.

Parents who took the chance and remained knew that we were using the West Australian testing system (WALNA) to assess our students' progress across the academic board. They also valued our reading, writing and maths age-testing and our honest reporting. When their children began to be successful, they had some confidence the improvement was real and would continue. They compared their children's work with that of friends in other schools, and Trinity College's waiting list continued to grow.

These parents also brought their friends and family to the Trinity Sunday celebrations. In the church calendar, Trinity Sunday is always around June – too late to attract enrolments. Yet people came in their thousands. The big chook shed only held 1800 people, so we installed large roll-up doors to enable one side of the basketball court to be opened up. About 6000 people came to these Trinity Sunday services, and we learnt to utilise good sound systems so those seated outside behind 500 prep schoolers could hear, even though they could only vaguely see into the shed.

Following the services all classrooms were opened, and every child – not just the best – had their work on display. Naturally, since winemaking was part of the agricultural science program, a wine-selling licence was organised for the day. About one tonne of wine was released each year and all sold out on the day. I believed academic excellence required the pursuit of excellence in every part of the life of the school, and winemaking was no exception.

Making (slow) progress

The poor academic results in our first four years were deeply disappointing, yet they were outstanding for our region. We appointed Barb Palmer, an art teacher from one of our neighbouring schools (Smithfield Plains High) to the staff, and she tried to cheer us up by pointing out that her school had celebrated when one student passed one subject, art, with a B!

Back in 1990, to win a place in most university courses, a student needed to be in the top 30%. By 1993, 67% of Trinity's Year 12 students were gaining a TER score that allowed their choice of a university course from a good range, so clearly progress was being made.

But the progress was uneven. In 1993 it was still being denied that girls were outperforming boys in Australian schools. In that year only one in four of Trinity's Dux students was a boy. We were not only failing, but our boys were even less successful.

To improve a Year 9 boy's ability and outcomes in mathematics, I found that when I insisted they play football for the school their results improved. At Year 9, boys needed to look successful to their peers, so they hid any academic weakness by messing around in class and not attempting their homework. By playing football I suspected they could be heroes on the field in front of their friends, who would look out for them and help them in maths. Boys becoming young men are natural hunters who need to succeed as part of a team. Regardless of the reason, their maths scores improved.

Postcode or school?

Is the problem of poor student performance a matter of the postcode where you live or the school you choose? Does the school you choose for your child matter? Will a bright child succeed at any school? If your family background is good, is success guaranteed? If a school is in a region of poor aspirations, should you look elsewhere?

To explain low general achievement in their schools, teachers will say, "Our students are from a low socio-economic background. What can you expect?" Indeed I heard this argument from a regional director of education back in the 1970s when talking about the slowly declining academic standards in schools in the northern region of Adelaide. This decline coincided with the introduction of a child-centred curriculum and open learning classrooms. I do not believe this was a coincidence.

The fact is that the problem is systemic. Our schools can and do fail. Personal stories from my daughter doing 'prac teaching' during her teacher training highlight the problem.

Our daughter Caroline, having completed an honours degree in history with English and Chinese sub-majors, returned from 18 months teaching in China to do a Diploma of Education at Adelaide University in 2004. Caroline was to undertake prac teaching at Smithfield Plains High School, not far from her old home at Trinity. To make the arrangements, she went at lunchtime to meet her supervising teacher.

Having lived in some very degraded areas of China, and knowing so many students who lived in the Smithfield region from her days at Trinity, Caroline thought she was well prepared for Smithfield Plains High. That evening, still in some shock, she described her visit to the English teacher's classroom as beyond her worst nightmare. In the silence that followed I said, "I thought you knew it was bad." Caroline replied, "I'd imagined the worst possible educational scenario before the visit. The shock was that this make-believe vision was true.

"After lunch I went with the teacher to his classroom to see an actual lesson in the school. Students were not following the teacher's instructions and telling the teacher to 'get f——d'. They called out, 'You can't do anything!' One student entered the classroom during the lesson with blood all over his face from a fight in the yard when he was supposed to be in that lesson. A student's bag was thrown out of the second-floor classroom window, and another student was stabbed with a compass. A boy walked in during the same lesson to shout at another student for f——ing his girlfriend."

This snapshot of what an experienced teacher had to contend with in the classroom for just 60 minutes may give the reader a hint of the reality. That reality may be why only half the students taxpayers supported in their schooling actually bothered to be present for this class. Students' non-attendance was a problem in state schools as a whole (and still is[53]). This is measurable, and is a superficial sign of the failure that underlines Professor Adey's concerns about disengaged students.

The facts from Smithfield Plains High School spoke volumes. Just three students from an enrolment of about 100 in Year 8 were able to gain their first choice for tertiary study (though this was an improvement from a decade earlier when the measure of success was for a student to pass a subject at Year 12). Caroline gave me the following data from the school. In 2000, from the 100 students in Year 8, 96 made it to Year 9 and 92 to Year 10 (probably by automatic promotion and compulsory school age 'attendance'). Only 69.8 were enrolled for Year 11. The school had appallingly low literacy skills among its primary school cohort – two-thirds of Smithfield Plains Year 8 students coming into Trinity had a reading age three to four years behind their peers. This highlights the need for parents to carefully select their child's primary school.

The vision that schools do matter and can make a difference was reinforced by wide publicity given to a report from Melbourne

University's Centre for Applied Educational Research published in December 1993. The *Australian* summarised it with the headline SCHOOL BEATS HOME AS SPUR FOR SUCCESS.[54] The nation's first large-scale study of teacher and school effectiveness had found that "Schools play a more important role in determining academic achievement than a student's home environment or socio-economic background". The effect of teachers and their classrooms on student learning accounted for between 28.7% and 45.6% of variations in student achievement. The effect of a student's background on their academic achievement was about 10%.[55]

The report indicated that performance in English at secondary level was more likely to be affected by the home environment than other subjects. This made some intuitive sense – students from non-English backgrounds were more likely to come from lower socio-economic backgrounds (though the study also found they were more likely to do homework frequently). But it may just have been related to junior primary teaching unsuited to students from poorer areas. The poor have little say in schooling. It is often given to them by a monopoly state education system controlled by the middle and upper classes. Early childhood programs that may be effective for middle- and upper-class students may be inadequate for those who have not already learnt the basics at home. I would challenge the view that the English skills of students from poor families will necessarily be compromised.

My experience and research as headmaster of Trinity largely concurred with the Melbourne University report. It showed that schools cannot blame students and their families for their lack of success. This research placed the lack of concern about schools being inherently wrong by educationalists into context. Our educational writers depend on the existing system for their bread and butter and have to make their critiques polite, careful and indeed acceptable. "Let's blame the family for lack of success," they chorus. I blame our schooling system and our schools.

1997 – a watershed year

In 1997 our initial group of students who enrolled at Reception in 1985 entered Year 12. We were looking forward eagerly to answering two questions: "Did our primary school program make any difference to their Year 12 results?" and "Did those who joined Trinity at Year 8 score higher grades than those who had joined at Reception?"

We found that primary education did affect Year 12 results, though not in all subjects. In the humanities, including English, students who had entered Trinity in Year 8 had 10% lower Year 12 grades than students who had entered at Reception. The overall 180 Reception enrolments had been non-selective and based purely on date of enrolment, whereas those joining in Year 8, who at the time were three years behind, had been offered a place in Year 7 which their parents had refused. The students who did not start in Reception achieved about 5% less in maths.

However, students joining us at Year 8 achieved the same grades in science subjects. Clearly our primary school science program offered no measurable academic advantage. We did not have primary school common testing of science; it was child-centred discovery learning, as in our feeder schools. The science curriculum as a rigorous study really only started at Year 8.

We had a lot riding on the 1997 outcomes. Was our publicity promising academic excellence just propaganda, or would we be able to continue to build academically? Any school that trumpets great educational success needs to be assessed carefully. Six questions need to be asked:

1. Did the school select students who were academic?
2. Did the school only allow students who would succeed to present for the public examination?
3. Did the fee structure of the school ensure that the only children attending were from families with the resources and knowledge to employ tutors, or to teach at home if their schooling failed?
4. Did only successful students start at the school in the final years?

Academic failure 169

5. Were the quoted results fudged, or were they indeed absolute measures of success against state (or preferably national) standards that mattered?
6. Were the results repeatable or just a particularly good year taught by teachers who have now moved on?

I put Trinity College's results under this blowtorch. In the same year as the 1997 report *Where Education Fails*, and in the same region that had the worst results in South Australia, students at Trinity achieved results I was happy with. I knew the 1998 results were likely to be even better. Did these results distort the truth?

Applying a realistic analysis, I answered the six questions:

1. *Did the school select students who were academic?* No. The enrolment at Reception in 1985 was open to all. The Year 12 group included students from Trinity's feeder primary school in Blakeview, drawing from the most socially deprived areas of South Australia. There was no selection of students. There was no interviewing of families. Enrolment was simply a matter of parents paying $20 to register interest and the school having a vacancy by the enrolment date. At Year 8, just four students had been granted a merit place.

2. *Did the school only allow those students who would succeed to present for the public examination?* No. From a 1993 Year 8 group of 182 students, 158 went on to Year 12. Some of our best Year 11 students had left when offered apprenticeships, and others had left when offered jobs following our Year 11 work experience program; but even so, 87% of our 1993 Year 8 group completed Year 12.

Trinity College Year 12 results 1997

Students in top 20% of state		
	State average	Trinity
Top 5% of state		14%
Top 10%		24%
Top 20%		46.9%
Top 30%		80.4%
	50	77.4
	1.58	23

Total Year 12s: 158
Enrolment at Year 8: 185

3. *Did the fee structure of the school ensure that the only children attending were from families with the resources and knowledge to*

employ tutors, or to teach at home if their schooling failed? No. About 30% of students were on 'school card'. This was used by the state government as the measure of poverty to provide free books to families in the state school system.

4. *Did only successful students start at the school in the final years?* No. The students started at Reception (five years old) or primary school, with half joining Trinity at Year 8.

5. *Were the quoted results fudged, or were they indeed absolute measures of success against state (or preferably national) standards that mattered?* The results were indeed a measure of success: the published TER scores were used. The school quoted the following results:

- 158 students sat for five subjects at Year 12 from a Year 8 group of 182.
- 90% were in the top half of the state.
- 50% were in the top 22.5%.
- 24% were in the top 10%. (This score qualified all these students to apply to study medicine.)
- 14% were in the top 5%.
- 6% were in the top 2%.
- 3% were in the top 1%.

6. *Were the results repeatable or just a particularly good year taught by teachers who have now moved on?* At Trinity the results of the previous eight years showed continuous improvement from a very low academic base. The following year the results were even stronger – so strong indeed that the 1997 results were overshadowed.

The value of academic study

Some university courses are losing their financial value when measured by the future salaries graduates earn. Some courses have high value for future employment and income potential. If your family values a university degree mainly for its usefulness in gaining a lifetime career, then TER scores matter. This means that attending a school with the

Table 3: **Trinity College Year 12 results, 1989–1997**

Trinity student results (% of total year cohort)

TER scores	1989	1990	1991	1992	1993	1994	1995	1996	1997
90+	2	0	0	1	5	6	6	8	24
80+	≥4	5	2	19	26	31	33	25	47
70+	≥21	19	43	59	67	72	76	67	80
Subject merit awards	1	3	2	8	11	9	13	14	23
Total Year 12 cohort	57	63	84	97	99	121	94	103	158
Original number Year 8	48	82	84	111	111	115	121	122	182

capacity to prepare students for success in public examinations is important.

In Trinity's 1997 results, 93% of those Year 12 students who applied for a university place were offered their first round choice. This figure rose to an apparently impressive 97% who gained a university course they had chosen after second round offers were made. However, claims like this need to be read with a suspicious mind. Ninety-seven per cent of what? All Year 12 students, or only those who passed Year 12 with a TER score?

Such a figure does not inform a potential student of the school accurately. There may have been 'career counselling' more interested in the future of the school than that of the student by advising them to choose courses that have very low entrance marks. If all students have such a course as one of 'their' choices, then schools will be able to claim a 90%-plus success rate.

Being the headmaster, I had the advantage of knowing the Trinity figures were genuine. For prospective parents, however, only the hard-core TER scores, which rank students alongside their peers, were accurate measures. *You need to know how all students performed, not just the top few.* The outstanding performance of the genius scholarship student gaining top of the state is no indication that your possibly average child will gain anything like a useful course of study, with results that will enable them to have real choices in the future.

Review of principal's contract

The academic performance of students at an independent school is a key criterion for determining whether the school board extends the principal's contract.

At the time of my first external review as principal in 1990, Trinity was no threat to other schools since the academic progress of students was still unproven. Typically, a review used survey tools benchmarked in a cross-section of state and independent schools. Trinity's staff, parents and students were surveyed by Professor Kym Adey and his colleague from the University of South Australia, Dr Schultz, and their report highlighted an outstanding school compared with major city colleges and state schools that were also evaluated.

At that time, Professor Adey's report on Trinity was politically helpful for me in gaining reappointment. To ensure the "spiritual life of the college" was also adequately reviewed, Father Gary Hillman, representing the Anglican Church, and Tony McGuire, a Catholic lay educator, were appointed, and their conclusions became part of the review. Gary Hillman wrote:

> I must say at the outset, that I believe the amount achieved at Trinity is almost miraculous and brings great credit to all involved in this exciting school, especially to the Headmaster, Mr Michael Hewitson, for his vision and drive. I found it to be a privilege to be able to look at another school and learn much in the process.

Tony McGuire agreed:

> We are very impressed indeed at the remarkable progress made by Trinity College in the very short time it has been in operation. A very great tribute is due to the Headmaster and to the staff, parents and students in what has been achieved. There is a sense of purpose very obvious in the school and dynamism that augurs well for future years.

Armed with these two reviews and a very strong enrolment program

Table 4: Trinity College Year 12 results 1998	
State average	Trinity
Top 1% of state	4.6%
Top 2%	8.6%
Top 5%	18.1%
Top 10%	24.5%
50	78
	28

(despite juggling argumentative politics about the size, nature and structure of the school), and despite the risks involved establishing a new campus at Blakeview, the review of my contract meant that I could seek a change that was most important for our family. It was not about money. Essentially, I offered to accept a very low salary in exchange for tenure, and a superannuation scheme that would match the lowest level possible in the Education Department of SA (namely, an Area School Principal, Class 1). My appointment was to run for 10 years until 2002 unless I lost the confidence of two-thirds of the council and a majority of the Anglican Schools Commission.

The school you choose does matter

Trinity's results illustrate how the school chosen does matter and makes a huge difference in educational outcomes. In fact, according to the Melbourne University study quoted above, the school chosen will be *four times* more important to a child's future than the socio-economic background of their family. The choice of school you make for your child will affect their performance, their moral values, their friendship groups and their choices for the future.

Trinity's very existence in the 1990s, along with its academic results way ahead of the state averages,[56] proved, without doubt, that where you live should not be an indicator of your academic success. Yet in 2012, after his first year as head of SA's public education system, Education Department chief executive Keith Bartley said he was surprised Australia was yet to fully recognise inequalities. Not enough had been done to bridge the gap between rich and poor in the education system, he warned.[57]

After three decades, nothing has changed. Why not?

In 1998 a second external review of Trinity was undertaken and by then the college was a threat to other schools and providers. Our 1998 results were so good we were embarrassed to publish them in the local papers, and the 1998 school magazine concentrated on just the As and Bs. What really pleased us was that the boys and girls achieved equally, with almost a quarter of all our students (24.5%) in the top 10% of the state (see table 4). Seven students gained a TER score over 99 and one, Michael Fyfe, achieved a perfect score in all five subjects and the top TER score available (99.95).

Trinity was now a real threat to the state system and we were about to be crunched from a surprising source.

Lessons learnt

1. Primary schooling in the core curriculum is an essential foundation in poor socio-economic areas for good Year 12 results. Time needs to be allocated as a priority to English, spelling, grammar and writing, together with number skills and mathematics.

2. Schools in poor areas have a tendency to dumb down their offerings and demands to the long-term detriment of their students' future options.

3. Teachers conscientiously try to raise the outcome for the least able 20% in educationally poor regions to the detriment of the top 20%.

4. Boys' education needs attention.

5. The strong professional teacher opinion that students in lower socio-economic regions cannot achieve the results of students from rich areas is incorrect.

12
The octopus grows
Trinity becomes a threat

The battle was not planned. However, a newspaper report describing my Trinity Sunday speech to 7000 people in front of the SA Premier and federal and state MPs from across the region was certainly 'challenging'.[58] The Gawler *Bunyip* reported:

> In his speech, Trinity headmaster Mr Michael Hewitson said that parents, teachers and senior students were "lighting the lamps" of our next generation ...
>
> "We are proudly independent and we are proudly public," he said.
>
> "We are certainly not a school owned by the state, run under the authority of the Minister for Education ... We are proudly independent, able to offer parents a choice of philosophic foundation for the education of the next generation.
>
> "We are proudly public. Three-quarters of our funding comes from the State and Federal governments ... We have based our fees and structures so that we are open to all, regardless of financial or socio-economic status. We are open to all regardless of religious belief.
>
> "I personally believe that public money should be conditional on public access to all schools in Australia receiving State or Federal funding."

Having just challenged the state system by proclaiming some success in our pursuit of excellence as a 'public school', and having claimed the right to public funding, my next statements picked a fight with all other non-government schools. Independent schools believe, as a sign of their independence, that they have the right to select their students, yet they receive public taxpayer funds with some tax payers having no access.

I believed that independent schools receiving public funds should not be able to choose only the easy to educate. Because each Trinity student received from the government about 60% of the money spent on a state school student, I thought it reasonable that Trinity could expect to have up to 60% of its enrolment come from a public list of children. This would not have gone down well with other independent schools.

In my speech I then 'challenged' the Members of Parliament:

> On the controversial subject of marijuana, Mr Hewitson said that sometimes lamp lighters get caught in their own light.
>
> "Mr Premier, our college has prepared a thoughtful challenge to our currently unacceptable marijuana laws," he said.
>
> "Given our desire to change these laws, we have prepared an alternative set of proposals for public discussion. Our college council is seeking a meeting with your Minister for Health."[59]

It was amazing how strong my relationships were with parliamentarians from all sides. I regarded them as friends and was able to confide in them, test ideas and discuss problems. I found our elected members reliable and trustworthy, but I understood the pressures they faced. The Australian Education Union (AEU) campaign was 'Public and Proud'. However, rather than evaluating and promoting the achievements of state schools, this campaign sought to politically pull down the schools that many parents preferred to choose.

The octopus and the public school dream

Trinity came under public attack by AEU members. The union invited all those concerned for the future of public education to attend a meeting at Craigmore High School on Wednesday, 24 September 1997.

From a pamphlet produced by Craigmore High School AUE members

Pamphlets were distributed about the Trinity 'octopus' swallowing Craigmore High School. The apparent organiser of the meeting appeared in the local newspaper to publicly attack "Trinity College's expansion proposals". They publicly stated that our students would be bashed up and that Trinity had jumped too far, too soon.

At a staff meeting I advised the staff that I would attend the meeting and why. "As a passionate supporter of public education, education for all and accessible to all, I wish to show my support. Trinity College is a public school, publicly funded with open enrolment, not for profit, supported by the church and legally owned by the local community."

The story of this battle is told in chapter 13. This chapter looks at the question, "Why did the SA state school teachers' union believe that Trinity was a threat to the very existence of Craigmore High?"

Growing pains

Blakeview had barely opened in 1991 when we were discussing other future growth options. New ideas were floated, such as a non-uniformed school with open, student-directed learning – the opposite to Trinity yet still in a caring Christian environment. We believed a small percentage of the population was seeking this type of school and there was plenty of land around Gawler. We discussed opening boarding schools, and to cope with the spreading demand for places at Trinity we considered adding more feeder primary campuses. For our senior secondary students, we explored the idea of a separate Year 11 class focusing on vocational education, and to make a dent on our waiting lists we considered a parallel co-located Reception to Year 12 school with 800 students.

By May 1991 we had written green papers for each proposal, costed and worked through. It all sounds so simple and professional after the event. However, there was genuine concern among some great supporters of Trinity. A public meeting held on 3 June 1991 needed careful handling, with genuine open discussion of all the ideas, and a vote by all on which ones should be recommended to the college council.

Father Mark, one of our chaplains, wrote a lengthy personal response to each idea, indicating he would listen carefully to those opposing his view and could change his mind. He wrote in the weekly newsletter:

> I clearly support the expansion of the College because I believe we cannot continue as a low-fee school offering the widest possible course structures to Years 11 and 12 without expansion. I also believe that, with the religious and values structure we have at the College, the more young lives we can shape and influence the better ... I am firmly committed to change only on the basis of the widest possible community consensus ... I urge all those who have views and doubts, to discuss these now and to prepare themselves to attend and contribute to the meeting in a useful and positive way, respecting the views of others as well as having their own views respected.

The vote was a clear majority for the establishment of a new co-located R–12 school.[60]

The decision of council to proceed resulted in the resignation of a close friend and supporter. He felt, as did many, that the enrolment list of 1000 might not be committed. The list consisted of people prepared to pay $20 and this did not guarantee they would follow through. Why risk a school of 1300 students to double in size? We could lose the lot! Wouldn't we put at risk the total future of the college by starting a parallel R–12? Many even believed the enrolment list was just propaganda and not real. They feared Trinity would have to borrow the total sum once again. In their view, the completion and consolidation of the original campus should not be interrupted.

Happy hour ideas

Like so many good ideas, the original move for what became known as the 'South' school came over drinks at a Friday afternoon happy hour or two in 1991. 'Brooky' (Stephen Brookman), our tech studies teacher and doer of anything, had established this custom; he was another Saints' old scholar and knew the advantage of community, habitually organising breads, dips and other food for the happy hour. Bright ideas and problems of the day were discussed, aired and even sorted. As a result, the future of the college was discussed. The problems for those trying to explain to distraught parents that their child could not get into the school became well known.

We were after small schools. We saw that an R–4 school of 300 was the maximum size if teachers were to know each other and their students. We agreed that a school covering Years 5–8 with 300 students was also the right size for everybody to know each other. On the other hand, a senior school for Years 9–12 of 450 was as small as one could have and yet have reasonable choice of senior secondary classes in Years 11 and 12.

French teacher Michael Liddle proposed: "If we have thousands on the waiting list, why don't we just open another school of 1000 on the other side of the footpath? We've bought an extra 25 acres of land for agricultural science. Why don't we see if we can buy some more paddocks for the ag science program and put a new school on the land we've already got?" There were obvious efficiencies of scale to this idea. I worked out that the chapel would be no more expensive for two schools to run than for one. Indeed, two schools would halve the depreciation and maintenance costs.

So the idea was born. We could have a parallel school. As with Blakeview, the new school would have the same core curriculum but its own style. What about school uniforms? We thought we would need different ones for each campus, yet a uniform that outside people would identity as Trinity College's.

The advantage of casual brainstorming on Friday afternoons with those who would have to make it work was that very practical solutions were worked through before the anticipated problems arose.

"How could we make sure that a student from the 'other' school could not be wagging it in ours?" (Teachers feared that students from the school across the footpath would hide next door, camouflaged in the same uniform.)

"Badges won't do, students could easily whack on the badge and sneak across undetected."

"So what about having different coloured shirts to identify campuses? They can't be so easily removed or swapped."

"That should work. We could keep the same blazer, tie and pants so that to all those outside the school, the students would all be Trinity; but to those in the know, they would be Trinity South with (say) blue shirts or Trinity North with white ones."

The colour of the shirt to identify the three campuses was just one of many debates. At the happy hours in the early 1990s we were naturally not limiting ourselves just to an extra school of 1000; we were already discussing a swimming pool, theatre, assembly hall and indoor basketball courts with sprung floors – even, perhaps, with after-hours community use. We had gone so far as to place them on maps, and I had drawn a sketch showing a pool with palm trees. The college was 'financially stretched', but we could dream.

The only source of reliable capital was parental donations. Schools not part of a school system or strong political grouping had great difficulty in winning any government capital finance through what was known as the 'Block Grant Authority'. The independently minded Anglican schools were not working together and were politically outmanoeuvred. Local South Australian rules were carefully crafted to ensure certain players would be successful in being granted these federal funds. At Trinity we used every other lever available so that we at least received grants to establish specialist facilities for the senior secondary program at Gawler.

Blakeview had to build a school without any federal or state capital funding. Indeed, in this poorest area of South Australia, the school, despite having the fastest growth and highest demand, received not one capital dollar. This school community built an R–10 school of over 700 students from its daily operating funds, which were only 65% of those of a state school.

During a visit to England I spent a week in the two King Edward Schools in Birmingham. They included a 1000-year-old boys' school and a separate 'Johnny-come-lately' girls' school, both sharing a library, athletics track and some technology facilities. The 'recent' girls' school was well over 100 years old and must have been a real social trendsetter when it first opened in the 1800s. The idea of making one of the Gawler schools for boys and the other for girls was debated and opened up for a whole school community vote. Overwhelmingly, both parents and teachers wanted co-educational schools, and each school to be separate.

Part of the selling of the South School concept to existing parents was a proposal to reduce the North School's Year 8 classes from

120 enrolments to 90. With 90 on the South Campus, the combined enrolment of 180 would have enabled some shared classes in subjects with smaller numbers of students, such as Year 11 and 12 Chinese and French classes. Financially, in strategic terms, the most efficient size for a senior secondary school was around five to six classes of 28 students at Year 11 and Year 12.

To further reduce the cost of education per student, we proposed maximising efficiency by having the South Campus start half an hour early. This would enable Lesson 2 on South to line up with Lesson 1 on North, and all other lessons would be offset as well. This would enable even more economic efficiencies. Instead of being used for six 50-minute lessons a day, school facilities such as the technology, metal and woodwork workshops and the library could be worked for nine 50-minute lessons a day. The ag science facilities, ovals and grounds would all similarly be able to gain 50% greater use.

With the prospect of well over $1 million per annum surplus predicted from this efficiency, the college council applied to establish this new school in two years' time.

South School blocked

Despite the application for a new South Campus of 900 students meeting every enrolment criteria of the government, its opening was refused by the state Minister for Education. Our first thought was that the AEU had heavied the minister so we asked him why he had refused. We learnt that other schools, particularly independent schools in the region, had written opposing the opening of the South School. The minister presented the documentation, which gave variations of the same reason – to quote from one of the independent schools: "Trinity is already the strongest school in the region and highly competitive. If approval is given to grant this extra campus, it would become even more competitive."

In Elizabeth, the second safest Labor seat in South Australia, state Labor had miscalculated. The young mayor of Elizabeth, Martyn Evans, had been knocked back for preselection in favour of a union nomination. Martyn ran as Independent Labor in a 1984 by-election, won the seat and now held the balance of power in parliament. With him and the archbishop in support, we went to visit the minister with a clear message.

I opened: "Minister, we have the enrolments. It is September; we want the school to open next year. The reason we have been rejected is that Trinity would be a better school if it were to have this campus approved. How can you, as Minister for Education, turn down an application that would enable South Australia to have a first-rate competitive educational unit? Why are you condemning this state to a second-class education by missing the opportunity to make a good school even better? How can you refuse this application, which follows all the rules? It is in a growth area, it has the enrolments and there is no demonstrable impact on any other single school."

Martyn held the balance of power. To secure a majority government, he was re-admitted to the Labor Party, and the school was approved.

By now it was late October and we faced the impossible task of building a school from scratch for 376 students by the start of the 1993 school year. How could we appoint staff, build facilities and furnish them in time? Michael Slocombe, head of Trinity's senior school, was appointed to lead this new venture. A late working bee was called for all parents to plant trees on the empty paddock – we needed the prospective parents of South to have a stake in their school and faith that it would start at the beginning of the next year.

Let me now tell the story through the eyes of one of the brave new staff members, Steven Ward from St Aloysius College, Adelaide, who joined us.

> I can remember the excitement that I felt at the prospect of becoming part of Trinity College's South Campus, an excitement that was only a little diminished when, one hot and dusty November's day a few weeks later, I accompanied an enthusiastic

Dr Slocombe around a paddock full of Salvation Jane which he assured me 'had the seeds of a school planted in it'. These seeds were then largely invisible, but he promised that they would, with careful nurturing over the Christmas holidays, have grown into the real thing by the time the New Year started. At the end of my tour I was casually asked if I cared to be a House Director. Of course I answered that I would be delighted and so as book day[61] came around in January, [I had] my first contact with my new House: Ferrier-Tebbutt.

The school was still being built on day one and temporary spaces had to be found. Teachers Bill Lokan and Roy Malone were housed with their Year 5 classes in the two sheep-shearing pens attached to the agricultural science block, with open slats displaying the earth beneath. The year began with a baptism of fire for the newly formed Clunies-Ross/Paterson House, which was also temporarily located in the shearing shed, and the hot February afternoons certainly tested the mettle of the members. The first-ever South Campus team event was the car tyre tube relay race that heralded the South Campus swimming carnival. The school was delighted when the already overheated Clunies-Ross/Paterson won the race. Students experiencing success in their school life is important, and the hot members of the shearing-shed House walked taller.

From the beginning we realised that South Campus, which had no capital and borrowed the lot to build the school, had to be financially in the black. From our learning curve at Blakeview we knew a two-stream primary school was needed. From a first-year start in the shearing sheds, the school jumped from 376 enrolments to 654 in the second year by double-streaming the primary school straight through the South Campus.

The campus had benefitted from the willing placement of a number of teachers from the original school (now called 'North Campus'). The curriculum was to be a college-based curriculum, so it was important that some of the established leadership was also on South Campus. Robert Smedley took on the challenging role of a daily administration teacher. He was a housemaster and headed geography across the whole school, and yet at the same time was to gain experience on South Campus with some primary classroom teaching.

Michael Slocombe wrote at the end of 1994:

> This year we have grown from 375 to 650 students and we have become a double stream school in Years R–7. That is something we have managed so smoothly that it is easy to underestimate the significance of the achievement. New students and their families have been incorporated into the life of the school in a way which would not have been possible if careful planning of resources had not occurred and if families, staff and students already at the school had not welcomed them.

Changes at the top

By 1995 the college had grown to well over 2000 students and it was time for me to relinquish my role as head of the North Campus to work with the college as a whole. For South to become a truly parallel school in its own right, the school leadership, bursar and principal needed to belong to them as much as to the other campuses. Richard Smith was appointed to head up the North Campus. He came from Victoria and was a very successful deputy principal in a regional independent college.

To be a principal, as the heads of the campuses were, you had to be at times unpopular, making the hard decisions. The difference between a deputy principal and a principal is that the deputy can give advice, then when unpopular decisions are made the deputy is able to say to staff, "Ah, the head said this, the head said that: I'm just carrying out the head's wishes." Richard made the courageous decision to serve as my deputy during 1996 when I resumed the year as nominal head of North. He gave me fearless and excellent advice, I would agree with him and he would then go and do it. Yet he was able to claim that the ideas were mine!

At the end of that year, however, it became clear that Richard's skill set was a little different from that needed in the position to which he had been appointed. The advantage of a multi-campus school came into its own when he was able to choose a position on South Campus instead. It was good to be able to fit positions to a person's real skills. Mr Kym Reynolds, who had come to Trinity as a biology teacher from Willunga High School and was chief biology examiner for the state, was an internal appointment who successfully took over the leadership of the North School.

Even though the college continued to grow, enrolment pressures did not decrease. The numbers applying meant that both North and South Schools went from three Year 8 classes to four by 1995. At the start of 1997 we had two R–12 schools of over 1000 students, plus Blakeview with 463 students.[62]

Nineteen ninety-seven was to be the year when South had its first Year 12 students and North had its first Year 12 contingent who had started at Reception with the Trinity College curriculum. The school's academic program would be either vindicated or a failure (I've already outlined its success in chapter 11). With growing waiting lists and 2500 students, the Craigmore High School AEU branch's view of Trinity as the growing octopus had well and truly arrived.

I will now disclose my main motive for seeking the expansion of Trinity. All the reasons I've given – unmet demand; economies of scale enabling better resources at a lower cost; the ability to give more children a caring yet disciplined and challenging school with values that have endured for two millennium – were all true, and were very large drivers of growth. However, there was one further consideration. If the college had remained a small school of, say, 1300 students, after I had left it could easily succumb to market pressures and seek to improve its resources by raising school fees, thereby disenfranchising two-thirds of parents living in the region. By growing to an inevitable 4000 students, Trinity became too big to rely easily on the rich; there were not enough of them in the northern suburbs of Adelaide. In my view, the school was able to offer the accessibility of Coles and Woolworths due to economies of scale, yet compete with the high-cost boutique and prestige city colleges.

Local council requests a Munno Para College

With huge waiting lists, Trinity was still turning away three enrolment enquiries for every student gaining a place. In the Munno Para Council area alone there were more than 1000 students on the waiting list. Local government can be very close to the community it serves, and Munno Para Council formally wrote to Trinity asking us to establish an R–12 campus of Trinity for another 1000 students. South Campus, while taking 1000 students from the waiting list in 1992, had failed to reduce it because another wave of enrolments was received as the wider community discovered many of their friends had been offered places at South.

The Trinity council decided another R–12 campus would be of no advantage to the existing students at Trinity. The alternative was a completely new school. We discovered that a new school would be more difficult to start because many on the waiting list made it clear their enrolment was for Trinity, not a new separate school.

I visited a developer, Alan Hickinbotham, and persuaded him to donate a parcel of land for a new R–12 school right in the middle of his new estate, Andrews Farm. It would be a selling point for a suburb that was otherwise isolated from services and schools (other than the nearby Smithfield Plains state schools, which were not meeting the aspirations of this community). After a great deal of planning, including developing a financial and building master plan for a new college, another public meeting was called by the Mayor of Munno Para for 5 December 1994.

We wrote to our waiting list in

Trinity College enrolments by campus, 1991–1997

Year		R–7	8–12	Campus total	TOTAL
1991	Nth	467	564	1031	
	Blv	237		237	1268
1992	Nth	468	594	1062	
	Blv	234		234	1296
1993	Nth	459	590	1049	
	Blv	256		256	
	Sth	284	92	376	1681
1994	Nth	467	591	1058	
	Blv	292		292	
	Sth	474	180	654	2004
1995	Nth	490	560	1050	
	Blv	324		324	
	Sth	466	294	760	2134
1996	Nth	500	555	1055	
	Blv	407		408	
	Sth	478	398	876	2338
1997	Nth	499	534	1033	
	Blv	463		463	
	Sth	507	502	1009	2505

Munno Para and over 300 came to enrol in a new separate school. It would run its own senior secondary program but would have up to five years support by Trinity. We also worked out a fall-back position: an R–4 campus that fed into Blakeview at Year 5.

All was now set to go, and approval of our application to open the school independent from Trinity seemed assured. It was in a growth area and we now had the political support of the state Labor government. With the CEO of the Munno Para Council on the board of the school, this would be a community school started by a local council with the ongoing support of local government. I was very pleased that my brother John, now the rector of the Elizabeth Anglican parish, became involved and because of his involvement on South Campus as a visiting chaplain, he was highly regarded.

Surprisingly, we did not hear from the federal Department of Education. On making contact, we discovered that the Catholic education authorities had, without notice, made an ambit claim for two new secondary schools in the area, one on each side of Main North Road. We were told that neither our application nor theirs would be approved unless we worked together.

This clever strategic move by the Catholic Education Office disappointed some and surprised us all. But I immediately saw an opportunity. Since we had the land, the enrolments, the local government support and the organisation needed to open, I thought that together we should seek to establish two new schools, one in Munno Para as an Anglican–Catholic joint venture within the Anglican Schools System and a matching Catholic–Anglican joint school south of Adelaide (perhaps at Seaford Rise, where we had also been asked to open a school and where we had been working with a steering committee), or even in the Port Adelaide area.

I was under a fair bit of pressure during this time when I noticed a small drop of blood in my urine. I immediately visited my local GP (the chair of Trinity College, Rupert Thorne). Within 24 hours I was in hospital and a bladder cancer had been surgically removed. The operation was traumatic and painful, but the next day I left hospital to attend an Anglican Schools Commission meeting in Adelaide that I thought was vital. Up for decision was whether this now joint venture school at Munno Para would be part of the Anglican system or the Catholic system.

The Anglican Schools Commission had for many years sought to establish a system of schools jointly funded by the federal government. The Catholic school system had worked this way over many years to great advantage. The advantage was that funding was calculated on the average needs of schools and students across the group. For many Anglican schools other than Trinity, such an arrangement, if implemented, would be of great financial advantage. Many of these schools were locked into low levels of government support and were just beginning to feel the competition from Catholic, Lutheran and new Christian schools charging far lower fees with greater government funding. The long-term strategic and financial gains of being part of a system would offset any immediate perceived loss of independence.

The existing Anglican schools were 'independent', and this independence was celebrated and very Anglican. While schools such as St John's Belair, Woodlands Anglican Girls School and St Peter's Glenelg would have benefitted in both the short and long term, no schools other than Trinity were prepared to be part of a new system, even though their financial liability should the system be in trouble was limited to $1000 and they could leave should they wish. Three schools were required to form a system with the support of their state-wide denomination. The idea of an Anglican system seemed doomed. However, after a great deal of lobbying and argument, Trinity successfully split its campuses into three legally separate schools, and, together with the Anglican Province of South Australia, successfully formed the SA Anglican Schools System.[63] Because there could only be one system per denomination per state, all the other schools were invited to join.

At the meeting to decide on the Munno Para proposal, I presented my reasons for insisting that the joint venture school, now named St Columba College, be part of the Anglican system. The principals of Walford (girls) and Pulteney (boys), together with some other schools including Woodlands at Glenelg, were adamantly opposed. I did not understand how much the once powerful Anglican independent schools were now struggling for enrolments. The reasons for their opposition were never stated, but it seemed that to them a new Catholic school was preferable to a growing Anglican system. The Anglican Schools Commission had effectively become a body to oppose the development of any new schools for fear they would take away 'their' enrolments.

Despite its successful opposition, Woodlands soon came under unexpected pressure when its numbers started to plummet. The school preferred to stay high fee, and its board did not seem to understand that it was on the edge of administration. They sought to amalgamate with Pulteney Grammar to become co-ed, but it was too late. Pulteney took the remnant of students and Woodlands closed.

With Woodlands closing, St Peter's Glenelg, an R–7 parish primary school, was invited to sell its existing site and buy the Woodlands property. Trinity invited St Peter's to again consider joining a new Anglican schools system. It was offered millions of dollars by the system to purchase the whole Woodlands site, with no down side. The St Peter's school council could not see what was in it for Trinity and declined the offer, preferring to sell more acres of land and property in one of Adelaide's wealthiest suburbs. The lack of trust was to me unbelievable. Their council was correct – there was nothing in it for Trinity, except a stronger system with the potential political influence needed to secure the long-term future of affordable and accessible Anglican schools.

As a direct effect of the lack of trust of Anglican schools in the Anglican school system proposed by Trinity, St Columba opened as a joint Anglican–Catholic college with a Catholic head and deputy as part of the Catholic system. To help with St Columba's foundation, my brother John shifted his two younger children there from Trinity South, and very sensibly St Columba later appointed him to chair the new council. John continued to work as a part-time visiting chaplain at South.

Fortunately the St Columba principal, Madeleine Brennan, a former nun, proved to be outstanding and used the weak Anglican influence to the school's advantage within the Catholic system. In fact, St Columba was a financial goldmine for the Catholic system because its students were from the most socially deprived region in Adelaide and received the highest level of government support. This significantly reduced the student socio-economic average of the Catholic system as a whole, enabling a secure high level of government funding across all Catholic schools. I was pleased over the following years for Trinity to discreetly support St Columba, including appointing members to its council who had skills and local knowledge gained from their time at Trinity.

A monopoly broken

By the start of 2000 the Gawler *Bunyip* reported:

> Nearly 19,000 children went to school in the local area for the start of term one last week, including 950 for the first time …
>
> For the first time, private schools in this area have attracted more 'first-timers' than public schools. Of those attending school for the first time about 500 are at private schools and 450 at public schools.[64]

Within 15 years, in a region that had less than 5% of non-state school students, the state school monopoly had been broken, with over half of all Reception students attending independent schools. The AEU saw this trend and believed that public education in 1997 was in crisis and needed defending – not by improving its educational offering to meet parental expectations but by opposing alternatives with all the forceful means at its disposal.

Non-government schools in the poorest region of Adelaide had within 15 years become the majority provider of education to new students. No wonder the AEU branch union at Craigmore High was worried. State schools need not have a monopoly on public schooling in lower socio-economic regions.

Lessons learnt

1. Not only are new non-government schools subject to the 'rules of the day'; if they are in lower socio-economic areas and have overwhelming public demand, they face additional political blockages.
2. Totally independent schools have no systemic protection, and to maintain quality will serve the wealthy.

13
All-out attack
Who really runs state schools?

The invitation in 1997 by the principal of Craigmore High School, Charles Jones, to visit his school was totally unexpected. The school was alongside our Blakeview primary campus, and as neighbours it was important for us to find out what he wanted to show us. We had developed an excellent working relationship with the new Blakeview state primary school now built along our other boundary, and I was a regular visitor there. Blakeview Primary principal Bob Kennedy was a sympathetic supporter of our work in Munno Para and a concerned and effective principal.

I had never been to the high school, so three of us from Trinity travelled down to meet Charles. We waited in the school's reception area, watching with interest as the frantic flock of Craigmore students and staff flew through. The buildings and front office design were replicated in state schools across South Australia, and with hard furnishings it had a slightly clattery, though certainly functional, feel.

Charles emerged, welcomed us warmly and invited us into his office.

"What Craigmore High and this region needs is a high-quality senior technical high school to engage our students and enable them to be employed," he said. "We lack this. I invited you here to sound you out. Would you be interested in opening a secondary campus at Blakeview? If you are prepared to extend into secondary schooling here, we could build and jointly share facilities for a senior secondary technical high school program."

My mind raced through the possibilities of raising the capital for such an expensive program. Charles had the support of his school council chair, whom we met, and we were told that the council was behind the project. Although we had many other competing projects, we were asked to buy 35 acres of land alongside the high school to enable this innovative and exciting concept to proceed. Such a joint venture would undoubtedly be an extraordinary gift to the Munno Para community and region.

Not only was the invitation to meet unexpected, we also found the principal of Craigmore High School a surprising person, with a quietly spoken English accent and international experience. With a Master's degree in chemistry from Cambridge University, he was an impressive principal with obvious integrity and vision for the future education of the students at Craigmore High. The land he suggested we buy had already been approved for subdivision, and if we were to secure some of it we needed to decide quickly as roads were about to go in. We also met some other senior staff at Craigmore High.

After considerable debate at Trinity about our other options, we decided this one required immediate action. The concept of a joint senior secondary technical facility and the necessary purchase of the land at Blakeview were included on the agenda for the next monthly council meeting.

Salisbury College of Advanced Education

As usual, Trinity was financially stretched, building South Campus and the Blakeview primary campus. We also had another major project on our books.

The Salisbury CAE had amalgamated with the University of South Australia, and its campus, originally a tertiary teaching and nursing training college, was up for sale. With our huge waiting list, we calculated we had a 1000 students living 24 kilometres away in the Salisbury area, and these students could form the foundation for a new college of 2000 students. Salisbury was also less than 20 kilometres away from Port

Adelaide, and we thought that many of the 1200 students enrolled for St Nicholas would be very interested to attend because a school bus trip would take less than half an hour. Trinity College council had made a formal offer to buy this university campus as a whole for $7.5 million. We had understood this was the only offer on the table for the board of the university to consider, and the price offered was in the ballpark sought.

We had originally been asked by the university to be part of a larger group of educational organisations to develop a hub of technological secondary schooling options for students in the region. We had numerous meetings with the university, and the then director of the Anglican Schools Commission, Tony Shinkfield, agreed to help us with the extensive and complex negotiations. One after another, the other invited schools and organisations dropped out with no cash to offer. Along with the university, we saw the need to provide practical and technical senior secondary education for the northern region of Adelaide. The university was concerned about the low number of students from the northern region who progressed to tertiary education.

We believed we could offer the university something worth more than cash. After considerable discussion about developing a new R–12 College of 2000 students, the university was offered a seat on the board of the proposed school. The new college would be technically and academically focused, and would enable the university to be involved in secondary schooling, developing strong links to its other nearby university campus at The Levels. The Levels was originally built to house an expanded South Australian Institute of Technology, which offered a wide range of degrees in engineering, mining and electronics. We made an offer of $4.5 million cash plus an extra $3 million payable on the school succeeding after two years. Trinity was risking $4.5 million of borrowed cash and its reputation to help establish this new college. The university would receive the money it was seeking as well as utilising the buildings to provide educational opportunities for the region they claimed to be their focus. The university would also have a flow of future eligible enrolments from a region that traditionally had so few.

Despite all these competing plans, Trinity's council decided to consider the request of the principal and council of Craigmore High to extend our Blakeview campus into secondary schooling and work to open a senior secondary technological high school as a joint venture. We knew we would have to choose between that and the 2000-student college at Salisbury since neither the council nor I were prepared to take on the educational risk of developing both at once, let alone the financial risks involved in borrowing sufficient cash.

Council resolved to ensure one of these two outstanding alternatives would proceed. Having worked for many months developing the concepts and finances, we decided to bring the Salisbury project to a head as the university seemed very slow in responding to our offer. A past Labor government minister was the consultant appointed by the university to promote the sale, yet despite our having a developed curriculum and financial master plan to back our formal offer for Salisbury, after two months we had heard nothing. The university was informed that it would need to reply or we would withdraw the offer to take up the small window of opportunity to buy the land next to Craigmore.

(By chance I later met the chancellor of the University of South Australia, Basil Hetzel, on a social occasion. I chatted with him about our offer for the Salisbury CAE and he seemed surprised. He knew nothing about it. I explained, "The university seemed so slow to reply we decided that you weren't interested." We later found out the offer had never been presented to the university council. There were suggestions that other secondary school providers had intervened to prevent this new school getting off the ground.)

With still no reply forthcoming, we decided to purchase the Blakeview land. The day after the Trinity council meeting, a deposit was made and we advised Craigmore High School. The next day the Craigmore High AEU branch phoned me to say they were writing to the Trinity council to oppose this initiative. It was interesting to note the perceived power of the teachers' union in the management of the school. Who was in control? The AEU members at Craigmore certainly believed it was neither the principal nor their school council.

Using the media, including local newspapers, they began a campaign to stop an expansion of our Blakeview campus into secondary schooling. They set up the Craigmore Organising Committee and produced pamphlets that were widely distributed through their parents and the press. They published articles in the *AEU Journal*, which resulted in the union employing a research officer to investigate Trinity.

They attacked Trinity as an undeserving recipient of public funding. We were siphoning off money from state schools. A cartoon was distributed showing a big American finned car labelled 'Govt money' sideswiping a broken-down VW ('State schools'), with the headline 'A fund and run'. Another cartoon showed an octopus called 'Trinity', obese with $7 million in government funds, swallowing Craigmore High (see chapter 12). If truth is the first casualty of war, then this was war. Trinity was actually receiving only $4500 per pupil, including parental fees and all government funding, compared with the state schools at the time receiving $5500 per pupil. Trinity was in fact at a financial disadvantage of more than 20%, and still had to use this money for buildings and capital works for which state schools received extra money.

The propaganda sent out by the local AEU committee was incorrect, but they did expect to win. They would have been buoyed by the success of another anti-Trinity campaign in the town of Kapunda.

Two's company, three's a crowd

Kapunda Council wrote to the chair of Trinity College formally inviting the college to open a campus in their area, 40 kilometres north-east of Trinity. This being the third local council to ask us to set up a school, we were not surprised by the unsolicited request. The 1992 Trinity master plan included one extra primary feeder school, and an extra primary

One of a series of three pamphlets produced by AEU staff committee at Craigmore High School

campus would enable parents to access a Trinity primary school since many children who were enrolled could not gain a place at the current primary campuses.

As a result of Kapunda Council's approach, Trinity indicated very clearly that we wanted to join in a partnership to open an R–7 primary school adjacent to the high school with the primary school as a joint campus. Pedare at Golden Grove was cited as an example of this approach; they shared with the local high school and a Catholic college. We made it clear that at Year 7 any Trinity parents wishing to remain in Kapunda for their secondary schooling would be encouraged to attend Kapunda High School, which was proud of its academic history.

We understood the local council's vision for Kapunda. They wanted their town to be an educational focus for those living in the region. Having a choice of schools would strengthen the community and ensure a future for the town's shopping and commercial centre. We were also committed to allowing any Trinity parents wishing to transfer to Trinity at Gawler at Year 8 to be able to do so.

I phoned Deane Rohrlach, the principal of Kapunda High, to discuss our co-operative desires. To my astonishment, I discovered he had not been approached. The Kapunda Council had not yet advised either the principals or councils of their two state schools of their approach to us.

A public meeting was organised by the Kapunda Council. Over 300 people crowded into the Kapunda Town Hall. A core of people from the state primary schools was "shocked and opposed" to an independent school like Trinity opening up a campus in town. "Two's company, three's a crowd" said the badges on the principals' and teachers' chests. To be frank, if it had been a school other than Trinity with such huge public demand, they probably would not have minded.

With opposition dividing the town, we made no immediate commitment despite the overwhelming interest expressed at the meeting by parents, the Kapunda Council and the local business community. We did agree to take expressions of interest from parents wishing to enrol their children. The local Anglican parish backed the project and offered us the use of its church hall and adjacent land. We reviewed this carefully and realised we could open a small Kapunda campus at very low capital cost.

However, despite the number of people from Kapunda who wished to attend Trinity (many of whom were already on our waiting list), we did not proceed. We were working hard to develop good relationships with state schools as partners in providing public schooling for all. We consulted parents whose children were already travelling 80 kilometres daily from Kapunda and found that most wished to stay at Gawler because their children had friends there. It was certainly easier to put on an additional bus from Kapunda than build a new school where other providers did not want us. Kapunda did lose out as increasing numbers caught the bus to come to Gawler. I was disappointed for the community, but we did not wish to buy into the problems between the state schools and their local council and further divide the community.

Local demand spreads

This kind of local demand spread further into distant towns with only a state secondary school.

Clare, 105 kilometres north of Adelaide, is a major country town in a wine-growing region. It had a regional high school yet the Education Department was cutting physics and pure maths classes from its curriculum. Teachers from the school visited me to enquire about sending their children to Trinity. After discussions with our school council, we backed them as we believed they should be offered places at Trinity so their children could receive what we considered a core academic secondary schooling. Without physics and maths, their children would not be able to undertake university courses such as engineering which required these subjects.

Parents in the town organised one bus, then two buses to bring their children down to Gawler. The first enrolled were the Clare High School teachers' own children, followed by other children whose parents were also concerned about the quality of their local education.

Families from Clare, having sent their older children to Trinity for secondary schooling, soon enrolled their primary-aged children to add to our R–7 waiting lists. I was not happy about five-year-olds leaving home so early in the morning to catch the 7.30 am school bus from Clare. At the end of the day they would arrive home well after 5.00 pm without having the opportunity for any sport or cultural co-curricular activities. In winter they would see the sun rise and set on the school bus. But this was a price many families were prepared to pay.

"The Debate"

The Craigmore teachers must have believed that if confronted Trinity would back down. In a series of leaflets handed out to Craigmore High

School parents, they called for an open debate. Their slogan was "Public and Proud".

A public meeting to support public education was organised. Having been president of the Whyalla Teachers' Union and active in union matters, I thought that by attending this meeting I would be able to help with a genuinely open debate. As principal of Trinity I believed public education was vital, and I also thought I would be able to dispel some myths to ensure that what was being debated was the actual plan for a partnership between our two schools. I particularly wanted to share the truth about funding of independent schools. Our financial books were already publicly open and reported each year to our AGM.

After announcing my intention to attend the meeting at a staff meeting, Michael Burvill-Holmes, a two-metre giant of a man, declared, "I'm coming too."

Wednesday, 24 September 1997 was a cold day. At 7.30 pm Craigmore High School was dark. The school seemed empty, yet Michael and I managed to make out a sign to the 'Library', the venue for the public meeting. We walked to a set of forbidding concrete stairs up to the second floor. As we climbed up between prison-like block walls, I was confronted by the bareness of the school. Rubbish had not been cleaned up and there was graffiti and other signs of disrepair.

I was suddenly very pleased to have accepted Michael's offer to come with me, though even now I did not realise how much I would value his presence.

Michael and I entered the meeting. I expected a crowd of hundreds, but the two of us made up more than 10% of the total number present. This included the whole 'Organising Committee' and an AEU employee who was attending. The meeting was duly opened, but the chair announced: "Mr Hewitson is not allowed to speak at this meeting. Any attempts by him to present Trinity College as a public school are phony. Trinity is a private, profit-driven enterprise and cannot be in support of public education." With a maximum attendance of possibly two others who had come to hear different points of view, I decided not to point out the obvious hypocrisy of the organisers in inviting open debate and then only allowing those who agreed with their position to speak.

Following the meeting, the union attack expanded on several fronts. As already mentioned, it included dire warnings that new students at Trinity would be bashed up by students from Craigmore High. The union also attacked Labor politicians, accusing them of only being interested in independent schools because that was where they sent their own children. They then tried to influence local government: councillors were personally attacked in leaflet campaigns and council meetings were stacked with rowdy visitors who interjected and then, when invited to speak, threatened student strikes.[65] The teachers mobilised their students and held noisy public rallies outside the council chambers.

Trinity College was also accused of bringing a drug problem to the area.[66] The union members assumed that we, "like other private schools", simply expelled students with drug problems. They displayed a total lack of interest in Trinity's extraordinary approach to changing the drug culture of the region. They also claimed publicly that Craigmore High did not have a drug problem.[67] I was personally attacked by Bill Cook, Craigmore High teacher and union organiser, for "recently advocating the legalising of some drugs". Trinity College, he claimed "had a drug problem".[68]

The plans to expand Blakeview into Year 8 in preparation for establishing a secondary school eventually went ahead, but the legal campaign by the AEU prevented the giving of planning approval for construction for at least two years. This delay should have sunk the venture. Following the bashing threats, many parents withdrew their children from Blakeview. Father Bart O'Donovan of Elizabeth Downs Anglican parish and his wife Prue decided to keep their son there along with 18 other strong families. With the Blakeview campus only approved for primary schooling in 1998, the 56 Year 7 students were all offered a place at either North or South Campus for Year 8. We then had to provide temporary facilities in Gawler for two Year 8 classes.

In the months before we opened the Blakeview Year 8 classes, about 20 students who were originally going to stay at Blakeview decided to transfer to our Gawler school. Our waiting list had previously been rock solid – if we offered a place (and the family still lived in the area), over 95% took up the offer. However, 40 students declined the offer of a place at the new Blakeview secondary campus, even though they said that if a vacancy occurred in Gawler, they would take it.

The union publicity had successfully scared off many families. Those coming included an unusually high number of children who were failing even the low academic expectations of many schools in the Playford council area.[69]

The next two years were not easy for parents, students or staff. In 1998 Michael Lucas, an enthusiastic scientist with an agriculture degree, and Ursula Turbitt, an old scholar and past school captain of Trinity, were outstanding Year 8 class teachers and our Blakeview students grew in strength.

Now we actually had two Year 8 classes running, we advertised for a head of the senior school at Blakeview. Linda Munns applied. Dressed immaculately and wearing high heels, she had excellent references and interstate teaching experiences in high-fee colleges. But I doubted she was tough enough to cope with Blakeview. The site was windswept and raining, and Linda's high heels came off as we sloshed up the creek to see the challenge first hand. She met the Blakeview Year 8 students back in Gawler, but I warned her that a large number of future students would be from families in the Playford area whose children were struggling in their existing schools. Trinity was the last hope for these families, and despite the parents' overwhelming support, the children would not be easy.

As 1998 progressed it became obvious that we would again have to set up temporary facilities in Gawler the following year, this time for four classes (two Year 8 and two Year 9). We advanced plans to build a new drama centre and classrooms at our North School to house the developing Blakeview senior campus, which would now number 108 students. To my delight Linda accepted the position of head and consolidated the senior school at North while eagerly watching as the Blakeview buildings were built. Bus trips for the senior students to Blakeview to attend their school assemblies enabled those who were having to spend two years in a holding school in Gawler to see the buildings go up and to look forward to moving.

The Education Department response

What did the bureaucracy do when there was this explosive demand for a competitor in an area where the Education Department had held a long-term monopoly? The lower socio-economic areas of the northern suburbs had previously only had state schools and a few Catholic primary schools.

In December 1997 the SA Department of Education, Training and Employment commissioned Harrison Market Research "to undertake research into the marketing of state education in Elizabeth–Munno Para District".[70] I quote from the statement of intent: "The final product of this research will be the development of a marketing template that can be used by the schools in the area." The research consisted of eight focus groups of parents in the district from both independent and state schools. These groups explored three broad issues:

1. Perceptions of the education options in the Elizabeth–Munno Para District.
2. Parental priorities for the education of their children.
3. Marketing strategies for education.

The groups were held between 9 and 11 February 1998. The resulting report described the following weaknesses:

- *Attention to basics.* "There appears to be a lack of attention to basics. State and private school parents believed that their children *in private schools* were getting a better grounding in the basics i.e. reading, spelling, writing and mathematics than they would in a state school. Considerable comment was made about

the need to get back to old-fashioned teaching methods such as correct spelling."
- *Quality of staff.* "Parents were uncertain about the quality and number of teaching staff. Many parents in both systems believed that private schools employed more teachers of higher calibre than did the state system" (because of private schools' direct involvement in the hiring and retention of staff). They believed that "non-performing staff in the state system would be moved, sending the same problem to somebody else at another school".
- *Lack of accountability.* Secondary school parents were concerned that otherwise competent teachers had to teach subjects outside their expertise, compromising the standard of education of their children. They found a lack of accountability in the state system because of the overarching jurisdiction of the system. "Parents believed it was not clear to themselves or staff in state schools who was accountable." Some parents said it was the system rather than the school letting them down, and that individual schools were probably powerless to change many things of concern to them.
- *Unclear standards.* "According to some parents, it appeared pointless to complain about children not reaching the required standard, because that standard was not stated clearly, and because neither schools nor individual teachers subscribed to the view that they had not done the job if children failed to meet parents' expectations."
- *Discipline.* "Secondary school parents suggested that teachers within the state system no longer had the authority to effectively discipline students. Various policies, behaviour management, harassment, stress and anger management, conflict resolution etc. were well and good on paper, but had no 'teeth' and were generally regarded as ineffective." Along the same lines, it seemed that in the state system, teaching students their rights without the corresponding responsibilities had gone too far.
- *Moral values.* "State schools do not provide sufficient grounding in

moral values." Even though the area of Elizabeth–Munno Para had few church-attending families, the report stated: "A large number of parents sending their children to private schools were looking for a school that taught Christian values. Private schools were seen to offer a strong moral and ethical grounding within a religious context. State schools, on the other hand, could only teach broadly accepted societal values without any underpinning framework."

- *Single-level classes.* There can be real strengths for some classes in having students from different year levels in the same class. However, the report stated: "Composite classes or multi-level class groupings generally got the 'thumbs down', especially from private school parents. Single level classes were one of the things they had been looking for when they chose an independent school."

The report then identified several key *opportunities* that were available to the Education Department and state schools:

- *Greater emphasis on basics in primary school, with evidence of achievement.* "This research suggests that most parents want schools to focus their main efforts on ensuring designated standards of literacy by the time a child reaches high school. If state schools publicly set those standards, and each school takes responsibility for achieving them, parents would have more confidence in the state school system."
- *Clearer school accountability.* The key thing was for schools to be individually accountable for their educational outcomes. "In parents' eyes the only acceptable educational outcome for their children is that they are able to read, write and calculate to a standard that will enable them to fully participate in society."
- *Preparation for work.* The report highlighted a need for "greater emphasis on preparing students for full-time employment, more career counselling, job placement services in community employment programs."

- *Technical education.* There needed to be "further specialisation of the state high school system to offer again technical high schools, boys' high schools etc."

The report concluded with two observations: (1) "If nothing is done, enrolments at independent schools will probably continue to increase … Decreasing enrolments will further stigmatise state schools and state school students" and (2) "[There is a] real risk that state school students will be regarded as the 'second rung' of society – that they are somehow less worthy of employment than other students."

This document went on to note that without real change, marketing could only achieve so much. The most powerful marketing tool was word of mouth. "One of the things that came out of the research directly related to promoting schools is the overwhelming importance parents place on talking to other parents about schools they are considering … More than that, everyone in the community is gaining an impression of the various local schools by listening to what other people are saying about them."

Craigmore High – from bad to worse

Craigmore High School principal Charles Jones was shifted to Mount Barker High. A new principal was appointed who worked with the staff. After even more changes at the senior level, in 2003, five years later, the Education Department carried out a long overdue review. *The Advertiser* reported: "The damning Department of Education review identified a staff culture of bullying and harassment."[71]

Indeed, the report was damning at all levels. Student outcomes were poor. The school had both low retention rates and low SACE rates. This was difficult to achieve – if most students dropped out of school, presumably the more able remained. The SACE (Secondary Assessment Certificate of Education) was so 'lowest common denominator' that every student who turned up should have passed. Craigmore's pass rate was 44%, but the fact that the state's average pass rate was just 73% pointed to problems that were wider than just one school. When this was combined with a mere 38% retention rate of Craigmore students to Year 12, the result was truly appalling.

With rampant absenteeism being measured, the students were clearly being failed. Both students and parents felt disenfranchised: "Students and parents told the review team that they were rarely involved in decision-making forums, and felt marginalised in important decisions about school life." If this was not bad enough, the staffroom was a hostile place for teachers, who felt unsafe being in the room with militant AEU members.

Despite all this, five teachers slated by the Education Department for transfer from Craigmore to other schools took their fight against this decision to the Supreme Court. Even the chief executive of the Education Department, backed by a lengthy, drawn-out review, was not immune to being legally challenged by thuggish, unionised staff. Who indeed was accountable for our state public schools?

The Harrison Market Research report was amazingly honest, and properly used would have proved extremely helpful to the Education Department as a whole. In 2013, however, the same problems and opportunities found in 1998 still existed. To this day, neither a technical high school nor an academically focused state secondary school is available to parents in Adelaide's northern region.

Lessons learnt

1. State schools too often have no one in control. Who is accountable in practice? When no one is accountable, student learning suffers.

2. Given the strong leadership on education from four very different local governments areas (Port Adelaide, Kapunda and Elizabeth–Munno Para), perhaps state governments are not the best managers of schools to meet local needs.

14
Industrial relations
Seven days a week

"You need to take this seriously because I can close the school down," warned the judge. The principal of Trinity had been taken to the industrial court by the non-government schools union (ANGEE[72]) and our staff union delegates.

Nineteen ninety-eight was looking good, and two distant, dark clouds had not yet been recognised. The Year 12 students held a great deal of promise because they included the first large group who had started with the college at Reception and completed Year 12 thirteen years later. Employers were phoning our dean of studies, Michael Liddle, asking to employ our students, and, as usual, by May he had run out of students prepared to leave school to take up employment or apprenticeships. Nineteen Year 11 and three Year 12 students had done so, but the remaining 161 had chosen to complete Year 12. It was a senior school made up of students who were totally embedded in a Trinity education mixing competitively with students who had joined the college at Year 8.

With so much hope and promise for the year, I had welcomed the introduction of enterprise bargaining because theoretically it meant we were not locked into state school work practices and salaries. In theory we would be able to tailor our wage and working conditions to the reality of the marketplace for the benefit of our staff, and hence our students. It was also an opportunity for ANGEE to recruit more union members. In practice, along with other heads of independent schools, I was ill-prepared for this change because we were dealing in a local school with a state-wide union that had many strategic interests which had nothing to do with the staff at Trinity. ANGEE raised the expectations of what enterprise bargaining would achieve for teachers.

The other cloud appeared at the time as a bright ray of sunshine. I had delayed a review of the school until after our 1997 Year 12 results so that the double-school model of a North and South Campus, with a shared Year 11 and 12 program, could be put to the test. The review was undertaken by Dr Viv Eyers, retired head of the SA Board of School Assessment, and Dr Tony Shinkfield, who had strongly supported Trinity over so many years. The fact that the heads of the two well-established and respected Lutheran colleges of Adelaide had resigned the year after their review should have been a warning. CEOs are supposed to know the results of a review before they undertake one, and we were very confident. As a senior leadership team at Trinity, we were to discover why knowing the result in advance was important.

Enterprise bargaining

It was neither wise nor planned to have a school review at the same time as our first-ever enterprise bargaining 'negotiation'.

Enterprise bargaining hit independent schools like a steam train. Independent school heads, with close working relationships with staff they cared for and protected, suddenly found themselves in a bitter guerrilla war with colleagues. Never before had I experienced the potential for the role of principal to be separated from staff and teachers. Enterprise bargaining was being set up across the state as a principal-versus-staff confrontation.

At Trinity I relied heavily on the advice and expertise of senior staff given at our regular weekly meetings, and they shared the load with excellent advice and deep insight. With our shared history of shoulder-to-shoulder support, our senior staff were able to rely on the staff of both Blakeview and the original North School. However, our South School was different. The head of South, Michael Slocombe, was an outstanding educator, but like me he could not easily read political trouble. He thought so highly of everybody that he believed all would 'play the game'. Most of the staff at South were new to Trinity and had never been in a school on the edge of bankruptcy.

Trinity was important to the union because it was already the largest school in the state and hence a key pawn in the quest to entrench union power. Being a low-fee school without crippling debts, Trinity was seen as capable of setting state-wide standards for non-government school salaries and conditions. It was also important to the union that the staff belonging to the union had a formal say in the running of the school through an enterprise bargaining 'advisory committee' that would have to be 'consulted' on decision-making in the school.

As far as the union was concerned, the head of Trinity was isolated and not protected by being a member of a state-wide system of schools. Catholic and Lutheran schools were systemic and individual schools in those systems were unaffected by the enterprise bargaining process. The heads of Lutheran and Catholic schools were able to align themselves with the staff, and for these heads it was not an 'us versus them' battle.

Trinity's financial accounts were available to all. By 1997 the college was making annual surpluses of over $1 million and accruing cash at the rate of around $2 million each year. The graph below shows how easily Trinity could be depicted as having plenty of resources to spend on staff. The graph also shows the $1 million per annum saving achieved with South starting in 1993. The two parallel R–12 schools operating with different timetables and sharing teaching facilities were an economic powerhouse.

However, the school had been expanding quickly, and the additional costs of long-serving staff, with higher salaries and accrued benefits, were not explained by the union. With new school buildings, furniture and teaching resources, the annual depreciation and maintenance costs were also going to rise as more assets aged. Ignoring these realities, the union described the million-dollar surplus set aside for capital improvements as "stuffing the cupboard with money" that should be paid out to the staff who earned it. The idea that a cash surplus was the best way a school serving a lower socio-economic community could provide buildings and facilities without borrowing the money was under attack. Drs Eyers and Shinkfield were told: "The school should borrow."

In contrast, I believed that a poor community could not afford debt because in the longer term the interest bill becomes an additional cost to be paid, probably by increased fees. As a result of higher fees, the poor would be priced out of the school. Throughout my term as headmaster, our fees had only risen in line with inflation, despite educational costs and salary increases being greater than the CPI.

With its secure financial base, Trinity had become an attractive place to work, and many new staff had made a career move to come. The very long-term future of the college was not an immediate concern to a number of new appointments. To be part of Trinity in the foundational

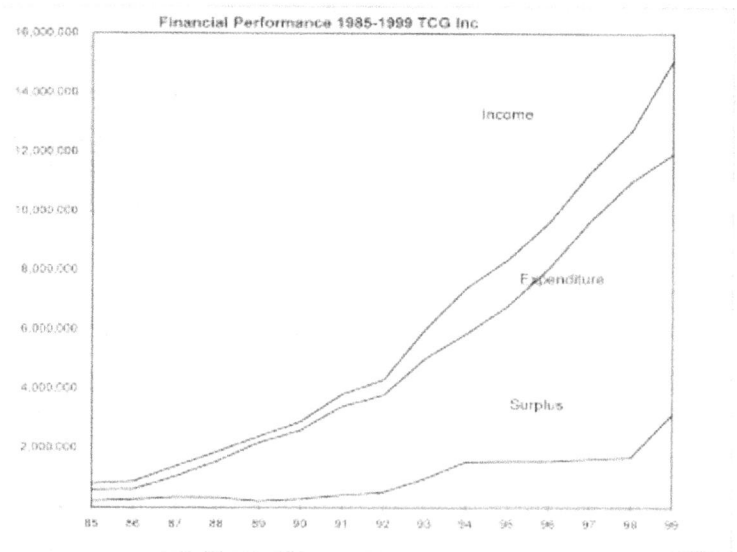

Financial performance 1985-1999 TCG Inc.

years meant such insecure and poor conditions that you would only have worked there if it was part of your 'mission in life'. For most new staff, accepting a position at Trinity was generally not a vocational call to 'mission' but a career stepping stone.

The school had one enormous advantage. Unusually for the headmaster of an independent school, my salary arrangements were transparent. Along with all our staff salaries, they had been tied to the Education Department salary scales. With the school's growth, the CEO of Trinity now received the same salary and retirement package as a 'Class A Principal' in the department. All other senior staff were also transparently on the award. The only way I would receive an increase myself would be through an enterprise bargaining agreement.

The 18 members of the college's senior leadership team were not in it simply for personal gain. The team included the heads of campuses, the heads of each school within each campus, and the non-academic leadership (the bursar and business manager). We discussed every step of the enterprise bargaining process and decided Trinity's approach as a group. Fourteen of our senior staff were eligible to vote on the agreement; the rest were considered 'management'.

During a subsequent divisive enterprise bargaining process, I managed to offer our staff the opportunity to make the principal's salary clearly part of the Enterprise Bargaining Agreement (EBA). The college council debated this offer with concern that it would limit their future ability to enter private arrangements with future heads, and it might also mean that the head and staff could at some future point line up against the council. However, the council voted to approve the offer because it would mean, in theory, that the staff, principal and college council would be working as one. It was an attempt to ensure negotiations would be non-confrontational because the process and agreement were for 'all of us'.

This, however, did not suit the union. They believed they needed an adversarial arrangement (which suited their understandable need for staff to join the union). My offer to also join the union was not well received.

A number of years later, after my retirement, my wife had an interesting conversation with another retired educator. "Where do you work?" the woman asked. "Trinity College," Ros replied. "Gosh," the woman said, "I worked in the non-government school teachers' union. How did you get on with the principal? He was the hardest and most impossible man the union ever had to deal with."

The original negotiator for the union was replaced and I was able to develop a sense of combative trust with her successor, Andrew Murray. When he started in front of the staff to hop into the headmaster's salary conditions, he did not know that they were on the table in public view. He was surprised because this openness of the principal's salary made it much more difficult to attack 'management' for hiding their salaries. Andrew quickly recognised the power of the 'us and us' proposition, and equally quickly rejected it. The head of Trinity College's salary would not be part of the EBA.

I still believe the school, staff and non-government schools union lost out from this since future heads could confidentially feather their nest, negotiate with staff and then raise fees, thereby pricing some families out.

Up before the judge

In independent schools across the state, the issue of staff remuneration for involvement in the co-curriculum program was an explosive time-bomb. My position was that I wanted our staff to be well paid and salaries to be competitive; but I also wanted to retain a sense of 'mission' whereby that something extra was professionally given to help keep fees down. Unfortunately, I also carried the baggage of my history. As the person responsible for paying the salaries, and having lived through a time when I did not know whether we would be able to pay teachers at all, I was extremely cautious about retaining capital resources and not over-committing. It would have been good to have offered a package of 2.5% above the award, even with our teachers having one week's extra holidays to cover the school's co-curriculum demands.

The lobbying, the stagnation of process and the lack of success in gaining an enterprise bargaining outcome were common in independent schools throughout SA. Many staff did not understand that the external union delegates' futures were not threatened if a particular school over-committed in enterprise bargaining and went broke. We were all beginners. Our deputy principal, David Smith, showed his political expertise in seeming to get an eventual resolution. The vote was taken with overwhelming support by Blakeview and North in favour of the negotiated EBA. However, the overwhelming majority of South School staff were unhappy with the agreement. At the request of the college's union delegates, led by the South representative, we were taken to court by the union.

The point at issue was that we were offering replacement teachers more than the award by giving them a year's contract. Normally, when a teacher took accouchement leave or leave for some other purpose approved in the award, their replacement teacher was considered a 'personal' replacement, meaning that when the teacher returned, the replacement lost their job.

We did things differently. With over 200 teaching staff, we expected 10% to be on leave at any one time, so the need for replacements was a daily reality. We had a pool of replacement teachers we regularly called on. However, instead of employing them on day-by-day contracts, we offered them whole-year contracts, which we would renew in June for the following year. This meant our replacement staff had continuity of work and effectively six months' notice for the following year. If absent staff returned early from leave for some reason, then we had to bear the cost of employing the contracted teacher as well as the permanent teacher for the balance of the year. It was a risk. On the other hand, when a contract teacher was outstanding, we could tell them we would love to make them permanent. Of the 10 primary replacement teachers who were constantly employed, all were made permanent within two to three years.

The union rep from South objected to this arrangement. He thought we should have a named replacement teacher for each staff member on leave so that when the staff member returned, that replacement teacher would lose their contract. The EBA did not provide for contract teachers who were not replacement teachers, and the union rep suspected we had more contract teachers than staff on leave. We did not.

We were put to the test. First we had to prove that there were no losers, and there were none; then we had to show that we had no more contract teachers than permanent teachers on leave. This was done, and the judge declared the matter resolved.

I tell the story of going to court to show the sensitive nature of enterprise bargaining. Without discussing the matter with us, the union and its staff reps acted because they were so sure we were doing the wrong thing. Our staff had been encouraged to have high expectations. It would have been great to have had a specific Trinity award where staff of excellence were offered above-award salaries or extra time; but the nature of a union-based, whole-staff agreement is lowest common denominator. It is about the protection of the weak. Anything one staff member gets, the others must have.

The review of the school by Eyers and Shinkfield progressed in an atmosphere of disappointment; with about half the staff committed long term, with a spirit of serving a mission, and the other half with a review panel to complain to.

The review

The report[73] arrived and I was stunned. It claimed to hold a mirror up to the school community, yet the reflected image was unrecognisable.

The review panel had started work in 1997. Initially I was warmly told that the parental response was quite extraordinary. A staggering 91% of parents expressed high to very high satisfaction with the college. No parent expressed even low satisfaction, let alone dissatisfaction.

Many positive parental comments were quoted in the report, such as:

"Dedicated and successful style, discipline helps to promote high standards of achievement with students' pride with the community."

"Brilliant, the staff is great, every child is important."

"Fundamental reasons for sending our children are being met, excellence in education and a caring Christian environment."

"If we were to ask would we have done as well elsewhere, I feel the answer is 'No' because the environment and general attitude in policy has enabled our children to fully realise their potential."

As the review progressed through 1998, however, I had to speak to the chair of the college council about the number of staff claiming that one of the interviewers, Dr Eyers, appeared to be only interested in negative comments about the school. The 16 senior teaching staff were uneasy and surprised by how little they were being involved in the process. The distance being kept by the panel was remarkable, as was the lack of attempts to seek information. Even support staff were not asked for information.

The day after receiving the negative report, I discussed with the council chair whether I should resign as headmaster. On re-reading the report, however, we realised it was distorted by false information. Checkable numbers and 'facts' were wrong.

The report claimed that forward enrolments were dropping. The reviewers wrote that "the pressure for places is now decreasing" and that "the school has declining enrolment numbers as you proceed forward into future years".[74] It was true that in 1997 there were only 116 enrolments for the 180 reception places that would be available offered in 2002 – much lower than the 400-plus chasing the 1998 places. For reviewers familiar with other independent schools, it was generally safe to assume that too few enrolments would always be a concern.

Unfortunately, neither the deputy principal in charge of enrolments, David Smith, nor his enrolment secretary, Rosemary Alexander, had been asked to check this information. The reality was this: being five years ahead, many future 2002 enrolments had not yet even been born. Yet by March 1998 all Reception places for 2002 had been filled by newborn babies and a long waiting list established. At Year 8 there were already 377 students enrolled for just 180 places, five years ahead. Enrolment applications had never been as strong.

On close examination, the report was also a false mirror of the academic results of the college. Dr Eyers was CEO of the State Public Examinations Board, with access to all the state figures for each subject. He stated that "the college had little to boast about as it was only marginally above the state average". To come up with this, he claimed he had taken a random sample of subjects offered by Trinity at Year 12 and found that its "marks for each subject were only 4% above the state average".[75] However, the so-called 'random selection' was actually a list of all the lowest performing subjects in the school. When the omitted 25 subjects were included, his academic evaluation of the college was two and half times too low. In fact, using TER scores, the 1997 results were a whopping 27.5% higher than the state average, and this in a lower socio-economic community where "education fails".

The report was clearly written to change Trinity to be more like the state schools from which its parents by and large had fled. It wanted the college to effectively be controlled by staff committees. The problem with this was the problem state schools had: nobody was accountable. Trinity staff already had enormous input into management and planning. They were able to develop strategic options and vote to select the school's strategic future. To the reviewers the school appeared authoritarian, probably because I as principal represented the collective view of the senior leadership team in the enterprise bargaining process that left some staff disappointed when the outcome fell short of union promises.

Fortunately the review process called for the report itself to be independently reviewed by a panel including the vice-chair of the college council (John Ragless), the secretary of the council (Professor John Thomas), the deputy principal (David Smith) and a number of other staff and council appointees. This panel unanimously rejected the report and recommended its rejection by the council.

Despite this expensive lost opportunity, the recommendations of the report still needed to be considered carefully by the council. One of its strong recommendations was for the college not to expand by adding any more schools:

> The resounding message of the college and college administration is that significant groups are of the very strong opinion that Trinity's growth rate must be curtailed. The council (92% of this group), teaching staff (18%), old scholars (17%), honorarium staff (32%) and paid non-teaching staff (29%) all place consolidation of the college as the one aspect of Trinity where improvement is most needed. Some parents (7%) also express concern about college growth.[76]

Parents still wanted an R–12 education, and I was convinced that to achieve this we needed a fourth primary school. Ninety per cent of our Year 7 and 8 intake had previously been unable to enter at Reception because we had no place for them. And so the risky idea of establishing a fourth R–6 school grew.

Other projects were planned, two of them particularly ambitious. A fourth R–6 primary school was already in our master plan, but two projects were ground-breaking. STARplex, a complex on our Gawler property with indoor pools, gyms, basketball courts, a theatre and much more, was planned as a commercial venture, and an Open Learning Centre for senior secondary vocational education, also at Gawler, would offer tertiary qualifications. However, with 92% of my council reportedly wishing consolidation, how could these proceed?

Gawler River School

The senior leadership team discussion of the possibility of a fourth R–6 school was unusually vigorous, and Ros Hewitson and Liz Hinrichsen were opposed. Ros and Liz were a powerful team – Ros ran the R–4 and Liz the 5–8 curricula and testing across the whole college – and they were strongly against developing "yet another school". Liz, heading the middle school at North, was one of a number of senior staff on the review oversight group who had unanimously rejected the Eyers/Shinkfield report. Yet unusually she referred to the review to underline her point: "This is a step too far. You are making enemies and the review clearly stated that 92% of school council were opposed to expansion."

Liz was supported by a battle-weary Ros: "Michael, we would be mad to do this."

Before presenting new initiatives formally to council, I always sought the input of our senior staff team, and I reflected their thoughts reliably and with total honesty in my council presentation. I respected their opinions, and if they opposed an idea, I believed they might well be right. With a fourth R–6 school, however, both state and federal politics meant it could be built now, and I believed that if we did not do it now it would never happen. I thought that once Trinity started to look inwards, nobody would have the courage to keep building in the future.

Rick Jarman, head of the middle school at South, and others argued in favour. "We already have 283 paid up Reception enrolments on the waiting list for 2000, more than a year ahead! It's the right thing to do."

"Look, Rick," Liz countered, "you have a vested interest because you would wish to apply for the head of this school."

"That may be," David Smith quietly chimed in, "but if these students can't come in at Reception, they will come in at Year 8 without having had our primary education. I support an R–12 offering to all our parents. I spend most of my life looking after parents who can't get into Trinity."

Bravely, with an interrupting dialogue from Ros, I pointed out: "We have an extra R–6 campus in our master plan, so if you do vote for this campus I will take it to council."

"You're mad!" said Ros. "Who's going to mop up after this one?"

I had no idea of how our senior staff would vote, but the vote recommended (albeit with an unusually large split) that I seek council approval. To my surprise, council overwhelmingly (though not unanimously) backed the preparation of a business plan and an application to the Commonwealth government for approval to open the new school in two years' time (2000). The planned site was at Gawler River, 12 kilometres west by car, in a region I predicted would one day be the centre of a very large Adelaide suburb.

Consternation at St Columba

Independent schools are used to believing they have a monopoly of independent education in their area. The Trinity proposal caused consternation at St Columba at nearby Andrews Farm.

In a letter on 14 August 1998 to my brother John, who was still chairman of the St Columba college council, I pointed out the history of the school. The reality was that Trinity's waiting list had contributed 500 students to St Columba since 1995, all from the region St Columba now saw as its own. I described Trinity's ongoing support for St Columba, and how St Columba's enrolments were struggling until Trinity wrote to its waiting list to encourage them to enrol. Some of the existing students at our Blakeview Campus also transferred with our blessing and support. We had nominated the very best people to the St Columba council: our deputy principal, David Smith (when St Columba was a primary school) and Robert Smedley, Trinity's head of geography and Blakeview (to assist with their move to become a secondary college).

We respected the St Columba principal, Madeiline Brennan, who was doing a fine job. We showed her our enrolment list – not one of the 240 then registered to attend Trinity at Gawler River was on the St Columba list (those on our waiting list who were prepared to attend St Columba were already doing so). By opening this new R–6 school, Trinity would greatly reduce its Year 8 intake, and far from competing with St Columba, would assist the growth of the new St Columba secondary college.

Many principals found *any* expansion of Trinity a threat. Although the

Gawler River Campus was to be an R–6 School, the steering committee for the school included not only people from the Gawler River region but also families from suburbs of Adelaide far beyond Trinity's normal enrolment. This troubled some high-fee schools, many of which were now struggling to attract students. The Anglican diocese contacted the executive subcommittee of Trinity to see if they supported the new projects (the Gawler River campus and STARplex) or whether "this was just Michael". Vice-chair John Ragless wrote to the archbishop and advised him of the strength of council support for both STARplex and Gawler River.

The steering committee of the Gawler River school met to consider the plans drawn up by the Reverend Chris McAleer, an experienced architect, South School chaplain and art teacher. We planned classrooms, an oval, a basketball court and a playground. The meeting finished and Chris and I were chatting when two parents came back from the car park to ask a question. "We have been talking with the others outside. We would like a chapel built into the design. Is this possible?" Only 18% of Trinity's parents were involved or connected loosely with a church of any denomination. As far as we knew, not one steering committee member was a regular church attender, let alone a practising Anglican. Nonetheless, the question should not have surprised us. The Eyers/Shinkfield review had shown that despite the irrelevance of the church in the lives of families attending Trinity, one of the four overwhelming reasons parents gave for sending their children there was the college's overt and committed Christian foundation.[77]

The steering committee met to write and review the prospectus for this new school, which now had a chapel/school assembly space, complete with a cross-topped spire on the roof of the classroom block. The prospectus, photocopied on cheap blue A4 paper, indicated that 137 enrolments had already committed from the existing Trinity waiting list, leaving only 13 vacancies. Those from the Gawler River region already at Trinity Gawler did not move. Rick Jarman was appointed as the prospective principal of the school.

Not all plain sailing

A working bee was held to clean up the car bodies and rubbish from the site and plant new trees. Working bees had become a tradition and provided a symbolic commitment to the new school, and once again new parents met others and became part of a real community.

However, it was not all plain sailing. By establishing a Gawler River campus we were unwittingly destroying another school.

When students who had applied to come to Trinity at Reception were not offered a place, we had no record of where their parents eventually sent them. Perhaps we should have worked out that these parents would look for a school closest to their first choice. This turned out to be Immanuel, the Lutheran primary school in Gawler. When so many Immanuel students who were on Trinity's waiting lists withdrew from Immanuel to attend Gawler River, the Gawler Lutheran parish publicly debated closing the school. We had not expected families living in Gawler to be prepared to travel out to the country to send their children to school.

The head of Lutheran Education agreed to meet me because I wanted to find out if he wanted our help to prevent their school from closing. I believed schools needed to compete for students to ensure that parents were offered a choice, but the quick and unexpected removal of a competitor would be bad for the community as a whole, and bad for the Lutheran Church. If we could give their school time to change direction and curriculum, then it would help to meet the overwhelming need for schools like Trinity. We worked very carefully to try to save the school, even freezing offers for new enrolments from the Lutheran school. This did not work entirely as hoped – a number of parents said, "If we can't get into Trinity from Immanuel, we'll transfer our children to Gawler East Primary and enrol to attend Trinity from there." However, the move did stop the mass movement of enrolments from the Lutheran school and allowed it to change, compete and survive.

It was a close call to achieve the Gawler River enrolments in an area without a large population and well serviced by St Columba. The new campus received very few existing Trinity students. When push came to shove, the closer location was met by the determination of parents' children and friends to remain in their existing school, even when a place back at Gawler in Year 7 was guaranteed. The new school opened with children travelling by bus from as far as Clare, 100 kilometres away, leaving home between 6.30 and 7.00 am and arriving home after 5.00 pm. Starting with 168 students and 51 at Reception, the school was able to grow steadily into a two-stream primary school.

Planning STARplex

In 1992 I enjoyed dreaming and drawing up plans for a community complex to be located on Alexander Avenue beside our North Campus. It would have a rock-climbing wall at the entrance, indoor palm trees overlooking an indoor heated pool, basketball courts, a gym and a

Students and staff of the Gawler River campus on the first day of school, 2000

theatre. At the 1992 strategic planning day for the college council, the proposal was a great catalyst to widen our thinking.

We had no hope of building a swimming pool, basketball stadiums or a gym just for school use mainly during school hours, and I wondered why other schools did so. So I asked the council, "Wouldn't it make more sense to use these facilities six days a week from 6.00 am till 10.00 pm, with community use enabling the financing and depreciation costs to be shared between a greater number of users?" If we facilitated such a community centre, it would break down the 'them versus us' feeling that Trinity was not really a school for the whole community.

At the time we were building Blakeview and Trinity South, but the idea simmered. The land opposite the college was to be subdivided and a sport, health and recreational complex such as we were envisaging would raise the value of the land. The developer agreed to sell the few hectares needed to build a megaplex cheaply. The college treasurer, Brian Carr, was a mover and shaker with high-level financial and management skills and was achieving great things as CEO of Tea Tree Gully Council. He encouraged us to develop an even grander design: "This is a once-only opportunity to buy the perfect site for the megaplex, and if all else fails, we can subdivide and sell!"

In 1997 the college council released discussion plans for three options:

1. Build a commercial complex for Sports, Training, Arts and Recreation ('STARplex') costing millions and risk all on it being a commercial success.
2. Build a school-owned double basketball court with a stage and retractable seating holding two thousand people that could be used for school speech nights.
3. Do nothing.

As principal I indicated in advance that I would support either option one or option two. Most staff supported the first option, even though they recognised this would consume the capital some thought should be spent on staff. We could afford the double basketball court stadium and this would cost the college per annum the equivalent of four full-time teachers' salaries (then about $164,000 a year) for 20 years. The STARplex option seemed potentially a bottomless pit, but in fact it could be limited, in the worst case scenario, to $2 million per annum over 20 years.

My worries about such a commitment were shared by some council members. Father Russell Simmonds argued forcefully that the school was over-reaching into areas it knew little about. We were risking the high quality of education offered to our students. The vigorous discussions were an important part of an effective board. However, the proposal was backed with a whole community vote. By a two-thirds majority, the school community voted to take the risk and committed to build STARplex.

Dale Martin, our business manager, put his hand up to manage STARplex when built and resign from his current role. With a young family, Dale now had real skin invested in this project, along with his CEO.

To further develop the concept, we visited successful community centres, mostly run by local councils in Victoria. We learnt that a climbing wall would be non-commercial. Out it went! We learnt we ideally needed four basketball courts with sprung timber floors; if we built two we would definitely go broke. Four it had to be! Physiotherapy and other support health services, child care, gyms, a café, a sports store and two indoor swimming pools, including an Olympic short-course pool, were essential. So final plans were drawn up and three interested builders were invited to tender with a design and construction price. Badge Constructions won the job. We added a concert hall with an end wall that opened up into the four courts to enable 8000 people to meet together on Trinity Sunday.

STARplex opened in June 2000 with 80 staff, Dale Martin as general manager and a team of five managers running the component businesses.[78]

Our financial risks had now increased dramatically. We ran STARplex, like our schools and the Montessori kindergarten in our original college headmaster's house,[79] as just another business unit. To run a school is to run a business. If the CEO/principal cannot provide the board with accurate financial statements for each and every operation, then cross subsidies start to occur and eventually the profitable arms are lost and the school goes bankrupt. Each of our schools hired STARplex at the same cost as other schools in the region. Because we took all the risk, each head of school was able to have first dibs at booking their preferred times. They also knew instantaneously what the cost to their school would be. This arrangement was far cheaper than any one school owning and running its own pool or theatre or courts. Schools can be more effectively part of their community by sharing their resources 24/7 at cost.

Lessons learnt

1. Industrial relations rules have an impact on quality education, for good or bad.
2. Schools with a mission based on the voluntary efforts of their staff and their communities challenge, and are challenged by, enterprise bargaining that seeks to focus on the benefits to individual union members and the union as an institution.
3. School facilities should be used 24/7, not just in school hours.

15
Flooded with money
Funding is not the main game

In 2012 there was still the belief that if we pumped billions of dollars more into schools across Australia all would be well. "The Federal Government is going ahead with sweeping reforms to the school funding system, planning to release its blueprint next month with the ambitious goal of increasing spending on schools by about $6.5 billion," *The Australian* reported.[80] However, the story of Trinity, a school that operated from 1984 to 1998 with just 65% of the money per child spent in a state school, shows that the quality of education is not just about the money.

The Grattan Institute, in a 2012 report written by a team headed by Dr Ben Jensen, made the point that spending on schools in Australia has increased while learning has declined.[81] I will concentrate on the solutions in the final chapter; however, Dr Jensen and his team have come up with some solutions learnt from Asia that overlap those in this story.

In another article in *The Australian*,[82] Dr Jensen summarised the situation as follows:

> In recent years, Australia has argued over and allocated substantial resources to public versus private schools, smaller class sizes, school autonomy and computers in schools.
>
> The Gonski review of school funding, teacher bonuses, hiring and firing teachers is not the main game. They are all important, but the evidence is clear that their impact on learning is at best negligible compared with the focus in the Asian systems.
>
> The lesson from Asia is that the only way to improve students'

learning is by improving teaching. Reforming teaching is about behavioural and cultural change, which means changing what teachers do, day in, day out, in every school.

Improving the quality of teaching is not only achieved by more teacher training, although this is important. It requires a vision and purpose being shared by the teachers, school and parents. Changing what teachers do requires a measurable curriculum that when taught well achieves strong academic progress for children. It requires the learning to be valued and assessed. The story of Trinity and similar schools underlines the important role parents play in achieving success. Truly successful schools are community-based, with parents, students and teachers accepting the vision and culture of the school and working together.

Dreams must be paid for

Schools do compete, and schools resourced at higher levels do have a significant advantage. High-fee independent schools that have about 165% of the funding of a state school are clearly able to spend more on each child's education. Most of this financial advantage may be wasted on resources that do not improve a child's learning, although some money is well spent.

At Trinity I was unhappy with our lack of spending in two areas. Both concerned children with lower academic inclination and, in some cases, lower ability. Our remedial and special education programs were poorly resourced. To fund and run an after-school sports and cultural program, Trinity intentionally chose to spend the available money on the 95% of students who did not require remedial education. In after-school music alone, each school had a primary, middle and senior concert band, string ensembles and choirs, with more than 500 students and 20 teachers involved, in addition to many instrumental teachers. School sport and drama groups were equally as valued – and expensive.

Money might not be the panacea, but it was clearly important to enable a quality education for all, if it was well spent.

We were very keen to increase our total income from 65% of the money paid for each state school student in order to expand our vocational educational offering. We had already started to spend on vocational and technical educational opportunities and planned a new campus for senior secondary vocational education. We dreamt about how we would provide a special education program to directly meet the needs of children with special learning difficulties, complete with specialist teachers and some small-group and one-on-one support. We also needed to be funded at the same level as other systems serving in the same communities to remain competitive in the longer term.

The 'system'
For decades, Catholic schools had been advantaged by their system. School systems were politically powerful and were recognised on a different basis from purely independent schools. This was well known. And yet even when independent Anglican schools were given the chance to receive the extra funding that being in a system made possible during the 1990s,[83] and even with a constitution written to protect the independence of each school, only Trinity was prepared to join a system of schools. The constitution limited the liability of any one school to $1000 should the system go bankrupt and schools would then return to fully independent status.

With this impasse throughout the decade, we believed our best chance to establish a system was to separately incorporate our three schools (three schools being required to found a system). To help our campaign, Archbishop Ian George and I flew to Canberra to put our case to federal education authorities. Later, when addressing the college community, the archbishop claimed to have done very little to advance the system cause, and that it was really up to 'your headmaster' to produce all the facts and figures to turn the tide. But logic and argument aren't all that is required in a democracy. The political presence of an archbishop taking the time to meet officials underlined the philosophical importance of education being open to all, serving the poorest in society through a school system committed to low fees. The archbishop's presence in Canberra, with his unrehearsed illustrations and stories from the diocese, increased confidence in the reliability of the data being presented.

We gained approval to separate Trinity College Inc. into a group of independent schools, each one a part of the "SA Anglican Schools System". Trinity College Inc. was not in itself a member of the system, just the three schools, North, South and Blakeview. The head of each campus now became a school principal, with the legal responsibilities of a principal. Because only Trinity's three schools formed the system, all Trinity's other activities, such as the Montessori Kindergarten and STARplex, were outside the system and therefore outside the government funding arrangements. Not being a member school, Trinity College Inc. was also excluded from the Commonwealth funding calculations. This made it easier to follow the strict guidelines for eligibility for increased federal government recurrent funding.

Flooded with riches

On 31 January 2000, a letter arrived from Dr David Kemp, federal Minister for Education, Training and Youth Affairs. We were advised that the SA Anglican School System would be raised from Category 10 to Category 12 for the purposes of Commonwealth General Recurrent Funding, effective from 1 January 1999. This meant we were going to be back-paid $1,219,554, and we were further advised this payment would be processed as soon as possible. We also calculated that during 2000 the re-categorisation would bring the school $1.5 million above what we had budgeted for. Trinity would receive a totally unbudgeted financial flood of $2.7 million, representing an unprecedented opportunity. It was beyond the wildest expectations of our business manager, Dale Martin, and our bursar, Wayne Smith.

We had increased our fees by 5% over three years to prove to the government that we had met its criterion requiring us to increase private effort by 5%. At the same time we had to have a well below average income stream and show expenditure increases beyond our control. It was almost a catch-22. We had been desperate to receive the same category as the Catholic system, Category 11, but our application had demonstrated that we qualified for Category 12 by the narrowest of margins, 0.002%. To qualify we had also shown that increased funding was needed because of the federal government's own wishes that we increase technology and computing across the school and introduce senior secondary vocational courses.[84] We had to demonstrate that our costs were rising above our income and were not self-inflicted.

Politically it was amazing to be treated strictly according to the rules. From 2000, Trinity received 75% of the state school funding level. Category 12 was the highest level of government support available for a non-government school. Once we received this increased funding per student, we decreased our fees by 5% to return the cost of sending a child to Trinity to an affordable level for families in the region. The fees were then the same as 1985 in real terms after CPI, up to half the disposable income of 95% of families in the region.

Open Learning Centre

We were thinking outside the square. I remember the beaming face of a young man who was finally experiencing real satisfaction, not just as a cricketer, but also in what he was learning at 'school'. It was at an information evening for the Open Learning Centre, where booths were showing off our senior secondary programs offered in 2001. The range of opportunities was wide – aviation, hospitality, electronics, painting and decorating, office administration, information technology, child care, youth work, carpentry and joinery, automotive mechanics, beauty therapy, tourism and horse racing. Our young man bursting with pride, professionally attired as a painter and decorator, was demonstrating his newly learnt skills.

Australian schools fail to educate at least a quarter of students. Many are children for whom a technical, applied, hands-on education – an education with direct relevance to qualifications – is important.

Coming through Blakeview was a group of students whose parents had sent them there despite union threats that they would be at risk from students at neighbouring Craigmore High School (see chapter 13). Those parents were so concerned about the state of their children's education that they accepted all the risks and challenges of this new campus. Only some of the 54 Year 8 students at Blakeview in 1998 were suited to traditional academic education. Some students were a year older and at the end of Year 9 took up work outside the school. By 2000, 47 subjects were offered at Trinity in Year 12, providing a wider range than almost any other school in South Australia.[85] However, this range was not suited to many of the Blakeview students, and still left many other students from North and South with irrelevant senior secondary education.

I believed our non-academic students should have just as good an education in senior secondary years as those who were university bound. Our schools seem to concentrate on producing university entrants, and with 70% of our Reception students qualifying for university by Year 12, I thought the balance was wrong. In our community we needed good people to take up trades and non-university professional options.

To run tertiary-level trade courses in our senior secondary school we needed to offer a 9.00 am to 5.00 pm program. The rhythm of learning for these students differed from the academic programs, which relied on intense lessons with follow-up study and homework. The time on-task was greater for the vocational students, but when they were not working, much less out-of-school study was required. It was quite obvious that those doing tech subjects could undermine the academic rigour of those doing university-orientated subjects.

The Open Learning Centre's students were unavailable for after-school sport and co-curricular activities and so were enrolled in STARplex, which offered day and evening access to gyms, swimming classes or individual programs, as well as many team sports with adults.

Students participated at least twice a week and their school fees covered these costs since they were often unable to be in the school sports' teams.

The traditional senior secondary school offering does not always engage academically able students either. The Open Learning Centre offered not only trade school pathways but also university qualifications. The college organised for academically able, technically inclined students to do two years at the Open Learning Centre as part of a Bachelor of Computing degree at the Douglas Mawson Institute or a degree at the University of South Australia. The Open Learning Centre was a different kind of learning, but certainly not second-rate.

Parents of the students attending the Open Learning Centre were overwhelmingly grateful for the way their students were able to grow and achieve. This group of parents was indeed the most appreciative of the Trinity College education their children received.

Time to go?

Should I continue as headmaster at Trinity or finish on the date I nominated when I started at the college in 1984? Ros wanted me to seek a new contract and do another three years. Our four adult children were unanimous in asking me to leave – they wanted a Grandpa for their own children. It was true that I had kept up a frenetic pace with starting the Gawler River school, STARplex and the Open Learning Centre, and planning was beginning on a teachers' college. Late in November 2000 I confirmed with the college council that I intended to finish on 1 February 2002 and not seek a new contract.

On Wednesday, 29 November 2000, the Gawler *Bunyip* announced: "Trinity College principal signals the end of a

The Bunyip, *29 November 2000*

stunning era". With the headline FROM A LOG CABIN TO FOUR CAMPUSES AND THREE THOUSAND STUDENTS, an accompanying cartoon took a shot at my labelling the school a 'dead duck' when I reluctantly took it on in 1984. At the time it was announced that I was probably going to take up the role of director of the Anglican Schools System. This was planned as a part-time executive officer position, working to build new schools across the state.

In the 2000 *Trinity College Year Book* I wrote:

> 2000 has delivered its promises and more. I am very pleased to report the sheer pleasure and joy of the students at Trinity College. This joy was so obvious that it was noted by the Non-Government Schools Registration Board in its official written report. Students with the sense of fun, students with the sense of purpose and love in their hearts, are a sign of an outstanding school. Students are striving for excellence; students are seeking to do their best. Students understand that values are eternal. They are prepared to grapple with the challenges of the Christian teaching. This is very much at odds with the world in which we live. Our students have lives which are built on a sound foundation.
>
> Many are waiting for a miracle, but the miracle is that we live in a universe of love. Some believe our world is seeking and accumulative. Some believe that the winner is the person with the most toys at the end of their life. Trinity College presents the winner as somebody who loves God, loves their neighbour and loves themselves. Our children learn that those who give, those who love and who build relationships, are enriched, as it's these relationships that enrich life itself.

I noted that the school's strong academic program, built from Reception, had been confirmed by the results of the West Australian Literacy and Numeracy Assessment, which we had participated in.

> In the year 2000, our students' results, across all campuses, are on average about 10% above those obtained in other non-Catholic, non-government schools. Our results are 300 to 400 % above the

state school benchmarks. We are 10% above independent colleges across Australia. In our case, every single student sat for the test. In some colleges, the special education students were withdrawn. It is quite clear that the standards at Trinity College are quite different and above the standards of many.

At our four schools' speech nights in December 2000 we were able to celebrate the successful opening of STARplex earlier in the year. Its operation was already proving a great success. The crèche and restaurant facilities, which would not normally be associated with a school, were benefitting our senior secondary students – we were able to offer VET and work education programs using them. Our early childhood studies courses had been integrated with practical sessions in the crèche as well as the Montessori Kindergarten. At the same time, the college was putting in place additional education resources such as a new electronics workshop, upgraded science facilities and a new IT skills centre, for which we had received a $500,000 federal government grant.

A new prospectus promoted Trinity, with over 3000 students, as indeed a 'small' school – or rather, a collective of 10 small schools coming together and sharing a senior secondary Year 12 program.[86] With the system being funded at Category 12 level, for the first time special education was being properly resourced. The Open Learning Centre had been born.

The year 2001 held a great deal of promise. After our speech nights we thought we would be able to enjoy a Christmas break and be ready for my final and concluding year as headmaster at Trinity College.

But tomorrow was another day, with an unexpected surprise and challenge.

Lessons learnt

1. Money does not make a successful school. Schools that are truly successful will be community based, with parents, students, teachers and the school vision and culture working together.
2. The separation and specialisation of the academic classes from the vocational classes helps both.
3. Senior secondary vocational education should take place during work-based hours, structured to prepare students for real work with real skills to match.

16

Fundamentalism and bankruptcy

The Investigator College story

The office opened at 8.30 am and Jo Statton, my secretary, buzzed to tell me that Dean Brown, the Minister for Health and Member for Davenport, was on the line.

"Michael, this is Dean Brown. I'm calling because Malcolm Buckby [the Minister for Education and our local MP in Gawler] gave me your name and hopes you can help us. An independent school in my electorate called Glendale has closed down. It's bankrupt, and I'm receiving desperate calls from parents concerned about their children's education."

"Oh," I muttered, more than just a little taken aback. "I've never heard Glendale."

"It's a school on two sites in Victor Harbor and Goolwa," Dean replied. "The problem arose last Monday [11 December 2000] when it was declared bankrupt and administrators were appointed. Liquidators have been called in and Peter Lanthoise of Hayes and Knight is handling the sale. I'm wondering if Trinity can take over the school."

I agreed to contact Malcolm Buckby and then phone back. Malcolm confirmed he had asked Dean Brown to contact me to "see if Trinity would purchase the assets and take over the running of Glendale". If the school was not taken over and rescued by another independent school, Malcolm was planning to purchase the school properties to provide extra classrooms for state schools in the region because they were all full. He hoped Glendale could remain as an independent school because it was meeting a demand for non-government schooling in the region.

Victor Harbor was almost a two-hour drive from Gawler. It and Goolwa were becoming extended dormitory suburbs about 80 kilometres south of Adelaide.

Immediately I spoke with our council chairman, Dr Rupert Thorne, and he called an emergency council meeting for 7.00 am the next day. I undertook to find out as much as I could beforehand.

Dean Brown had given me the phone number of the principal of Glendale, Louise Levy. I didn't have to ring her because she was already on the other line. Could we help?

My mind raced in two directions at once. I knew Trinity was not interested in running a school in Victor Harbor and Goolwa because it would be of no benefit to our existing students and families. So I informed Louise that we would have no interest in making Glendale's sites another two campuses of Trinity College. Knowing nothing about the school or its community, I asked her, "If Trinity were to try to re-establish an independent school on the Trinity model and owned by the people of the region, would parents be prepared to continue in 2001?" We discussed what this would mean and Louise immediately spoke to her staff. She rang back within five minutes to say they would start phoning school families immediately.

Early that evening Louise informed me that they had been able to speak to one hundred families and all but one had indicated they would continue with Glendale. Louise said she expected a minimum of 520 enrolments the following year.

I had never met the principal or any of her senior staff, and I was still surprised that I had not known the school existed. Now I had the school's published financial statements to consider. Could they be trusted? We had to start our financial modelling somewhere, but clearly the staff of Glendale might have been a little too optimistic about the future. I told Louise I would be happy to plan for 450 students because their school had closed down not just for the year but for good, and as a result Glendale parents would already have looked elsewhere. "You have probably already lost some students," I said. Louise was extremely confident and strongly spoken, so we compromised to plan for 480 students.

Agreeing on the enrolment numbers was critical for re-engaging staff and calculating future finances, to say nothing of reporting to the Trinity council. Louise agreed to use the same student-to-teacher ratios as Trinity (one full-time equivalent teacher for every twenty-five primary students, one for every eighteen Year 8–10 students and one for every fifteen Year 11 and 12 students.) Needless to say, this was a far larger number of students per teacher than had existed at Glendale. But Glendale had been overspending for a number of years, and for the coming year had budgeted for a deficit of $827,000[87] and was going deeper into debt. The immediate cause of bankruptcy was the withdrawal of Commonwealth funds following an enrolment audit; but the school had no financial reserves, and with growing recurrent debts had been forced into administration.

The enrolment audit had discovered that the school had presented false enrolment numbers and gained extra funds from the Commonwealth government. The federal Department of Education had called in forensic auditors and withdrawn funding. Louise immediately blamed the bursar. This worried me because I knew that school principals had to sign the forms going to the government. At Trinity we knew exactly how many students were in each of our four schools because our classroom roll-books matched the names and numbers being charged school fees. Louise suggested she had blown the whistle on their figures, and the audit was conducted as a result of her expressed concerns about the school's financial management. Clearly the lie of the land was messy and the truth would be hard to know.

At 7.00 am the next day, the Trinity College council met. It insisted that all documentation was to be examined by an external lawyer versed in property matters. The commercial viability of the school was to be examined by Trinity's chief executive (me) and the bursar, in consultation with the treasurer, and a report given to the council. The council resolved it was prepared to commit $3 million to purchase the assets, and acknowledged a further liability of up to $2 million to the Block Grant Authority (the body administering federal government capital grants to South Australian independent schools).

This repayable debt was important for the future of Glendale. If the property was not used as a school, then $1.45 million would be immediately repayable to the government, along with the advance received on a promised grant to build at Victor Harbor. The Victor Harbor site was residentially zoned land with only a farmhouse. The school's primary school buildings were temporarily on land owned by the Victor Harbor CRC church. The Goolwa school was already built so it could easily have been turned into an aged care facility or retirement village.

The Trinity council confirmed its aim to re-establish an independent school owned by the people of Victor Harbor and Goolwa. I contacted a relieved Louise and asked her to organise meetings with staff and parents for the following Friday when we could share our plans and confirm enrolments. The administrators agreed with the arrangements and encouraged me to proceed.

Heading for disaster

I walked under the grapevine-smothered pergola through the still, cool morning air to attend the Trinity staff meeting. Each year, with speech nights over, we held our end-of-year Trinity staff meeting to farewell our departing staff and welcome new staff coming the following year. It was a celebratory chapel service, followed by a few talks and presentations and an extended, languid lunch. The lunch was held in the central quadrangle of the North School, a former creek bed with the feeling of a picnic area shaded by the gum trees planted 15 years earlier.

Our staff were told the facts as I knew them. Trinity, through the Anglican Schools System, was prepared to try to re-establish an independent school owned by the people of Victor Harbor and Goolwa based on the Trinity College model. I asked the staff, "What do you think? Our council needs to know your reaction before they sign on the bottom line. If we don't help, I've been told the school will become two state school sites. The Education Department schools in the area are full, and Goolwa Primary School across the road could use the classrooms."

The informal and immediate response from our staff was overwhelming support. They knew this would cost resources for Trinity, but they were also proud of their achievements in establishing four schools with so much parental demand in the northern region of Adelaide. Our senior staff felt empowered though certainly not confident.

If the messy problem at Glendale had only been administrative it would have been easier, but the troubles went deeper. Unknown to us, student enrolments had already split into three, with some committed to stay, some transferring to a Christian school in Strathalbyn and some to a new Lutheran primary school opening in Victor Harbor. It was not a matter of rescuing a unified school; it was already irreconcilably divided, with battles raging for control. The school community had not allowed for diversity. It was winner take all. We were heading for disaster.

We engaged the Gawler firm of Bolton's as our lawyers. Tony Piccolo, our business manager, in a whirlwind devoted entirely to the 'Glendale project', gave positive reports on the willingness of the Commonwealth government to bend the rules to enable Glendale to reopen as part of the Anglican Schools System without the required waiting times.

We reported to the Trinity council that the school would just be financially viable with 480 students. Given Louise Levy's predicted outcome, there would be a very small financial surplus with 520 students. With my instincts suggesting there was worse to come, I advised the council to be prepared for as few as 450, which would lead to a loss of $174,605. The council was also advised that key Trinity College staff had volunteered to help over Christmas at no cost to the school.

Before the Friday meetings in Goolwa, Peter Lanthois, the administrator, phoned. "You are no longer the only ones interested," he told me. "Two other players are now in the market."

"Good!" I said. "Now we can have Christmas."

Without a pause Peter replied, "No, please stay involved. We don't know if they have the cash."

"OK," I said. "We'll still come down on Friday as planned."

Louise kept phoning to encourage us to stay with the project. Then another phone call came from Peter with more problems. "You won't be able to take enrolments at the meeting," he said.

I quickly responded, "Then we're pulling out now. There is absolutely no point in purchasing a school without students."

Twenty minutes later Peter was back on the phone. "We've reconsidered. You can take expressions of interest at the meeting but not formal enrolments. Temple Christian College and Annesley College have also been invited to speak at the meeting, and we have shifted it from the school to the Goolwa Fire Station."

In a state of partial shock and with no idea of what was happening locally, I agreed that we would come down and take expressions of interest.

I travelled down early on the day to address staff and give them a chance to ask questions. I can still visualise them spread around their staffroom with a cluster sitting right at the back. The raw emotion was obvious and deep. Suddenly they had no school, no Christmas pay and no future at Glendale. They told me that some of them had also lent their savings to the school and these would be lost too.

A question came from the back corner of the room. "Is the science curriculum at Trinity 'Bible Christian' or evolutionist?" I knew this issue would be important to some in the school, both teachers and parents, but I was determined it was not going to be divisive.

"From my Christian tradition", I explained, "the Old Testament describes two different creation stories with a different order of creation in each. Yet I understand that other Christian traditions read the first two creation stories as one." I told them about a night years before when, as a 22-year-old air force pilot officer, I chatted with another officer over a bush campfire and first heard a viewpoint other than my own. He could not understand how I could be a Christian and accept evolutionary theory, and I could not understand why not. I went on, "From my background Darwin is a hero of the church; he was supported by the Archbishop of Canterbury and is buried in Westminster Abbey. However, if Trinity is involved, while we would be teaching evolutionary theory, we would respect parents who chose the school for its creationist curriculum and would not seek to attack their family teaching."

I understood that some present would not regard Trinity as Christian, but our rule of engagement was clear: we would not be presenting the Bible as a 2000-year-old science textbook (I did not add that to do so, I believed, devalued the Bible as well as science).

I was very pleased when carloads of Trinity office staff and teachers, including deputy principal David Smith, arrived at the Goolwa campus. They were armed to take 'enrolments'. There was a large turnout. The meeting had been effectively reduced to two players: Trinity College and a partnership of Temple Christian College and Sunshine Christian School, represented by Pastor Neil Milne from the Adelaide Crusade Centre and Brian Hagger, principal of Temple Christian College Mile End (Annesley had not officially withdrawn but was unrepresented). I knew Brian well as we had both been members of the Anglican Church at Aldgate, and he had sought my help in the late 1980s when Temple, with falling enrolments, had been threatened with closure. I respected and trusted him and was pleased he was there.

Our two visions were presented to the meeting. Pastor Neil outlined a future for the school under the direct pastoral oversight of the Adelaide CRC Church, as a school with selective Christian entry that would provide

Glendale with direct curriculum continuity with the past. I outlined Trinity's vision for an independent college of excellence, open to all, in a disciplined and caring Christian environment, owned by the people of Victor Harbor and Goolwa. "Although Glendale had a creation science curriculum," I explained, "Trinity accepts evolutionary theory as science. But we would ensure that parents who had chosen Glendale because of its past teaching would not have their family positions undermined." I emphasised our commitment to a partnership between parent, teacher and school, and our belief that parents had the prime responsibility for their children's education.

At about eight o'clock that night our Trinity travellers adjourned for an evening pub meal, my shout. I wanted to thank our staff for their commitment and loyalty, way beyond the call of duty. I was very relaxed because I was quite sure we were not going to be given the responsibility of running Glendale. Our bursar, Wayne Smith, was not so certain, but I believed that the Temple/Sunrise group was the body with most to gain by helping and most to lose by not doing so. "All they have to do is offer one dollar more than we do for the minimum amount the liquidator is prepared to accept and the school is their responsibility. We won't compete," I said.

My calm was soon shattered. Over the next week it transpired that Annesley had neither the money nor the interest claimed by the administrator. It also transpired that although the Temple/Sunrise group had a great deal of interest, they did not have the money. As a result they were hoping to enter into a deed of arrangement with Glendale's creditors to keep trading. We were the only ones at the table offering to pay for the assets.

Encouraged by the administrator, we signed and lodged our letter of offer just minutes before the deadline.

Even though we were committed, however, it was still not a done deal. The administrator had to put the offer to the creditors to vote on. A meeting of creditors on the following Friday had to decide between the two offers on the table. We were not involved in that meeting and had no say on the outcome. About 250 creditors, including investors, staff and parents of the school, attended. They were told the meeting had been accelerated because one or both of the offers would be withdrawn if a delay occurred. Our letter would certainly have been withdrawn. Even though the administrator recommended the Trinity offer, it was no foregone conclusion because Pastor Neil Milne was offering to sort out the issue of repaying creditors, and investors in particular, by way of a roundtable discussion and private arrangement.[88]

Further, the Victor Harbor site had re-entered play because the Victor Harbor CRC was purportedly telling families that they would not allow "Trinity" to use the classrooms on their land. We had followed up this rumour because the school had listed the existing Victor Harbor classrooms on its property register. They had been paid for by the school and were the only classrooms available in Victor Harbor. John Bolton, our property lawyer, in a detailed written report on 21 December, advised us that in his opinion the school did have the right to lease the Victor Harbor site at the CRC. "Even though the lease has not been registered, the school has been using an unregistered lease document for a period of 20 years with a right of renewal for a further 20 years."

The creditors voted in favour of accepting the Trinity option.

A poisoned chalice

We had apparently signed up for a school with no guaranteed enrolments and a staff who had not committed or been signed on. Starting on 23 December, we had to meet with staff, carry out teacher interviews, gain $20 enrolment guarantees for students and find a home for the Victor Harbor school. (While we might have had the legal right to use the classrooms at Victor Harbor, it would have taken six months to enforce this, and unless the school opened in four weeks it was dead.) We were in off the deep end, with more surprises, challenges and twists and quirks to follow.

Would the school be able to open? Trinity was now committed for over $4 million. We had the required $2.45 million to pay for the assets in the bank and budgeted a further $500,000 to pay ongoing Glendale wages and recurrent operational costs. The BGA was due to be paid back $1.45 million if the school closed and had to be sold.

To succeed we needed to connect strongly with churches across the region, so I decided to invite both the Anglican Bishop of the Murray and the Uniting Church Moderator to be 'visitors'. Constitutionally the school would be like Pedare, an Anglican–Uniting Church school which otherwise had the same constitution as Trinity. However, we were a long way from surviving until an AGM, so to give us local advice I set up an advisory group consisting of members of the previous board. We knew almost nobody and were operating on trust, knowing that this was a necessity.

Poisoned chalices are either taken up stupidly, perhaps in ignorance, or accepted as unconditional gifts in an act of sacrifice, knowing that there will be strife and tears. We knew we were heading for trouble. When all are claiming innocence, a newcomer making many hard decisions on the run is an easy scapegoat for players in the previous debacle to blame. Glendale had gone bankrupt because it had claimed more enrolments than existed, and everyone was blaming everyone else. It was not just the principal and bursar blaming each other; the recent short-term chair of the Glendale council told me of the battles with, and problems of, his predecessors. "We never had the chance to run the school," he said.

We were too busy to be involved with the past. First, enrolment days were to be held in the Anglican parish hall in Victor Harbor and at the school in Goolwa. Then staff had to be arranged. Teachers were offered a year's probation for a permanent job while the existing senior staff were taken on trust and offered a year's contract with the understanding that if all worked well, their positions would be confirmed at the end of the year. Louise was offered the position of acting principal, with the principal's position to be openly advertised mid-year. It was my hope she would apply and be able to be given a five-year contract.

As acting principal, Louise was to recommend to me all staff to be retained and their fractions of time. As CEO of Glendale, I retained the authority to control finances and the appointment of permanent staff. I set up panels to meet and interview Louise's recommendations. We needed to ensure they wanted to sign up for a permanent position with twelve months' probation. By re-employing existing staff, we were taking over their long-term payout liability from the administrator. This would increase the payout to creditors. Brian Webber, retired head of Prince Alfred College, had a holiday house in the area; he joined the panel, along with teachers from Trinity. We were trying to build mentor and support bridges between Glendale and Trinity staff. All Louise's recommendations were appointed, ensuring she had the best chance possible to win staff support and loyalty, as well as ensuring her accountability.

Then there was our other immediate problem. We had nowhere to teach at Victor Harbor. I made the strategic decision that Glendale, being an R–12 school, had to have a primary campus at Victor to survive. The Goolwa township was too small to support a quality independent senior secondary school and Glendale needed feeder students from Victor Harbor. The CRC pastor and one-time chair of Glendale sent a letter to his congregation on 19 January 2001 to defend his church's position not to allow Glendale to continue to use its classrooms. The classrooms were transportable, but the verandah posts had been fixed to the CRC's land and therefore, they argued, were church property.

The Victor Harbor enrolments looked very sick. The previous bursar of Glendale, Graham Pope, had been appointed to Murraylands Christian School at Strathalbyn, and over the Christmas holidays, 34 of Glendale's Victor Harbor students had unexpectedly enrolled there (a free bus would run them from the CRC to the school). Should Glendale fail to reopen in Victor Harbor, I was told the church was planning to open a new primary school using the buildings on their land. With our dire need for students in Victor Harbor, my vision for an R–12 school was promoted to ensure the local community knew we were serious about developing a college of excellence locally.

The Lutheran Church in Victor Harbor had also just opened a new primary school next to their strategically located church to serve the whole region. This new school had none of the baggage of Glendale and was well planned, and even before Glendale had become bankrupt it had accepted Glendale students for the following year, especially from the non-fundamentalist end. The Lutheran school was to be a feeder school for Tatachilla Lutheran College at McLaren Vale, a 30-minute bus drive away. This new primary school and Tatachilla together was a strong R–12 alternative to Glendale.

Still, the Minister for Education wanted us to continue, and authorised Glendale to enrol a maximum of 535 students and the Lutheran school 100.

In a bankrupt school, trust is a rare commodity

Given that money and reliable statistics had been a concern for the previous school, I decided that Trinity's bursar, Wayne Smith, would handle all the funds. The Glendale administrative staff reported directly to him by phone and email. Enrolments were finalised by our enrolment secretary at Gawler, Rosemary Alexander. These were people I could trust and they worked hours beyond the call of duty.

We had a school desperate for every enrolment, and this put the pastor of the CRC church in a powerful position. Should he take out the CRC children, I estimated 30 to 40 others would follow. We had budgeted for 520 enrolments and realistically anticipated 450, but with just 420 the future was bleak.

We had to prepare a fully documented curriculum for the whole R–12 school in order to gain approval from the SA Non-Government Schools Registration Board before we could open in February. We had publicly planned to continue the curriculum offered by Glendale but had difficulty obtaining full documentation for it. Louise was working with her senior staff team, and after one meeting she asked me whether they could adopt the Trinity College curriculum. I explained that this would entail a commitment to regular testing, including common testing across the school. The rigour would be foreign to the staff. Would they cope? With some reluctance we agreed, out of necessity. We advised the registration board on 10 January that the school would adopt the Trinity R–7 curriculum at the request of the Glendale staff,[89] and that we would meet with the board tomorrow when the Glendale team presented their primary and secondary curriculum. Such was the rush that I stated we had not yet seen the secondary curriculum and would look at it for the first time, together with the registration board, at the meeting!

Meanwhile, enrolments were still struggling. Goolwa, which had new enrolments coming in because of Trinity's involvement, was just holding the planned numbers, but numbers at Victor Harbor had collapsed. To try to secure our enrolment base, we advertised the introduction of the Trinity curriculum. During January, Ros and I, together with Kym and Sue Reynolds, stayed down in Goolwa to meet parents, implement the curriculum and support the Glendale leadership team. We gained quite a number of new enrolments, including past Trinity families who had moved into the area, but still the 520 looked like a mirage.

What were our options? On the one hand, our lawyer advised us that we did not have to proceed with the project and could demand our money back because the assets we had bought included the classrooms at Victor Harbor and these were unavailable. On the other hand, business manager Tony Piccolo located some expensive mining site transportables to house five classes that could be put on the land at Victor, alongside the farmhouse, to open in February.

With just two weeks before school started, Malcolm Buckby phoned to ask how we were going. It was good to tell him the facts, describing the huge gamble we would be making if we proceeded. He said to let him know as soon as possible if we were going to pull out as the Education

Department was making contingency plans to buy the Goolwa school to house an expanded state enrolment. I told him that I would need to present the facts to our college council for their decision.

With only 420 enrolments we were heading for a slow crash. Yet I had grown too close to the community to make the call. I was committed to the people and students. Every trip there I took a trailer load of furniture and desks. Past Trinity parents who had moved to Victor Harbor and Goolwa were full of hope. We had met so many people of goodwill. The fundamentalist families in Goolwa were committed because they understood we were for real, and they hoped they would not be let down. Moreover, the effort of the previous four weeks had been herculean. Provisional registration, approval to build a new school site, approval of temporary classrooms and toilets, funding approvals, an application to go from Reception to Year 12 at Victor, the development of a new curriculum, the sorting of legal staffing arrangements and the appointment of staff had all been completed in a month.

With only one week to go, I woke up to attend another pre-breakfast emergency council meeting. The heading on my report was: "There is nothing in this for Trinity." I presented the now very sick budget and the overall 20% shortfall in enrolments. I was pretty sure we would withdraw from Glendale. Trying to distance myself from the people and the work that had been done, I could see it was the rational thing to do. I gave out a sheet with the progress we had made and a list of all the negatives, fully expecting a vote to withdraw.

But a surprise awaited me. One member of council, 'Jono' Sims, a lawyer and South Campus parent, gave an impassioned speech about the impact the new school would have on the community. He talked about a family he knew who had now enrolled in the Goolwa Campus; how Michael could, if all else failed, go down and run the school himself; and how, while we might lose financially, the people in that region deserved to have a school like Trinity. I was amazed. Jono was normally so rational and calculating, but this speech burned with emotion, vision and giving.

I phoned a very surprised and relieved Minister for Education to let him know that the council had voted to continue.

The head of the Victor Harbor campus, Jim Dunbar, rallied the parents and teachers of the town. Together with members of his Uniting Church congregation, they built a playground, installed a portable toilet block and classrooms, rolled out some grass, put in paths and refurbished the old farmhouse to accommodate a library and offices – all in six-and-a-half days. To the people of Victor Harbor, it was a miracle.

On 23 February 2001 the Bishop of the Murray and the Moderator of the Uniting Church joined together to celebrate the fact that the campus had opened on the first day of term, with 114 students.

The school opens

Superficially we made a flying start. We had the miracle of the Victor Harbor school rising from a paddock. It had happy students in class, expectant teachers and a hum for the future. The Goolwa campus opened with 307 students, greater numbers than ever. The politics of the CRC church in Victor Harbor had little effect in Goolwa.

However, there were still many challenges to be overcome. The staff, having been through trauma and disillusionment, were wondering about their future pay and were also concerned about the school's changed direction. Parents at Goolwa were complaining about one of the best teachers in the school. I was dragged into these matters. I had to deal with the complaints to retain the confidence of a group of about 14 Goolwa parents.

In a gracious act, Louise wanted me to have the principal's office. I insisted that she, as acting principal, operate from the principal's office, and that when visiting the school I would use one of the smaller counselling rooms.

Louise organised an official launch of the new Glendale College. I suggested the Newland Uniting Church in Victor Harbor as a good venue to build bridges with the extended Christian community. Students were bussed in from Goolwa and we all robed up in a gesture of understanding for Louise, who having grown up in the Anglican Church sought to honour the birth of a new school in this way. In my talk I underlined the transitory nature of my leadership as CEO of Glendale, using a parable and describing the physics of geese flying in V-formation. I was out in front taking the headwind but would soon retire and take my place at the back of the line. With so much extra energy required at the front, I thought my time in this school as leader would be short.

I did not then realise how much stronger those headwinds were going to get. The unfamiliar Trinity curriculum soon caused problems among the primary school staff. The core reading, writing and arithmetic programs were tested and the emotionally exhausted teachers had to cope with unfamiliar accountability. For Victor Harbor principal Jim Dunbar and his wife Robyn, our curriculum was counter-cultural. Jim was working with a school campus of which he was still head but with a curriculum style opposed to his own natural conviction.

By the end of March, Louise and Jim had stopped talking to each other when it came to the problems at Victor Harbor. A circuit breaker was needed and I knew a retired primary principal who might help. The past head of Trinity's Blakeview Campus, Kevin Whittington, was happy to assist. Louise endorsed the concept of his presence in the school to provide a mentoring role. She had wanted Jim shifted to Goolwa but I asked her to be patient. I hoped that given time and Kevin's gentle support, Jim could oversee the change to a rigorous curriculum in the Trinity style that most people in Victor Harbor who remained with the new school wanted. I did not relish having to choose between Jim and Louise. I wanted both to succeed.

Kevin was very sympathetic towards the Victor Harbor staff given the loss of the past, the exhaustion of teachers needing a holiday and the delightful, friendly atmosphere of the school. He wrote to me, "They need helpers not police persons – praise not criticism because they are very fragile at the moment." However, Jim was most concerned about Kevin and clearly did not welcome his help in implementing the advertised curriculum. Barely 10 days after Louise welcomed Kevin's involvement, I received a note from her: "I am most concerned that Kevin Whittington's presence is increasing pressure on staff. While I know you have the best interests of Glendale at heart, I must insist that he not visit Glendale College at present. The staff are implementing the curriculum quite well and things are running smoothly. Kevin is very kind and he means well, but I am sure you will understand our dilemma. Please support me in cancelling his visits to the College over the next four weeks."

The changes were welcomed by some, possibly most, parents. I believed it was important for Glendale's parents to share a vision for the future beyond the present mess. Many parents were very, very happy, taking the trouble to write me letters of strong support expressing thanks for the changes happening in the school.

Having won approval from the Minister for Education, we announced our strategic commitment to develop two R–Year 12 schools at Victor and Goolwa. In April we announced the appointment of school chaplains. The Victor Harbor chaplain was the Reverend Mark Bowey, rector of Victor Harbor Anglican Church, whose own children were attending the Victor Harbor campus. The chaplain for Goolwa was the Reverend Phil Pynor, who had pastored the Uniting Church at Goolwa and Nankita for the previous three years.

I decided we needed to resolve the question of a long-term principal by the end of Term 1 rather than mid-year as planned. The past had to be confronted and a long-term CEO for the school appointed. Given the widening divisions between Jim and Louise, either Louise needed to be confirmed as CEO with a five-year contract to make the calls herself or a new head needed to be appointed. By now Louise apparently had a long list of complaints about me. Supported by the rector of Victor Harbor Anglican Church, she tried to persuade the advisory committee to back her to take full control of the school. The Archbishop of Adelaide was asked to meet with Louise and her deputy and spoke with me about refusing the request. I asked him to go ahead because I needed to know what their concerns were. But all I learnt was that the archbishop had told them no one else but Michael was prepared to help their troubled school.

To prevent fragmentation, I had to be prepared to keep confidences from everyone at the school and take all the hits without the opportunity to defend myself. Being an absent CEO at the best of times is tricky, but to be an absent CEO in a climate of mistrust is a disaster. Everybody blames everything on the absent CEO, and he doesn't even know what the issues are. The school steering committee could be receiving continual complaints about my purported actions and I would not know. Parents who did not like the changes and reduced resources for their children would also blame the absent CEO. Members of the advisory committee and others making suggestions for me to make certain hard decisions would not be quoted and would quietly agree with those who complained. By keeping confidences, I was being presented with information that stripped me of any and every reputation and ensured that I became the target of all.

An April newsletter, written by me, was sent out to parents inviting them to visit Trinity College on Trinity Sunday 3 June 2001. There they could see multi-campus schools and a community coming together, as well as every child's schoolwork on display. I described our plan for R–12 campuses at both Victor Harbor and Goolwa totalling 1200 students. I gave notice of the decision to advertise the position of principal for Glendale College earlier than planned.

I had to bite the bullet about the past and come to an assessment of Louise. Could she grow the school and enable it to succeed in the future? I encouraged her to apply for the permanent position and told her I could not guarantee we would get any suitable external applicants. Letters in her support came from parents concerned about yet another change to their school, and the Year 12s signed a collective petition.

The day after driving down to Goolwa and back to ensure the distribution of the newsletter and inform staff of the decision to advertise the position of principal earlier, I was due to go to Port Augusta, a round trip of 600 kilometres. Geoff Gordon, the first chairman of the Trinity College board, came with me. Father Mark Thomas, the first chaplain of Trinity, had mooted the idea of an Anglican College for Port Augusta and the surrounding region. Interest was very strong and we set up a board for this new school, Flinders College. We were planning an R–Year 6 start to the school and enrolments were flowing in. I was grateful for Geoff's company on the road. It was good to be able to talk through the Glendale problems. There was no baggage at Port Augusta as at Glendale – just sheer pleasure in working together. Trust was there in bucket-loads.

On Sunday, when I got back to Gawler, I was informed of a secret meeting of the Glendale steering committee to be held that evening at Victor Harbor. Louise had organised the meeting and clearly "mutiny was in the air". I did not attend. The chair of the steering committee, Phil Pynor, our Goolwa chaplain, demanded I be removed as CEO of Glendale.

This was unanimously rejected by the Trinity College council and our chair, Rupert Thorne, gently advised him of this in formal correspondence.

A new head selected for Glendale

Rupert Thorne, David Smith and I drove down to Goolwa for the interviews. We had set up a panel for the selection of a new head. It was large; the locals had to own the new principal. There were two people from the Victor Harbor campus and three from the Goolwa campus; and because the rector of Victor Harbor refused to have any part of it, I had been able to have the rector of Strathalbyn appointed to represent the Diocese of the Murray. He was a past teacher and principal with a younger wife and a young child who had spent a year at Murraylands Christian School.

We had a group of strong applicants to interview. A number on the existing school staff had also applied. Given the history of the school and the need to make a clean break, I took more political hits by deciding that only external applicants would be interviewed. Following the six interviews, there were clearly two very strong applicants, either of whom I believed would succeed, and both had three votes from the non-Trinity selection panel members. One, an Anglican, was preferred by the people close to Victor Harbor. The other, Don Grimmet, from a Uniting Church background, was well known to me and had been encouraged by Phil Pynor to apply.

To ensure local ownership of whomever was appointed, Rupert agreed with me that those of us from Trinity College should leave the meeting. I knew both candidates were outstanding as I had thoroughly checked their backgrounds and talked at length with people I trusted from their schools and churches. The two communities now attending the school actually wanted two different kinds of school, yet they depended on each other. There would be quite a number of parents not represented by the panel in both schools who were keen to see a rigorous academic school – tighter, more demanding and challenging – whilst others wanted a school that was gentler: clearly loving and with greater latitude given to students. Both of the short-listed applicants, planning for their own children to attend Glendale, wanted a basic academic rigour. It was a measure of my confidence in both that I was prepared to leave the selection panel to make its own decision.

The new principal-elect was Don Grimmet, commencing in 2002. This left the rest of the year to be seen through. Louise Levy engaged lawyers to establish terms for an early pay-out, based on the fact that she had a right to serve to the end of the year. I responded by encouraging her to serve out the year alongside Don, indicating we had no intention of breaking our contract with her. I acknowledged that she indeed had much to offer. She also wanted me to "bite the bullets" that would lead to the removal of the head of the Victor Harbor campus, yet I believed Jim Dunbar and his wife, who had given the sacrificial service to that school, deserved support.

On 18 May 2001 I sent home with the children a newsletter to all parents. With honesty I congratulated Louise on her work and acknowledged the support she had within the school community and her role as a Year 11 and 12 teacher. I also explained that once the position was ready to be openly advertised, she had declined to be an applicant. Even though we had no way of knowing if the school would attract strong applicants, she did support the need "for an outstanding educator who had none of the history of Glendale". My offer to her of a senior position at Trinity College Gawler was declined and she returned to her previous school in Victoria.

Given that Don Grimmet was released by his present school to attend Glendale College once a week to prepare for the following year, the need for me to spend time in the school was coming to a close. It was time to hand over. To ensure the new principal-elect was not undermined, my deputy, David Smith, was appointed as CEO until Easter 2002. David confirmed, "There are things happening in Glendale that are not known of or approved by Don. The issue is to pick the battles to fight and in so doing help him to gain knowledge about what is happening and hence control of his school."

Very early on David was involved in negotiating a new enterprise agreement with the staff. Quite surprisingly, the staff, or at least the vocal ones, would not accept the same pay rate and overall deal that the staff at Trinity had agreed to, even though the Trinity pay model was inclusive of co-curricular commitment, which wasn't a feature at Glendale. Pleasingly we had developed at Trinity a positive working relationship with the union's Andrew Murray and between us we were able to help the staff see sense.

To the astonishment of all, Glendale finished $300,000 in the black in that first year. The change to a new principal was expensive, the school numbers dropped a little and expenditures went up, so a year of loss was to be incurred in 2002. But the transition had taken place. Don had his own children attending the school, lived in Goolwa and was philosophically close to the aspirations of many in the changing Glendale College community.

The strategic plan for R–12 schools at Victor and Goolwa was implemented as planned, and the school grew to well over 900 students within the next decade. With no pressure from Trinity the new steering committee asked to change the name of the school and so 'Investigator College' was named after the ship that gave the bay on which Victor Harbor sits its name. The region was discovered and mapped by Matthew Flinders in the HMS *Investigator* in April 1802. The people of Victor and Goolwa finally had a non-government school owned by their community, giving parents a choice.

Lessons learnt

1. It is important to understand that non-government schools can and do go bankrupt and into administration.
2. Changing teaching practice and culture is far harder than producing curriculum documents. The committed leadership of a principal is vital, backed by a leadership team.
3. Graduate teachers did not have the skills to teach numeracy and literacy using phonetic spelling and the rote learning of number skills.
4. What matters in schools is what happens in the classroom. The culture and history of each school contributes to this. These are matters parents understand and it is best left to parents to choose which schools their children should attend, not just governments or systems.

17

Change and real teaching

Do the lessons of this story stand up to teaching today?

Having retired as headmaster/principal at the end of January 2002, I knew the school would run well for the rest of the year. It had good staff, strong finances and not even an enterprise bargaining agreement to cause a ruffle. With new leadership the past's penny-pinching ways quickly changed. Cut flowers were on the front reception desk. New financial contracts were put in place for some senior staff, and over the year an extra 25 non-academic staff were appointed, creating a more institutional bureaucracy.

I retired determined not to be involved in the running of the college. Originally Ros and I planned to move to the suburb adjacent to Trinity. However, Wayne Philp, a member of senior staff, said, "Michael, if you live there and the bell goes two minutes late, you'll be around in a flash to find out what's wrong! I'd move far away." I knew instantly he was right. We moved across Adelaide to Unley, where I had grown up as a child.

Open Learning Centre

The flowers arrived at the front door with a basket of goodies. It was a gift from the staff of the Open Learning Centre. They had been awarded the top Vocational Education Training Initiative in South Australia and were on their way to Sydney to represent the state for the national award.

The centre was established to provide a career-, trade- or business-focused education for students who mostly were not academically inclined. All students won, not just those attending the centre but also those in the traditional academic program, who were no longer diverted by those not academically inclined. I expected the Year 12 results to improve even further once students who had previously left school before Year 12 were in a separate program tailored to their interests and needs. With the support of my successor, headmaster-elect Luke Thomson, a purpose-built campus for the centre had been completed on our Gawler site during 2001. It had 37 students that year, but under the leadership of entrepreneurial head Marion Gaertner-Jones it started 2002 with an enrolment of 83, growing to 120 by the end of first term. Students studied and trained in 13 industrial areas and accessed 42 tertiary certificates.

However, winning the award was a bitter-sweet moment. Luke had already decided that the Open Learning Centre would be wound back and become a reduced range of choices within Trinity's senior secondary college. The rhythm of learning, which matched workplace realities and was spread from 8.00 am to 8.00 pm, clashed with the traditional academic senior secondary timetable. The centre was to be handed over to the college's Montessori Kindergarten.

Change, which was the prerogative of my successor working with the council, was certainly on the way.

The dream of an Anglican Teachers' College

By 2012 the failure of teacher training courses across Australia to provide competent, skilled teachers had become widely recognised. An open letter to the country's education ministers signed by 36 educators, scientists and clinicians called for a "vast shake-up at all levels of teacher training" to ensure children were taught to read properly.[90] The letter was prompted by results in the Progress in International Reading Literacy Study, which ranked Australia 27th in children's reading abilities. To the shock of many educators and governments, the study revealed that almost a quarter of Year 4 children in Australia failed to meet the standard of reading for their age.[91]

The decline in reading skills was reported on page 1 by *The Australian* under the headline: BELL TOLLS FOR CLASSROOM REFORM AS PRIMARY STUDENTS HIT LOW IN INTERNATIONAL READING TESTS.[92] In the same issue, Kevin Donnelly, director of the Education Standards Institute, wrote: "Australia's substandard results in the Trends in International Mathematics and Science Study and the Progress in International Reading Literacy Study are an indictment of those academics, subject associations and teacher unions that have argued during the past 20 to 30 years that all is well with our education system."

In 2002 this view was not so widespread, but it was a concern at Trinity. The lack of preparation that new teachers received to teach primary school reading, writing and mathematics was evident amongst our own staff. Those who could effectively teach these basics had been trained over 30 years earlier.

I had another major concern. Most of our new teaching graduates believed that truth was relative to the individual. Their philosophical foundation was the discredited philosophy of a 19th-century parlour game. I felt we could run teacher training to produce teachers who had a philosophical position on the purpose of education and the meaning of life, if any meaning exists at all – and, if not, an understanding of how this would impact on the learning and resilience of children. Nihilism leads to superficiality or despair. I was concerned that our new teachers were ill-prepared to meet the spiritual needs of children.

An Anglican Teacher's College offering a post-graduate Diploma in Education had been on the agenda for about two years. To establish it seemed straightforward. Adelaide Diocese had the expertise on hand: Jeremy Seward, Trinity College treasurer, was helping establish tertiary business courses in universities throughout Australia, and Archdeacon Peter Stuart, head of St Barnabas Theological College, had the necessary academic theological and philosophical skills.

However, development of this teachers' college stopped, along with that of Flinders and Rayner Colleges,[93] when neither the diocese nor

Trinity was prepared to extend their risk to any more new ventures. The diocese had substantial financial guarantees in place for three schools and mounting litigation due to the paedophilic behaviour of a youth worker. Trinity had a new principal and felt Glendale was risk enough. The idea was shelved.

Perhaps one day in the future, the Anglican Schools System in South Australia will once again be empowered to grow to fulfil the promise that school systems offer.[94]

The power of systemic independent schools

The major strength of a system is the capacity to plan for the state's educational needs for the next 100 years. An individual school council just looks towards the needs of its school, possibly a decade ahead. Individual schools rarely seek to meet national objectives or even new needs in 'distant' suburbs or towns. Even schools that are loosely connected to a church organised on a state-wide basis are better than an isolated school.

Systems can better handle school failures such as Glendale College and Woodlands Anglican Girls' School. In a system, Woodlands, instead of closing, would have been able to evolve to meet new needs. With the Anglican Schools System, the mechanism to enable the evolution of Glendale to Investigator, as an independent college owned by its community, was legally straightforward.

Financially, Trinity College, the South Australian Anglican Schools System and Investigator College were secure, with no bank loans and cash in the bank. Trinity was in the recurrent black with over $2.5 million operating surplus each year. Over time it would need about $1 million of this to cover increasing long-service leave and salary costs as the schools matured. By being members of the Anglican Schools System, the four Trinity schools received about $1.6 million extra in recurrent grants for 2002 alone.

In 2002, Investigator, with a new head with strong political support and a $300,000 surplus from the year before, was building on the Victor

Harbor site to develop an R–12 campus with the help of a Block Grant Authority grant of around $800,000. With Investigator repaying the system loans at prime bank rate, and Trinity receiving the same interest rate it had when the money was in the bank, I felt able to focus on other things.

The Lutheran Schools Association (LSA) in South Australia demonstrates the ability of a system to strategically plan and plant new schools, and to enable failing schools to regenerate, evolve and contribute to the educational needs of families. The Lutheran primary school in Gawler survived not just because Trinity helped after the unexpected impact of the opening of our Gawler River School, but also because the LSA decided the school was important to their system and enabled Trinity to work with them. Port Augusta now has a Lutheran systemic primary school, and parents throughout most of South Australia have a Lutheran school that they can choose.

Back to teaching again

Decades before, I had planned to teach again during my retirement. I hoped part-time teaching would enable time to prepare my lessons, read widely and try new things. Would my notes and the ideas I wrote down during my time as director of the Salisbury Education Centre and headmaster of Trinity stack up, or had I romanticised teaching like an out-of-touch tertiary academic?

My first encounter with teaching again was hardly smooth sailing. Brian Hagger from Temple Christian College invited me to teach Year 11 and 12 physics along with some junior science for the remainder of 2002. I refused because I would not have employed myself for this role – I had taught Year 11 and 12 chemistry, biology and maths, but only Year 11 physics. Two weeks later I was asked again. Brian indicated that he felt God's hand was in their offer. This time I said, "Although I wouldn't employ myself, you are clearly stuck, and if I can do the first six questions in last year's public physics exam, I will do it." Physics seemed to have been dumbed down; the first six Year 12 questions were at the Year 11 standard of a few decades earlier, and some covered material I had taught in Year 10 at Eyre High School in 1970. "Temple was founded on a literal interpretation of Genesis," Brian said, "but you will be safe to take physics."

Within two weeks, I hastily met with him straight after a lesson. "Brian, it *isn't* safe for me to teach physics," I explained. "During the last lesson I was explaining how the earth's Magnetic North and Magnetic South poles have switched over, with the North Pole becoming magnetically a South Pole, and the South Pole becoming a North Pole." I reported the ensuing class discussion:

"The last magnetic shift was very recent," I said, "around the time of the last ice age."

A hand went up. "When was that, sir?"

"Oh, only around 25,000 years ago, and the ice age ended only about 15,000 years ago."

Another hand shot up. "Don't you believe in the Bible, sir?"

In response I chose to give the students an insight into modern physics: the uncertainty principle; quantum mechanics and chance; how the observer actually physically alters the scientifically measurable results of an experiment. I pointed out to the class that none of this is described in the Bible. "For me, the Bible is a collection of books telling sometimes contradictory stories containing eternal truths; the Bible is not a science textbook to be changed according to the results of the next experiment." This lesson took an hour, and the class was so quiet a feather falling would have clanged loudly as it landed.

Brian put his hand on his brow. "Oh, the daughter of the head of the creation science movement in South Australia is in that class."

We were both braced for an onslaught from parents, but not one complaint was received. I believed physics students should know and be able to describe the subtleties of the universe, the nature of time, the nature of quantum mechanics and the contrasting Einsteinian perceptions of the universe. All Year 8 science students should know that by looking into space we look back in time, and when we look deep into space the light we see is sometimes 13 billion years old.

Many parents at Temple had chosen the school because of its biblical creationist tradition and I believed they deserved my support. So in my later teaching at Temple, I prefaced my lessons by saying: "In my Christian tradition, this is the way we see it. Some of you will come from homes that will see it differently." By stating this, I was able to present with clarity and intellectual freedom how, in my Christian journey, I saw things, and also affirm that students and their families deserved to be supported in the Christian schooling of their choice.

The following year I was supporting remedial students when Temple's biology teacher was hospitalised. She would be away for three months. On the last day of the school holidays I received an urgent phone call: "Would you teach Year 11 and 12 biology for a whole term?" I discovered that I was to teach "genetics and evolutionary theory". A quote sprang to mind: "God moves in mysterious ways, his wonders to perform." I was teaching in a most unlikely school, and I was teaching the subjects many would have least liked me to teach. I thought God must be laughing.

Bringing boys up to speed

When the advanced Year 9 science class entered the room, I was in for a surprise. There were only four boys out of 30 students. Temple, along with most schools, had educationally lost two-thirds of the boys who should have been in this class. When I had previously taken the bottom class the position was the opposite, and I had then thought the school must have had more boys than girls.

I offered to take an all-boys Year 8 class for both science and maths to "bring the boys up to speed". The class I taught was set so I had boys in the upper 70% ability range. I learnt so much, and I rediscovered that boys can be extended, challenged and succeed.

When undertaking science 'pracs', the boys were told not to read the instructions. Many female teachers were horrified. But that's the way males work, I explained: "If all else fails, read the instructions." Play in these classes was allowed and encouraged – I thought play was "good fun experimentation". It was noisy; students might be climbing on the benches and all talking at once. However, when we worked as a whole class, discipline was rigid. If danger was imminent I gave three clicks of the fingers, all stopped work and all eyes were on me. In one lesson, a preceding class had opened up many of the gas taps. I switched on the mains and my students were about to strike matches when someone said, "Sir, our gas taps are already on." Fortunately, three clicks, silence and all faced me before we blew the lab sky high.

Being an unusual teacher at Temple meant I relied on the strong support of the two successive school principals. In mathematics boys who completed their work were given puzzles or games of chess to play. Students who had previously done little homework during primary school put in extra time to get ahead so they could play chess in class. I learnt as I went. Within a couple of years I discovered that students could learn maths by guessing the answers. Most students did not have to be taught the rules. When we did a new chapter, students were encouraged to guess the answers and leave a space for the method equal to the number of marks given for the question. They then filled in the empty spaces to earn the marks and check their guess. When they could do their maths in their own way, we learnt the rules that they were supposed to use. To me all this was normal.

In South Australia, the education gap between boys and girls has increased.[95] In 2011, 98% of girls who started Year 8 in 2007 made it through to graduate, but only 78 per cent of boys. This is a 20% difference, compared with a 15% difference in 2000. Not only were there far fewer boys, with presumably the less able 32% having dropped out; they were also outscored by the girls. Almost 90% of girls who completed the SA Certificate of Education (SACE) in the previous year earned a university entrance score compared with 81.4% of boys.

A 2012 review of the new SACE revealed the compulsory subject, the 'Research Project', provided "an 'inherent advantage' for female students, most of whom achieved As and Bs, while almost half the male students received Cs."[96] In 2009 I attended the teacher workshops to prepare to teach the Research Project. The subject was so obviously feminised it was misnamed. Most marks were not awarded for the outcomes of the project or for research, but for writing up how you felt about the process and outcomes.

To review your research is valid, but what boy whose project was to design and build a chair could care less about writing up how they felt? What mattered to a boy was the chair, its function, its form and its strength. I had a student research "how to manufacture bio-fuels; how to test the quality of these fuels by measuring their viscosity, their ignition temperature and their thermal output; and how to test his bio-fuels in engines". He was able to strip and remove car engines and do up an old car from scratch. He successfully manufactured bio fuels using different processes and tested their efficacy. A brilliant project with brilliant science, all written up – and he scored a C. He had not heeded my advice to address how he felt about the project in terms that spoke to a "50-year-old female teacher who did not understand science".

Because the Research Project is so biased, I need to make a sexist comment to illustrate how as a subject it is skewed against young men. Fortunately, being the first year of the subject, my C student was able to rewrite and resubmit the same project the following year. His rewritten project could indeed have been written by a 50-year-old female teacher, and he scored an A. Another boy in the class did follow my advice. He examined the effect of microwaving water on the growth rate of plants, complete with stories about how his mum felt. He was rewarded with a merit certificate, full marks and a presentation at Government House.

We need to enable boys to succeed. These boys who were brought up to speed in Year 8 matched the girls in Year 12, and the academic standard achieved by the school in Year 12 increased for both.[97]

Mouse traps and space ships

In 2004 I was given a mixed class of Year 8 boys and girls. The way girls learnt was different. They were less happy to guess an answer in maths; they wanted the method. In science I had to ensure that the girls had time to read the suggested method. I found I preferred the co-ed classes.

The formal maths and science curriculum could be covered in less than half the time available. I worked according to the precepts I had preached to my staff at Trinity:

1. Set new work for homework (not just finishing what should have been done in class). Otherwise the slower students feel punished and the brightest students learn to bludge because they have no homework at all. Ensure students spend some time on homework but not too much – play time at home is important.

2. Spend time and ensure the basics are rigorously taught and tested. (In the top maths class, students who had not been taught their times tables at primary school took the opportunity to remain back after school while I taught them their times tables.)

3. Ensure student exercise books are neat and inspire personal pride. Given that I spent so much time outside the core science curriculum, the work in their exercise books demonstrated that the core had been covered.

4. Spend half your time on experimental learning, exploring, taking chances, following up special interests and learning by play.

Over time I discovered that Year 8s could read and describe to the class the content of the latest scientific research from scientific magazines written for adults (generally with a uni degree and a lot of background knowledge). By the second semester, most could not only read these scientific papers but could critique the research against the knowledge of the day and other scientific papers. I was amazed by their ability and discovered that our dumbed-down science courses were not allowing our more able students to flourish.

In class we had many hands-on experiences. Pracs were formally written up. Scientific definitions were learnt by rote so the words could be accurately used. In one experiment Year 8 students were given a mousetrap and asked to design and build a 'car' powered by it. By showing them examples from the year before, the girls soon learnt to match the boys, racing their contraptions to see how far and fast they travelled.

Temple encouraged me to teach science through research projects. Older students were scattered across the school: in the chemistry lab (running alpha, gamma and beta rays through 'the alternative skins of a Mars space ship' or titrating and distilling chemicals), in the tech studies facilities (with one student fashioning blades to improve the way we do wind power) and in the music suite (discovering how learning is improved or not with different types of music playing while performing learning tasks, or exploring the nature of beauty ['Is it in the eye of the beholder?']). Having been in my class in Year 8, these students could design experiments.

They also learnt that the Year 12 'Research Project' could be done without any real research. Students could fulfil the basics by choosing topics with easy-to-get information. But those who opted for genuine research discovered that scientific research requires persistence, because often the experimental design has to be modified many times, with no guarantee that any future experiment will work. For example, how do you design the seating and harness for a jet fighter plane turning sharply with a force on the pilot of many Gs? Look it up on the internet – or carry out original experiments to develop the knowledge required to do the design. One student used eggs in a harness on a home-made big dipper ride. It took many, many hours of work to perfect a design without every egg breaking. This student's results were stunning and counter-intuitive. Do you think the egg was stronger sitting end on or lying down?

Teaching is about time spent on-task, a good knowledge-based core curriculum and time to develop student capacities to think beyond the square. I encourage teachers both to ensure the core curriculum is learnt and to spend about half of their time on developing students' critical thinking and passion for understanding and learning. Wisdom is not taught by rote learning. Education involves some risk. Teenagers need to be able to make a mistake as part of their learning, though they also need to learn that there are consequences to mistakes. Avoiding risk and the possibility of making mistakes is itself a big mistake.

Being low fee, Temple was not (and still is not) socio-economically selective. However, it is not open to all tax-payers because it focuses on church-going children. Unlike some schools it is not academically selective, and being located in the centre of a large city, this enrolment bias is part of its marketing attraction to some church families. Temple's newer Salisbury North campus does have an open enrolment policy because the requirement for all students to attend a church would not work in that lower socio-economic location.

Temple had the basics right. Teachers had their own classrooms and students came to them. There were formal disciplinary procedures that worked for the teachers in the school. The timetable gave English, maths, science and history/geography plenty of time, with 230 minutes per week given to Year 8 English, maths and science each. The children were unconditionally loved and cared for in family groups from Year 7 to 12.

I was very pleased that the first cohort of co-educational Year 8s I taught in 2007 for both maths and science graduated in 2011, with 35% of the school's students receiving an ATAR score (Australian Tertiary Admission Rank, the old TER) of over 90. Year 12 results depend on outstanding Year 12 teaching based on a sure foundation built up over many previous years.

Christian schools are generally founded in prayer and God's discerned will. It was very rewarding to have the opportunity to teach at both the start and end of my time in education, and it is as a run-of-the-mill classroom teacher with no special authority that the lessons of this book have been learnt and tested.

In life and death

The sky was dark and became black as we drove to the funeral in the Barossa Valley. The rain started not with a whimper but with heavy splatters on the windscreen. It grew heavier, the wind blew and we slowed down, hoping we would arrive on time.

The funeral was for a 30-year-old Trinity old scholar who had committed suicide. From a farming family, he was a young man suffering from severe depression and perhaps more. Thinking of others, he had cocooned himself in his doona and shot himself in the heart, leaving no visible damage. The funeral was to be a godless affair because, as Mum said, "The last five years of his life were spent in rejection of God."

The room was packed with both friends of the parents and some 60–70 Trinity College old scholars, some with their spouses and very young children – his friends. The dignified service was a celebration of the young man's life. The celebrant made the points that could be made in such a ceremony, which in a way was hopeless. He said: "If you are feeling pain now, know that it is because, in life, the necessary outcome of all human love is sorrow and loss."

My mind raced with the thoughts of a headmaster dedicated to giving young people a sense of hope and purpose. Trinity had underlined the biblical injunction to love God, love your neighbour and love yourself. To my mind this man had certainly loved his neighbour and had demonstrated this by the care he took with his final suicide. But we seemed to have failed him in his not loving himself, and in not knowing the joy of life and a God of love. You know in your logical mind that the basis of suicide is a mental disease common in our affluent society, but …

The love of God and the joy of life have an eternity that this celebration lacked. His godmother gave the eulogy. It was a very Christian eulogy, an intimate and personal portrayal of a life lost, finishing with the words "God bless you". The wake following was one of discovery for me as I learnt about the lives, joys and successes of many old scholars.

The suicide took something from his close, loving family. He was a good worker and his father enjoyed working with him on the farm. When I spoke with Dad, there were all the ifs and buts. "If only," he said, "I had made the appointment a week earlier and taken him to it." I replied, probably very unhelpfully, "Perhaps if you had the suicide would have happened a week earlier." There could be no ifs and buts.

The drive home took another hour-and-a-half and on the way we called into our local supermarket. There a young lady named Kate and I exchanged a glance of recognition. "How have you been, Mr Hewitson?" she asked. "How has your day been?" I told her about the funeral and my sense of failing the young man. Her deep sympathy was telling, and she shared how she had lost her father to a terrible cancer. She also told me she had just submitted a thesis for her PhD on the effects of the drug ecstasy, and followed this up later with an email linking me to her research.

This encounter enabled me to reflect on this terrible death. I recalled that at the wake an old scholar named Troy had introduced his young baby and wife. He had gained his doctorate in grape research, wine oenology and viticulture. I met a hairdresser now living and working in Adelaide's western suburbs and I was proud; she also had the joy of living and pride in her achievements. I met a range of old scholars who shared this same joy of living, and I hoped that they also had a sense of eternity, a love greater than human love which, by necessity, does indeed end with loss and sorrow.

Word-of-mouth is the best judgment

In this book I have said a lot about what makes a school succeed and what parents should look for in choosing a school. More than once I've posed the question: Why in its early years did Trinity College, without advertising and with very poor resources, have such a large waiting list? My answer would indeed be complex; however, two simple things stand out: how do parents report the school, and how do others meeting children from the school see the school?

I received the following letter on 10 December 1996. It was written by the father of one of our female students to whom some awful things happened – unprofessional, shameful deceit involving a teacher outside of school, the student and her family. Yet this letter clearly showed forgiveness and I believe the family would have spoken well of the school to others.

> Dear Michael,
>
> You are probably not aware yet that our youngest daughter, C——, will be leaving the College at the end of this term, rather unexpectedly … This morning C—— was informed that she had gained a place on [a hairdressing] course commencing February next year. She was one of fifteen candidates selected from a field of 60, ranging from students through to mature adults. I am quite sure that her selection was helped by the grounding she gained at Trinity …
>
> We have always been proud that our children attended Trinity and have always appreciated the education the girls have received, both academically and socially. You have always been 'at the helm' and as such we have never had any concerns re. policy etc. at the College. On a more personal note: We appreciate the care and understanding you showed the family during the B—— episode. I am sure, from feedback we gained at the time, that you were personally involved in looking after the welfare of A—— and C—— … We deeply appreciate that. Finally, our thanks to all involved with our children at the College. I am sure that, although they probably don't realise it at the moment, the College will be with [our children] throughout their lives and many times in the future it will have a beneficial impact on their lives.

The second comment I would make is that the best ambassadors to a school are the students themselves. As headmaster I sometimes received letters from strangers who noted how well Trinity College students behaved in public. The following letter came to me in March 1994 via Les Leske, the Baptist minister in Elizabeth:

Dear Les,

When delivering the Easter leaflets yesterday, a young lady overtook me on the Fairfield Road and I offered her one, which she accepted graciously, and told me with a smile that she lived a few doors ahead so that would save me one delivery.

As I passed her gate, she then offered to deliver the remaining leaflets on Fairfield Road as she obviously noticed my greying hair ... "It's a bit hot for you today, isn't it?" she asked.

I asked her if she went to church and she said she went to Trinity College and attended as many services as she could at the school. I was impressed with her friendliness and readiness to help, and as I collected my car and drove off, I could see her tall figure marching resolutely along Fairfield Road with my leaflets.

I wondered if we should contact the college and thank them for their influence on at least one of their older students. It's not the first time I have heard of a pleasant incident in relation to this school.

It is my experience that the most important way communities judge schools is by word of mouth. It is also my experience that word-of-mouth and parental information is extremely accurate five years after the event. Parents make their enrolments for the future based on their knowledge in the present. Schools change and leaderships change, but the stories of the past linger.

Lessons learnt

1. Most new graduate teachers from university lack a philosophical foundation for life to share with children.
2. New graduate teachers are often poorly trained to teach primary school children reading, writing and mathematics.
3. Systemic schools offer leadership to independent schools that looks beyond the next decade to the next 100 years. They allow strategic planning for schools to be where people live.
4. Schools which provide the teacher with a classroom, some defined authority to control the learning environment (including disruptive behaviour) and support to enable the teacher to flourish benefit student learning.
5. Parents and students themselves are the best advertisers for a school, enabling communities to value the school.

18

Rescuing Australian schooling
Educational excellence for all, in every postcode

> *More money thrown at a non-performing system of schools has not, and will not, increase student access to quality schooling.*

In this book I have highlighted the fact that Australia's schooling performance is truly appalling.[98] It is so bad that in recent times both sides of federal parliament have spoken out detailing our poor performance.[99] "International tests [in 2011] showed our Year 4 students performed the worst out of all English-speaking countries in reading literacy, with nearly a quarter not meeting minimum international standards."[100, 101]

Over four decades parents have consistently shown they want schools to offer their children at least three things: the basics taught well, a safe and therefore disciplined environment, and good values. Many parents in Australia cannot send their children to a school with any one of these.

This book has highlighted how, over 40 years, schools have failed in lower-economic areas. In each decade we have had Directors General of Education in various states lamenting this poor performance and telling us it is going to be fixed. Yet nothing has changed. Various educational innovations have been introduced which have disguised this poor performance and lowered standards for all.[102] Yet still leading non-teaching educators, validly critiquing the narrowness of individual studies,[103] are quoted by those with a vested interest in maintaining the status quo despite the overwhelming evidence that it is not working.

Because schools in our lower economic regions are failing, Australia is losing future talent, planting seeds for social decay and reducing the quality of education across *all* schools. Our top students have lost international competitiveness. "Fewer high-performing 15-year-olds are reaching the top literacy and mathematics levels than in 2000."[104] Clearly our answers to the question "How will our children learn?" are inadequate.

In the decade to 2010, real per-student recurrent spending on schools rose by nearly 50 per cent.[105] Australia has not been alone in increasing spending on education. Ben Jensen of the Grattan Institute notes: "Many OECD countries have substantially increased education expenditure, often with disappointing results. Between 2000 and 2008, average expenditure per student rose by 34% across the OECD and 44% in Australia, yet student performance has fallen."[106]

This lack of relationship between per-student spending and student performance is one of the core weaknesses of the Gonski report, which advocates additional annual spending of $5 billion a year (on top of an estimated $6.5 billion). Apart from the political need to ensure that no school is made worse off by the change to funding formulas,[107] the case to justify such a massive increase has not effectively been made. Money alone is no answer.

It is so frustrating. We now have growing public understanding that our schools are failing, yet the answers being suggested in isolation will also fail. Most proposed solutions will cost a lot of money. Even though a few schools with really talented teachers will produce some bright stories that divert attention from the real issues, we need to address the problems of four decades of educational misdirection. The issues are:

1. School governance – who is actually responsible for a child's education?
2. Teaching – quality and review.
3. Curriculum – content and assessment.

Former Australian Prime Minister Julia Gillard presented "A National Plan for School Improvement" in September 2012 to the National Press

Club. Her critique and the need to act matched the findings of this book.[108] But how to achieve this change was not addressed. This book proposes changes that actually alter the way our children are taught.

The key issue is school governance. Who is responsible for a child's education at school? All political parties have voiced an answer.

Prime Minister Gillard's response was "Give more power to the principal". She combined this with the introduction of school improvement plans, measurement of student academic progress, longer school days and a concentration on reading, writing and maths. While all of this is good, it is insufficient and could just create another bureaucracy to supervise school improvement plans that talk about great outcomes and achieve nothing.

The then Shadow Minister for Education, Christopher Pyne, opened his contribution to the debate with a warning:

> What has been delivered [in the federal government's 'education revolution'] is a masterclass in wasteful spending and appalling mismanagement, all without any tangible impact on what actually matters: improving how and what teachers are teaching so student outcomes are improved. But perhaps we shouldn't be surprised – after all, the fate of the 'education revolution' was predicted over 90 years ago by Franz Kafka, who wrote: "Every revolution evaporates and leaves behind only the slime of a new bureaucracy" … [A Coalition Government] will give principals and parents a real say in the running of their school. The future of our government school system depends on it.[109]

Again, this is well and good. But how can you empower principals and give parents a real say in the running of their school? Without the key reform I will outline later in this chapter, this change will only improve schools where the principal and parents agree on the need to lift basic academic standards. Non-performing state schools will have no pressure to change because most parents in the poorer postcodes have no schooling choice – the state school is a monopoly.

Three alternative futures

There are three alternative futures for our schools and hence our country. In the first we continue as we are – a 'continue talking and spend more' future. In the second we return schooling to a command economy – the state schooling monopoly continues but with state-controlled order and inspection as described in chapter 1. This is a 'schools by command' future. In the third we move to an approach which empowers parents with genuine information and choice about the schooling they can choose for their child. This is a 'schools by demand' future.

The first option in my view is no option at all. The second is the better solution if you believe government knows what is best for the education of our children. The third relies on parents bearing the prime responsibility for the education of their children (albeit by choosing one of the state-approved schooling alternatives). In my preferred solution the second and third alternatives are combined, with one other crucial ingredient: the principle of parental choice being the best measure of schooling quality.

Future 1: Continue talking and spend more

The first alternative future is to continue as we are – spending more and more money to achieve less and less. This is the easy road to follow. Without significant change, however, our future will follow the laws of entropy. We will decline into disorder.

As we continue to dumb down our schooling and reduce our academic rigour, our nation will lose the vigour and competitiveness to survive.

To continue as we are would mean continuing current policies regarding independent schools. Present support for non-government schools does little to encourage genuine schooling competition in poorer regions. The story told in this book describes in detail why establishing strong, competitive non-government schools is politically difficult. Government policies protect existing providers, both government and non-government, from real competition. Existing educational providers argue that a closed and empty school built with public money is a waste of precious educational resources, but I disagree. The bigger waste is to have this empty school filled with students learning the hidden curriculum described in chapter 2: how to avoid contributing to society, how to collect social services and how to demand their rights.

Current non-government schools policy effectively favours the establishing of small, non-mainstream schools with strong communities based on different cultures. These schools will not necessarily engage in our national values (the rule of law with the same laws for all; our democratic system of government; free speech and an open press). Conflicts from overseas could become part of Australian life. Our long-term future could be as a nation of separately competing tribes, squabbling over diminishing resources.

Future 2: Schools by command

If public schooling remains the sole 'right' of state governments to run, then we require a framework to measure school performance. This implies the return of school auditors, filling the role that school inspectors filled in the 1960s. In this scenario Education Department schools are still the only option for most parents, but the government adopts criteria for measuring school performance such as those developed by the Australian Council for Educational Research (ACER), claimed to be the first nationally consistent way of judging school improvement.[110] The ACER approach "identifies nine elements that research shows lead to improvement in teaching and learning, covering the setting of goals, teaching methods, using data and the school environment".[111] The federal government in late 2012 indicated such an assessment of school performance based on the ACER model was part of its school improvement plan.

This model could certainly be used in my preferred strategy to improve schools and classroom practices. However, giving parents a choice of school is a far better tool to measure the quality of classroom teaching than the proposed measures used in a monopoly state school, thoughtful as they are. I would certainly apply these methods, but with an important additional aim: to give parents more information to decide which school to send their child to.

The problem with bureaucratic tools is the capacity for manipulation, with the kinds of actions proposed being a mirage and not real. Even worse, how could these tools be applied without monitoring by auditors? (The original ACER framework "envisaged schools being assessed by trained auditors, like the old-style school inspectors", but the federal government's 2012 proposal made no mention of external auditors.[112]) Will such a framework be a face-saving but meaningless paper trail of doctored statistics in lieu of real action, or will Australia's governments ensure they are valuable tools backed up by inspectors' audits? And will the evaluation outcomes be part of the public information available to assist real parental choice?

There are also things you cannot assess by formal measuring. How can you measure the way a school addresses whether life is meaningful and why? Or whether it teaches children that each individual needs to overlay his or her subjective purpose on a meaningless universe? Formal measuring cannot uncover a school's hidden curriculum.

Future 3: Schools by demand

I believe parents should have the prime (though not the only) responsibility for the education of their children, and government should have a role through the provision of diverse, measured and quality-reported schooling. This solution is based on the story of this book – the story of a teacher in the most difficult state schools; a director of an education centre in a lower economic region of Australia, working with teacher training and curriculum development that changed children's lives and behaviour; a founding headmaster of the largest school in Australia.

The best way to measure school performance is by parental demand. A school's recurrent government income would then be based on student numbers. Schools which did not provide the schooling parents were seeking would reduce in size and be challenged to change their offering, or to close so that their assets could be reused. This solution would involve the government enabling schools which parents, both rich and poor, would choose for their children.

In the USA, charter schools have been very successful in changing educational outcomes in the poorest communities. Charter schools are fully funded public schools free and open to all, just like our state schools. A charter school, however, is autonomous, with its own board. The Commonwealth government could look at the potential for enabling independent state schools similar to charter schools in Australia.

State governments could offer the best of both models. Each state school could choose whether to become an independent state school (reliant on student enrolments for funding and run by a board that appoints a principal responsible for staffing, students and curriculum) or a systemic state school under the authority of a Director of Education for systemic state schools, with a defined core curriculum, core content, common testing of the core and school inspectors. Teachers would be given professional freedom once the core curriculum is taught and be expected to expand beyond the core.

The state system would compete as a whole with other providers and be funded on the basis of student enrolment plus an additional budget for the school's overseeing bureaucracy. The state and non-government systems could be encouraged to establish technical high schools at either senior secondary or secondary school level. The director of the state systemic schools would not be the head of the Education Department because the departmental head would have oversight of *all* schools receiving state funding.

Parents do measure quality

Chapter 13 illustrated the failed governance structure in our state schools. There are no excuses for continuing as we are. The Trinity story shows that parents understand this.

Parents know that schooling matters. One indication of this is how real estate costs have risen near schools that are well regarded.[113] State schools vary greatly in quality and the price of housing and rents also rises near good state schools.[114] The cost of renting or purchasing real estate in areas with good schools demonstrates that families with children are assessing schools and are seeking those that will deliver for their children.

While this trend shows how families are valuing schooling, and this is to be praised, it also ensures the poor are financially locked out of 'well regarded' schools.

Research has shown repeatedly that it is children from families with low socio-economic status who are most at risk of school failure.[115] Children from lower socio-economic areas cannot even successfully go from school to work.[116] School absence has been a problem in lower socio-economic areas for decades.[117]

However, as this book has shown, this result is not inevitable. "Although children of low socioeconomic status may begin school with significantly different experiences and skills than their middle-class peers, research indicates these children can catch up."[118] The experience in East Asia demonstrates this:

> Nor is it just the smartest children who are benefitting [from Asian education advances]; in fact slower and disadvantaged students are less likely to drop out of school in Hong Kong, Shanghai and Korea, where the gaps between the top and bottom of the spectrum are smaller than in many other OECD countries. In Australia, the bottom 10 per cent of students is 13 months behind their East Asian counterparts.[119]

In these Asian countries,

Increasing performance and [educational] equity has been achieved with high and increasing participation. For example, 30 years ago about 40% of young Koreans (aged 25–34) finished secondary education. Now the figure is 98%, ten percentage points above the OECD average.[120]

I believe there is a way to change education in Australia to become once again internationally competitive and to reach out to all children, both rich and poor, and it should not cost another $6.5 billion annually to achieve it. We must change the way we offer schooling, especially in our poorer regions.

What can Australia do?

It is the ability to offer a real choice to parents that will lift the education offered by all schools in a region, as well as some of the key attributes for the success of schools that matter.

I mentioned earlier the development of charter schools in the United States. America has found that a monopolistic public education has educated children so badly that it is opening fully publicly funded schools independent of the state government systems. It is my contention that Australia should do something similar.

Let me report a story about a group of kindergarten to Year 8 charter schools in Minnesota. David King, a journalist with *The Australian*, reports on a school offering parents in Minneapolis a very different choice:[121]

> There's a crisp intensity inside the kindergarten class at Mastery, a new charter school in Minneapolis that's turning stereotypes about demography and destiny on their heads.
>
> In a room adorned with pictures of Martin Luther King and Jesse Owens, two teachers circle 21 little boys as they practise sitting up straight and making their way to a carpet where they'll read a book. "We are college-bound scholars, and I need 100 per cent," says one teacher.

There's no slouching or horsing around here. "Sit up and SLANT," says the teacher, and the boys, all five years old and all black, bolt upright.

The place is heavy with unwieldy acronyms. SLANT stands for Sit up, Listen, Ask and Answer Questions, Nod your head, Track the speaker. It's a skill set drummed into the kids from day one and they'll carry it through their years at the school.

The task may be too much for young Treyvon, whose attention begins to wander. He foolishly starts talking to a mate. "Do you need to go back to the 'take a break' chair?" his teacher asks. He stops immediately.

Eventually the boys get the hang of sitting, then standing in an orderly fashion and there's high praise for them.

"That's what we do at Mastery – we go until we get 100 per cent. We are scholars going to college."

While five years might seem a little young to be focusing on sending a child to university, a college education is the expressed goal for every child who attends the Harvest Preparatory Academy, really a cluster of five schools, including Mastery, which caters for about 1000 students from kindergarten to Year 8.

They are run by Minneapolis-based educational pioneer Eric Mahmoud, whose charter schools, publicly funded but run independently, are closing the achievement gap in Minnesota, a state where it was among the widest in the nation. Almost all the students at his Minneapolis schools are African American and 90 per cent qualify for a 'free or reduced lunch', meaning they receive financial assistance to attend school. The school has a big migrant community, reflecting the recent influx of families from Somalia, Ethiopia and Eritrea. On the day I visit the school, 10 students are in care facilities because they are homeless.

Homelessness is not confined to America. In 1986 I suspected someone was camping in the large concrete pipes in the Trinity College playground. I discovered it was one of our students. A low-cost school uniform hides obvious poverty.

Eric Mahmoud gave three reasons for the charter schools' success: "Belief, time and data."

Belief. "We are completely confident and we completely believe that our children can achieve academic success at a very high level," Mahmoud says. The schools believe every child has the capacity to succeed. However, I notice they have another even deeper belief. There is a hidden curriculum at play, namely, that the education of these children is not about 'me' (the individual) but about the local community. Their teachers tell them that when they graduate they will be valuable and can return to their communities and continue to make a difference for good.

Callie Lalugba, the principal of Mastery and Harvest, says: "We don't believe that you are born with a certain intelligence and that you can stay there … We want students to complete college and come back and help your community and have an impact on your community. They are constantly hearing that from the time they get into kindergarten up to the eighth grade."

Trinity's hidden curriculum was similar. The same messages about students' capacity to succeed, contribute and make a difference were underlined by the teaching "Love God, (or, for the secular person, value the cosmos), love your neighbour and love yourself". These new charter schools and schools like Trinity both share a belief that every child can succeed and should live a life that contributes to the greater good.

Time. Time is about time on-task. Harvest Preparatory Academy has a year-round calendar from August to July, and the day runs from 7.45 am to 4.45 pm (except on Fridays when it finishes at 2.00 pm). This gives students about 35% more classroom time than other schools.

The Trinity story was of a school which spent 20% more time teaching core academic subjects. The school day at Trinity included extra 'after-school' times because I believed that, with so many families where both parents worked, schools should offer a comprehensive 8.30 am to 4.30 pm program combined with the provision (at extra cost to parents) of an integrated before- and after-school learning centre from 7.00 am to 6.00 pm.

Data. All the core subjects at Harvest are loaded with data and tested on a weekly basis. The teachers prepare common tests and have regular feedback discussions on Friday afternoons. Indeed, reading the story of the Mastery school gave me a sense of déjà vu. To cover accumulated learning Mastery has six-weekly tests; Trinity had term tests. Teachers discuss remedial programs to enable students not performing to keep up.

> By the end of the school year the tests are long and cover a vast range of material. The tests arm the teachers with information about what students are learning or struggling with, and allow them to plan intervention when students fall behind, or share techniques that work ... The tests are created by the teachers but are in a format similar to the all-important Minnesota Comprehensive Assessments, the reading, writing and mathematics tests that measure and benchmark the school against the state's academic standards.[122]

Is all this worth it? King's article reports that the students at Harvest's schools "outperform the state average in maths and reading in every grade, and the latest estimate is that about 80 per cent of the kids who have been at the school will go on to some kind of college."

Only half of Trinity's program was data-driven, with documented core curriculum in all subject areas. To ensure growth in learning, the curriculum was organised by the school over 10 years. I believe schools should offer more than data-driven programs, which is why the other half of the time was teacher-directed, open-ended learning.

The publicly-funded charter schools in America's most deprived communities are making a difference.

Schooling not the answer for all

Chapter 17 mentioned a student who left school at the age of 15 and successfully continued her learning as a hairdressing apprentice. This shows that some students are better off leaving school for work at the end of Year 10.

Forcing children to remain at school until 17 increases the costs of schooling, and because this is essentially forced learning, many teenagers rebel (though other reasons are often given, including lack of relevance, motivation or even ability). By forcing these teenagers to remain at school we also reduce the effectiveness of senior secondary schooling in poorer areas. Academic students are distracted by their conscripted school peers. Compulsory schooling after the age of 15 is probably against the national interest.

I would allow, and in some cases encourage, students to leave school to take up an apprenticeship or full-time work. Why can't students who are able to gain work or apprenticeships be allowed to leave for paid employment, with the signed approval of parents and perhaps the school principal? For the purposes of governmental statistics, students who have left school to undertake apprenticeships or full-time work and who are endorsed annually by their school until the age of 17 should be regarded as continuing their education. This should become the measure of the percentage of 17-year-olds remaining in lifelong learning.

Teacher training and development

In an editorial in February 2012, *The Australian* commented on the real issues in education:

> Too much of Australia's contentious and long-running education debate has centred on peripheral matters: funding, class size, the public versus private debate, buildings and laptops. The experience of four of the world's best school systems [according to OECD measurements of outcomes in key learning areas] – Shanghai, Korea, Singapore and Hong Kong – suggests these issues are far less important than the selection of teachers, their training and mentoring and educational research into what actually happens in the classroom rather than social theory.[123]

According to the editorial writer, the Grattan Institute's *Catching Up* report makes it clear that "the [overseas] gains cannot be attributed to rote learning or cultural differences. The achievements are not driven by ruthless Tiger mothers driving their offspring to exhaustion."

I have some sympathy with the claim that the lesson from Asia is that the only way to improve students' learning is by improving teaching. Reforming teaching is about behavioural and cultural change, which means "changing what teachers do, day in, day out, in every school".[124]

While teacher training is important, however, it will only lift the quality of Australian schooling if we also change the way we "do schools". When a principal's job depends on choosing good teachers to attract enrolments, he or she will look for quality staff from other schools and tertiary institutions that prepare highly competent teachers. The systemic state schools could once again offer scholarships to the most able school graduates in exchange for a bond of three years to teach in any systemic state school.

Julia Gillard summed up the kind of teachers we need so well:

> Nothing matters more to the quality of a child's education than the quality of the teacher standing in front of the classroom. I want that teacher to be someone who loves the job, who is of the highest calibre, who got the best training and support as a new teacher, who continuously hones their skills, who is delighted to have their skills measured and areas for improvement highlighted.[125]

Clearly entry scores into teaching must be lifted to an ATAR score of 70; it is not good enough for those who do not succeed academically to become our future teachers. Tertiary institutions lower their standards to accommodate those with ATAR scores below 50%. I also support Ms Gillard's claim that improving teaching involves "requiring more classroom experience before graduation and higher entry requirements for the teaching profession."[126]

For teachers to love their job they need to be able to support the vision of the school in which they work, because teaching is about doing more than you are paid for. It is about giving to children 'skills for life'. This book has detailed the beneficial educational outcomes of schools where the parents, the teachers and the vision of the school work together. The hidden curriculum is what really matters.

Chapter 1 of this book highlighted the important role the annual inspection and review of teachers played in state schools of the 1960s and '70s. Teacher training should not stop when a teacher begins to teach. Ms Gillard supported this change: "All our teachers will be reviewed annually in their school, a thorough ongoing assessment of their skills and where they need to improve."[127]

A new kind of school for Australia

How can Australia's federal government actually achieve the following aspirations spelled out by Julia Gillard[128] and totally supported by the story of this book:

1. More power for principals, including over budgets and staff selection.
2. Every school to have a school improvement plan and be held to account against it.
3. School children to be asked to face up to being measured and urged to improve, and adults to be asked to do the same. Every child falling behind to get a personalised learning plan.
4. Children to be able to spend longer in the school with breakfast clubs and after-hours activities.
5. Reading, writing and maths to be the foundation stones, taught, tested, improved.
6. Principals to be empowered to lead their schools, making decisions that get improvements unencumbered by stifling bureaucracy.

Ms Gillard stated, "There's no button you press for school improvement – schools are human organisations – but the change-makers need to know you're on their side."

This book is about the political 'button' to achieve real change and school improvement. It is about giving parents a real choice of schools, especially in the poorer regions of Australia. The federal government could invite all educational providers and others, such as state and local governments, to run schools with a per-student income equivalent to the state Education Department cost. These would include some fully government-funded independent state schools. Independent schools with high levels of public funding would respond quickly to a new source of funding. The proposed 'independent state schools' would also respond quickly or lose both funds and enrolments.

These new 'independent state schools' could be reconstructed state or independent schools. In my proposal they have characteristics similar to those Ms Gillard outlined:

1. They are run by a school board of 10–12 governors that represents the local community as well as the wider state interests. This board appoints a principal on five-year renewable contracts responsible to the board for staffing, students and curriculum.
2. They run a full 7.5-hour daily program, including breakfast clubs and after-hours cultural and sporting activities.
3. They have a core curriculum that is sequential and explicit, with reading, writing and maths as the foundation stones.
4. They practise regular weekly and semester testing, with semester results and *My School* results reported to parents.
5. They are open to all, with fees no greater than those of state schools.
6. They have their property and assets vested in the school. Schools that go bankrupt have their assets returned to the state.
7. Teachers have in-school improvement programs, including annual reviews and incentives.

These new schools are needed in the poorer regions of Australia.

A real choice

According to *Australia in the Asian Century*,[129] released by the Australian government in December 2011, making our education system one of the world's five best is crucial to making the most of opportunities created by Asia's economic growth.[130] The real question, wrote economist Henry Ergas, is what that would involve:

> It is not by being welfare states that the Asian economies have lifted millions from poverty towards affluence, but by making individuals and families bear the primary responsibility for their fate. With both sides of Australian politics committed to vast increases in social spending, it is high time we learnt to take Asia seriously.[131]

This book is about the dramatic improvements in student learning and social behaviour that occur when the community offers a diversity of schools for all parents and teachers to choose from. It is about how this choice is needed most in our less affluent regions where education is failing. Given this choice, the story describes how parents can choose the type of schools our government says it is seeking to establish.

We need to reclaim the prime importance of parental responsibility in making our education system one of the world's best. We must not throw the baby out with the bathwater because international comparisons also highlight our strengths. However, we can empower parents by giving all families, both rich and poor, a real choice of schools that parents would choose.

Lessons to learn

1. Parents are the best evaluators of schools. Monopoly schooling can fail, and parents in poor areas should also have a choice of schools.
2. Schools may not be the best place for some students to learn. Teenagers over the age of 14 should be able to take up full-time apprenticeships or work that is authorised annually by their school principal as an alternative to compulsory classroom attendance. Students so registered should be included in the list of people completing their secondary education.
3. State education departments could fully fund independent state schools where enrolment is open to all.
4. Both existing state and non-government schools should be able to apply to become independent state schools. New independent state schools in the independent sector should be able to open in poorer areas if they have demonstrable parental demand and accept all students in the same manner as state schools.
5. Public student performance testing for all these schools should be mandatory and the results publicly reported.
6. Any community group, from local governments and churches to not-for-profit charities and educational associations, may sponsor independent state schools.
7. New schools are needed that offer more than just core academic skills. Schools need to offer values for living, encourage student exploration and innovation, and provide students with entrepreneurial opportunities.
8. To ensure a diversity of philosophical and religious traditions is offered through publicly funded independent state schools, there should be a separation of church and state. Proselytising of any faith system (including atheism) should not be allowed in state schools. But cultural practices, both religious and non-religious, can underpin the value system each school claims to teach.
9. New schools that parents wish to choose for their children are needed in lower-economic areas. Values matter, and schools need to overtly state their value systems for parents to choose.

Appendix
How to choose a school for your child
What parents can do.

Parental choices are a better guide to quality of education than government ordinances. Parents must actively choose the school for their children. Your choice matters because schools are different and different schools suit different children.

When choosing a school for your child:

1. Meet the school principal and ask about issues that concern you about the education of your child. Find out:
- What is the school's discipline policy?
- Are classes mixed ability, open learning or traditional (with set student places and streamed-ability groups)?
- How will the school meet the academic needs of your child, whether gifted, with special needs or of average ability?
- How will your child be looked after in pastoral care? Who sorts out problems for individual children such as bullying?
- What will be the role of technology and computers in your child's learning?
- Does the school offer cultural and sporting opportunities in a co-curricular program or do these activities take up part of the normal school day?
- Are you allowed to see around the school on a normal day? (A number of parents asked me on such visits to see the student toilets because at their child's current school the toilets were almost unusable.)

2. Look for a school that not only talks about its educational practice but actually implements it. Some children need personalised learning based on their particular interests, with

teachers acting as advisers, but most benefit from a structured program. Does the school:

- maximise time on task? (How much formal time is devoted to core subjects: reading, writing, maths and science?)
- hold high expectations? (Does the school regularly test and report results to parents? Can you sight the tests?)
- establish a school climate supportive of academic learning? (Does the school measure student academic progress and achieve results? The most public are the Year 12 results and the limited NAPLAN results published on the *My School* website, www.myschool.edu.au)
- have strong parental involvement and support? (Ask other parents. Word-of-mouth removes spin and public advertising. Can you view children's work?)
- expect students in Year 2 to successfully write their own creative one-page story?

3. Whose values will your chosen school teach? Ask the fundamental question: Will my child grow up right?

4. As a parent and principal, I would want my children to have all of the above and something more. I would want to know that the teachers will explore, expand and experiment, not just sharing examinable content, but giving my children resilience and the skills to learn and discover.

5. Ask other parents, especially those who share your values. Are the students unconditionally loved, even when this is hard?

6. Observe the behaviour of students and old scholars away from the school.

The government is not good at picking winners in industry or education. I would insist that members of parliament back your right as a parent to choose a school that supports your family's need to educate your children. If there is no school in your region you would choose, contact your member of parliament. You may need to become involved in starting one

Endnotes

1 *The Advertiser*, June 2007.
2 *The News*, 16 February 1977.
3 *Alcohol the Experiment*, a worldwide literature search by Heather Brown (SA State Library) on post-1975 indexes, published by Salisbury Education Centre, December 1978, pp. 123–166.
4 W. De Haes & J. Schuurman, *International Journal of Health Education*. Vol. 18, No. 4 supp: October/December 1975.
5 *The Advertiser*, 15 September 1977.
6 ibid., p. 5.
7 *Alcohol the experiment*, p. 138.
8 ibid., p. 116.
9 ibid., p. ii.
10 *Australian Journal of Alcohol and Drug Dependence*, Vol. 5, No. 4, November 1978, p. 105; L.H.R. Drew, 'Education about alcohol in school', *Health Promotion in Australia*, Commonwealth Department of Health. Report 1978–1979, pp. 175–81.
11 The New Webster's Dictionary, Vol. 2, defined secularism as "supreme or exclusive attention to affairs of this life". It defined 'secularist' as "one who theoretically rejects every kind of religious worship", or one who "believes that education and other matters should be conducted without the introduction of a religious element."
12 M. Hewitson, *Into the '80s: Towards a state school education reflecting the pluralistic needs of state, children and family*, Salisbury Education Centre, March 1980.
13 ibid., p. 13.
14 Commonwealth Department of Education, "Choice and Diversity" newsletter, March 1980.
15 Personal correspondence, John Steinle to Michael Hewitson, 29 June 1980.
16 Pamphlet calling a public meeting about Hills Christian Community School, December 1980.

17 Personal email, Lynn Arnold, 14 February 2013: "One other area probably needs clarification too; and this represented a hard political lesson for me at the time ... namely the reference to Cabinet support [was] correct ... but only to an extent. I had not, at that stage, taken a formal submission to Cabinet. Rather I had discussed it with my colleagues and gained their concurrence to my proceeding with the enquiry. However, later, after my rolling, one of my Cabinet colleagues did counsel me, saying that the case I had put to Cabinet may not have been as transparent as I had thought I was being. The whole episode was a very powerful political lesson to me on the need to be complete in the briefing one provides to colleagues whose support one is wanting on issues likely to be controversial ... Regretfully, I admit now that I was not complete in my briefing. And the real pity of this is that, as a new minister of only 15 months or so in Cabinet (and 35 at the time), I let enthusiasm for a cause get in the way of its successful evolution and thus effectively participated, albeit unintentionally, in killing the idea."

18 The 'whale' is actually described as a 'large fish' in the Old Testament.

19 'Parental' meant at least three parents, plus grandparents, old scholars and paid-up members of church congregations who were affiliated with the school – six of the twelve-member council in all.

20 *The Bunyip*, 29 November 2000, p. 1.

21 This wording is based on a headline in *The Australian*, 29 December 1993. See chapter 11.

22 Carolyn Jones, "School beats home as spur for success", *The Australian*, 29 December 1993, p. 1, citing the director of the Melbourne University Centre for Applied Education Research, Professor Peter Hill.

23 Jemma Chapman,*The Australian*, 17 February 2004.

24 *Parents' and Community Members' Attitudes to Schooling*, survey, Department of Education, Science and Training, 2003.

25 These tables list the most important factors to parents across Australia when choosing a school in 2003.

26 Littleford & Associates, 'The effectiveness of schools and the longevity of heads", August 2000.

27 Possible after-school detentions included: (1) Week-night detention, with a

note sent home and signed by the parent before the detention was done. (2) Friday after-school detention for an hour, with a similar note to be signed. (3) Saturday morning detention for two hours for students who had been given two Fridays in one week from two different teachers. For a very serious breach of discipline, the principal had the authority to issue a Saturday detention.

28 Bob Dufford SJ, "Be Not Afraid", based on Isaiah 43: 2–3 and Luke 6: 20ff.
29 The 85% figure was from federal and state governments and the 15% balance was from school fees. In total this was still only 65% of the amount each state school child attracted in recurrent funds alone. From this 65% we had to cover the capital costs as well.
30 Proverbs 29:18.
31 And still is. As former Prime Minister Julia Gillard stated in her speech, "A National Plan for School Improvement", at the National Press Club on 3 September 2012, "we particularly need to improve the education of our poorer children".
32 *The Adelaide News*, 29 March 1989, p. 22.
33 *Portside Messenger Press*, 30 September 1987, p. 1.
34 *The Portside Messenger*, February 1989.
35 Errol Simpler, "Parents back Christian studies", *The Weekend Australian*, 11 March 1989, p. 5.
36 All student names in this chapter have been changed for privacy reasons.
37 Richard was accepted by Blackfriar's, eventually graduated and went on to study medicine and become a doctor.
38 "Cannabis ... use precedes the development of schizophrenia by six times." Dr Pols writing in *Australian Medicine*, reported in *The Advertiser*, 6 April 1996, p. 13.
39 A national survey of 29,700 students in 1996 and released in 1998 reported cannabis was the most commonly used illicit substance, with 36% of 12 to 17-year-olds using it at some time and 55% of 17-year-olds. In addition, 20% of all students had used cannabis in the previous month. Reported in *The Advertiser*, 9 March 1999, p. 33.

40 *Drug and alcohol use among SA school children (1996)*, Drug and Alcohol Services Council, March 1999, p. 3.
41 "Families linked to drugs", *The Advertiser*, 31 August 1996.
42 "Your Shout", Book 1 of series *Alcohol: Its science and sociology*, M. Hewitson (ed.), Rigby Publishers, 1980.
43 "What's Brewing?" Book 2 of series *Alcohol: Its science and sociology*, M. Hewitson (ed.), Rigby Publishers, 1980.
44 *The Sunday Mail*, 20 April 1997.
45 "College's legal marijuana plan" half baked", *The Sunday Mail*, 27 April 1997.
46 Leah Manual, "College call for drug law change", *The Bunyip*, 9 April 1997.
47 Letter to Malcolm Buckby, MP for Light, in response to our paper, 21 September 1996.
48 This study was funded by a grant from the National School Drug Education Innovation and Good Practice Project, a Commonwealth Department of Education, Training and Youth Affairs-funded initiative under the National School Drug Education Strategy. All Trinity College schools (South, North, Blakeview) and other selected schools across Australia took part. Results were contained in a report sent to me as principal of Trinity in 2001.
49 "There is no doubt that child protection issues are a significant factor in men's attitude towards teaching, generally, and that this factor is magnified in relation to primary teaching. The community attitude towards male primary school teachers is a troubling paradox. People say they want more male primary teachers in schools while many harbour suspicions about men who want to work with children." *Boys: Getting It Right*, House of Representatives Standing Committee on Education and Training, 2002, 6.83.
50 "Findings from 'Staff in Australia's Schools 2007', a project commissioned by the former Department of Education, Science and Training (DEST), suggest that the proportion of male teachers in Australia's primary school classrooms, for example, could be as low as 21%.". ABS, *Where have all the male teachers gone?*, 2010.
51 TER = Tertiary Entrance Rank; ATAR = Australian Tertiary Admission Rank. A score of over 95 means that a student is in the top 5% of Year 12's Australia-wide.

52 Katherine Thornton, *The Messages of Its Walls and Fields: A history of St Peter's College, 1847 to 2009*, Wakefield Press, 2010, p. 8.
53 *The Advertiser*, 11 January 2012, pp. 1, 3.
54 *The Australian*, 29 December 1993, pp. 1–2.
55 The report stressed the importance of the early years in developing literary skills. Early Childhood Education, Reception, and Years 1and 2 were key.
56 Trinity academic results compared to the top 10% of the state and compared with a state median TER score of 50.

Trinity Year 12 results compared with SA state results, 1997–2002

	1997	1998	1999	2000	2001	2002
% with a TER score above 90 (top 10% in state)	24	24.5	18.6	14	17.2	13.2
Median TER score (state median = 50)	77	78	77	72	71	72

57 "School boss warns of class divide", *The Advertiser*, 21 May 2012.
58 *The Bunyip*, 28 May 1997.
59 ibid.
60 The votes were: 16 – no expansion; 5 – expanding existing two schools; 184 – expand, with 116 for a co-located R–12 campus and 66 for a new school at Williamstown.
61 A day before school starts at the end of the holidays when students/parents meet their class teacher and housemaster and pick up their book orders for the year.
62 Trinity enrolments by campus on page 187.
63 See chapter 15.
64 *The Bunyip*, 9 February 2000, p. 20.
65 "Trinity campus clash", *Messenger Press*, 29 October 1997, p. 1.
66 ibid.
67 ibid.
68 ibid.

69 The City of Playford was formed by the amalgamation of the Munno Para and Elizabeth councils in 1997.
70 "Development of a Marketing Template, State Education Pilot Project Elizabeth–Munno Para District", 4 March 1998.
71 Charles James, "Report finds Craigmore failed students", *The Advertiser*, 23 September 2003, pp. 1, 4.
72 Now the Independent Education Union of South Australia (IEUSA).
73 "Trinity College Evaluation 1997–1998", a report for the college council prepared by V. Eyers & A. Shinkfield.
74 ibid., section 1, p. 7.
75 ibid., section 4, p. 16.
76 ibid., section 3 conclusions and section 7, p. 13.
77 According to the report, parents' reasons for sending their children to Trinity were:
   1. It had a Christian emphasis.
   2. They liked the academic curriculum.
   3. Firm discipline was anticipated.
   4. They simply felt their child would be better off than in a government school.
78 *The Bunyip*, 7 June 2000, p. 37.
79 We started the Montessori Early Learning Centre around 1992. It accommodated approximately 60 students and a staff of about five under Director Sue Reynolds.
80 Justine Ferrari,"Gonski reforms overhaul of schools to cost $6.5bn", *The Australian* , 23 July 2012.
81 Ben Jensen, *Catching Up: Learning from the best school systems in East Asia*, The Grattan Institute, 2012.
82 Justine Ferrari, "Lessons from Asia show way forward for schools ",*The Australian*, 17 February 2012 .
83 Des Parker & Gordon Young, *Strategic planning, South Australian Anglican Schools Commission*, December 2000.

84 We were already planning a new senior secondary campus called the Open Learning Centre offering part and full tertiary qualifications in the areas of business, multimedia, entertainment, horticulture, electronic engineering, automotive mechanics, furniture manufacture, hospitality, small business management, tourism, community services and health.

85 Locally, a new Catholic secondary school called Xavier College had been established in 1996 and was running a comprehensive school with a focus on vocational education training.

86 Four R–4 schools with 300 students each; four 'middle schools' of 350 each; and two senior schools of 450 each. The total, with no extra intake, was a school of 4000 by the time the younger students got to Year 12.

87 Letter, M. Hewitson to Non-Government Schools Registration Board, 27 December 2001.

88 *The Times* (Victor Harbour), 29 December 2000, p. 1.

89 Letter, Ms Heather H. McDonald to Non-Government Schools Registration Board, 10 January 2001.

90 "An Open Letter to all Federal and State Ministers of Education" <http://resources.news.com.au/files/2012/12/21/1226541/996513-aus-news-file-open-letter-to-education-ministers.pdf>.

91 Justine Ferrari, "A decade of lost action on literacy", *The Australian*, 22 December 2012.

92 Justine Ferrari,*The Australian*, 12 December 2012.

93 Rayner College was another attempt to establish a school in Adelaide's north-western suburbs.

94 A decade earlier the Sydney Diocese invited me to explain how to achieve a system and how to open new schools affordable to all. I made a number of visits. After very similar difficulties with their existing independent schools, the diocese backed the project, and despite many failures was eventually able to start with the bare minimum. The Sydney Anglican Schools Corporation has flourished, with 17 schools in 2012 and planning for more. <http://www.sasc.nsw.edu.au/our-schools>

95 Sheradyn Holderhead, "School finds single-sex learning the key to improving males' performance", *The Advertiser*, 31 August 2012.

96 Sheradyn Holderhead, "Gender gap as boys struggle with SACE", *The Advertiser*, 20 July 2012.

97 While the research projects were supposed to be the students' own work, teachers could be so supportive that the project could be their work rather than the students'.

98 Cf. Finding 1 of the Gonski review of school funding: "Australian schooling needs to lift the performance of students at all levels of achievement, particularly the lowest performers. Australia must also improve its international standing by arresting the decline that has been witnessed over the past decade. For Australian students to take their rightful place in a globalised world, socially, culturally and economically, they will need to have levels of education that equip them for this opportunity and challenge." Gonski et. al, *Review of Funding for Schooling: Final Report*, Australian Government, December 2012, p. xxix.< http://foi.deewr.gov.au/system/files/doc/other/review-of-funding-for-schooling-final-report-dec-2011.pdf>.

99 Prime Minister Julia Gillard, "A National Plan for School Improvement", National Press Club, Canberra, 3 September 2012; Christopher Pyne (Shadow Minister for Education, Apprenticeships and Training), "Achieving Teacher Quality: The Coalition's Approach", Sydney Institute Address, 16 July 2012.

100 Peter Garrett (then Minister for Education), "School critics must study harder", *The Australian*, 29 May 2013.

101 International results show that our students are two years behind Korea by age 15 in reading, maths and science. In 2011, how schools across the whole of Australia, including the wealthier postcodes, are performing was illustrated by the performance of our Year 4 students and Year 8 students against international benchmarks in maths, reading and science. A close look at the following link will give a detailed, balanced overview of results in all areas: <http://www.acer.edu.au/timss/overview>.

102 An obvious example of this is how we are changing the way we measure our Year 12 students, with more and more emphasis on school-based assessments, avoiding the rigour of public examinations and independent scaling of these marks.

103 For example, Alan Reid, "Raising the level of educational debate", *Professional Educator*, Vol. 13 Issue 1, March 2013, pp. 5–6.

104 Ben Jensen, "Spending billions is the wrong fix for our failing schools", *The Australian*, 23 February 2013.

105 Judith Sloan, "Why I don't give a Gonski for more school spending", *The Australian*, 28 August 2012.

106 Ben Jensen, *Catching Up: Learning from the best school systems in East Asia*, The Grattan Institute, 2012, p. 2.

107 Gonski report, Recommendation 19: "... no school will lose a dollar per student as a result of this review".

108 The Prime Minister stated: "The first truth is we have to aim higher for every child in every school. Four of the top five schooling systems in the world are in our region and we aren't in that coveted top five ...

"The second truth is we particularly need to improve the education of our poorer children. These are not children raised in extremes of violence, neglect or disadvantage. Just kids whose parents pack their lunch, take them to school on the way to work and expect they're being taught to read and write while they're at school. And they're not ... By Year nine, the average child from the same battling family is two years behind children from the most-well-off quarter of Australian homes in reading and maths ...

"And the third truth is we are failing our indigenous children. There are about 18,800 indigenous school children in very remote Australia. Today in very remote Australia the average indigenous child is still reading below a Year three level in Year nine."

109 Christopher Pyne, "Achieving Teacher Quality: The Coalition's Approach".

110 Geoff N. Masters, *Teaching and Learning School Improvement Framework*, ACER, 2010. <www.acer.edu.au/documents/C2E-Teach-and-learn-no-crop.pdf.>

111 Justine Ferrari, "Test tied to school funding", *The Australian*, 6 December 2012.

112 ibid.

113 Majella Corrigan, "Blackboard Jungle now has an exclusive address", *The Weekend Australian*, 3–4 February 2007.

114 ibid.

115 "Socioeconomic status", North Central Regional Educational Authority

<http://www.ncrel.org/sdrs/areas/issues/content/cntareas/reading/li7lk13.htm>, citing M. Knapp, & P. Shields, "Reconceiving academic instruction for the children of poverty", *Phi Delta Kappan*, 71, 1990, pp. 753–58.

116 S. Lamb & P. McKenzie, "Patterns of success and failure in the transition from school to work in Australia", LSAY Research Reports, 2001, Figure 5.3.

117 Sheldon Rothman, "School absence and student background factors: A multilevel analysis", *International Education Journal*, Vol. 2, No. 1, 2001, pp. 59–68.

118 "Socioeconomic status", North Central Regional Educational Authority <http://www.ncrel.org/sdrs/areas/issues/content/cntareas/reading/li7lk13.htm>, citing Purcell-Gates, McIntyre, & Freppon, "Learning written storybook language in school", *American Educational Research Journal*, Vol. 32 No. 3, 1995, pp. 659–85.

119 Editorial, "A salutary lesson from the world's top school systems", *The Australian*, 17 February 2012.

120 Jensen, *Catching Up*, p. 10.

121 David King, "Lesson for all as US schools think again", *The Australian*, 1 September 2012.

122 ibid.

123 Editorial, *The Australian*, 17 February 2012.

124 Justine Ferrari, "Lessons from Asia show way forward for schools", *The Australian*, 17 February 2012.

125 Gillard, "A National Plan for School Improvement".

126 ibid.

127 ibid.

128 op. cit.

129 *Australia in the Asian Century*, Issues paper, Australia in the Asian Century Task Force, December 2011. <asiancentury.dpmc.gov.au/sites/.../asian-century-issues-paper.pdf>

130 Henry Ergas, "Truth about tigers and school", *The Australian*, 29 October 2012.

131 ibid.

www.ingramcontent.com/pod-product-compliance
Lightning Source LLC
Chambersburg PA
CBHW052052230426
43671CB00011B/1882